Sexual Harassment on College Campuses
Abusing the Ivory Power

A revised and expanded edition of
Ivory Power: Sexual Harassment on Campus

SUNY Series, The Psychology of Women
Edited by Michele A. Paludi

Sexual Harassment on College Campuses

Abusing the Ivory Power

Edited by

Michele A. Paludi

State University of New York Press

Published by
State University of New York Press, Albany

© 1990, 1996 State University of New York

For information, address State University of New York Press,
State University Plaza, Albany, N.Y., 12246

Production by Cathleen Collins
Marketing by Theresa Abad Swierzowski

Library of Congress Cataloging in Publication Data

Sexual harassment on college campuses : abusing the ivory power /
    edited by Michele A. Paludi.
        p.   cm. — (SUNY series, the psychology of women)
    Rev. and expanded ed. of: Ivory power. c1990.
    Includes bibliographical references and index.
    ISBN 0-7914-2801-X (alk. paper). — ISBN 0-7914-2802-8 (pbk.
alk. paper)
    1. Sexual harassment in universities and colleges—United States.
I. Paludi, Michele Antoinette. II. Ivory power. III. Series: SUNY
series in the psychology of women.
LC212.862.S49   1996
370.19'345—dc20   95-15813
                                                               CIP

10 9 8 7 6 5 4 3 2 1

For college students
from whom I have had the honor
of being called Professor:
Thank you for teaching me.

Contents

Acknowledgments

I would like to thank the following family friends, and colleagues who help guide my thinking in research, training, and expert witness testimony in sexual harassment: Rosalie Paludi, Lucille Paludi, James Tedisco, Fr. John Provost, Rita Stapf, Reverend Richard Campbell, Marianna McShane, and Anne Levy.

I also thank Lois Patton at SUNY Press for encouraging me to edit a second edition of this book. She understands my need to continue to educate campuses about sexual harassment.

About the Editor

Michele A. Paludi, Ph.D., is an internationally recognized expert in academic and workplace sexual harassment. She is the editor of *Ivory Power: Sexual Harassment on Campus* (Albany: State University of New York Press, 1990), coauthor of *Academic and Workplace Sexual Harassment: A Resource Manual* (Albany: State University of New York Press, 1991).

Dr. Paludi is currently writing *Sexual Harassment of Adolescents by Teachers and Peers* for SUNY Press.

Dr. Paludi is Principal of Michele Paludi & Associates, Consultants in Sexual Harassment, and offers education and training in issues related to sexual harassment at schools, colleges, and organizations. In addition, she is an expert witness for academic and court proceedings involving sexual harassment.

For her research, training, and investigative work, Dr. Paludi received the 1992 Progress in Equity Award from the National and New York State Chapter of the American Association of University Women. She is also the 1988 recipient of the Emerging Leader Award from the Committee on Women of the American Psychological Association. And the YWCA awarded Dr. Paludi their 1992 Woman of Vision Award for Advocacy. Dr. Paludi was named the 1994 Woman of the Year by the New York State Business and Professional Women's Organization.

Dr. Paludi's book *Ivory Power* was the 1992 recipient of the Gustavus Myers Center Award for Outstanding Book on Human Rights in the United States.

Dr. Paludi is the author of nine books on sexual harassment, psychology of women, and gender. Her coedited book *Psychology of Women: Handbook of Issues and Theories* was recently named the outstanding academic book in the United States by the American Library Association.

Dr. Paludi was a member of Governor Cuomo's Task Force on Sexual Harassment.

Contributors

Stephen Arlington is an attorney with McClung, Peters, & Simon in Albany, New York.

Maryka Biaggio is on the Faculty at Pacific University.

Arlene Brownell is with International Learning Systems, Inc., in Golden, Colorado.

Richard Campbell is the Minister for the Scotia United Methodist Church in Scotia, New York.

Darlene DeFour is Associate Professor of Psychology at Hunter College, where she is also a member of the campus's Sexual Harassment Panel.

Louise Fitzgerald is on the faculty at the University of Illinois at Champaign-Urbana.

Dorothy O. Helly, a founding member of Hunter College's Sexual Harassment Panel, is Professor of History at Hunter College.

Fredda Jaffe is a family therapist in Seattle, Washington, who offers training on sexual harassment for victims and perpetrators.

Anne Levy is on the Faculty at the Eli Broad College of Business at Michigan State University.

Bernice Lott is Professor of Psychology and Women's Studies at the University of Rhode Island.

John Provost is Pastor of St. John the Evangelist Church in Schenectady, New York.

Kathryn Quina is on the Faculty in the Psychology Department at the University of Rhode Island.

Vita Rabinowitz is Associate Professor of Psychology at Hunter College.

Helen Remick is the Affirmative Action Officer at the University of Washington in Seattle.

Jan Salisbury is owner of Salisbury Consulting in Boise, Idaho, and offers consulting in team building and diversity as well as sexual harassment.

M. *Cynara Stites* is a Clinical Social Worker at the University of Connecticut Student Mental Health Service.

K.C. Wagner is Director of the Women and Work Institute of Cornell University's School of Industrial and Labor Relations.

Barbara Watts is Dean of the Law School at the University of Cincinnati.

Sue Rosenberg Zalk is the Ombudsperson at the City University of New York Graduate Center and a member of Hunter College's Sexual Harassment Panel.

Preface to the Second Edition

Since the publication of the first edition of *Ivory Power* in 1990, I have left academia full-time and started my own consulting firm in upstate New York that deals with education/training, policy development, grievance procedures development, and expert witness testimony in sexual harassment—both academic and workplace sexual harassment. Through this consulting work I have met hundreds of students, faculty, administrators, and university employees who have shared their experiences with sexual harassment—as victims, friends of victims, perpetrators, and individuals charged with investigating complaints of sexual harassment.

Throughout each of these aspects of my work I have been reminded of an experiment in social psychology to which I was introduced as an undergraduate and graduate student. The experiment, conducted by Solomon Asch in 1952, concerns social influence–how people alter the thoughts, feelings, and behavior of other people. In short, it is an experiment in conformity, of when we change our behavior in order to adhere to social norms. In Asch's experiment, a participant would enter a laboratory room with six people and be told the experiment concerns visual discrimination. The task was simple: Individuals were shown two cards. On the first card a single line was drawn. On the second, three lines were drawn and numbered 1, 2, 3. One of the three lines on this second card was the same length as the line on the first card. Participants were instructed to call out, one at a time, which of the three lines was the same length as the line on the first card. Unbeknownst to one of the seven individuals—the real participant in the study— the remaining six were confederates of the researcher and they had prearranged a number of incorrect responses. For example, five of these confederates would say "1" when the correct answer was "3." The question was, when confronted with five people responding with the objectively incorrect answer, would the participant conform to the erroneous group judgment or not conform? Asch reported that this experiment was a discomforting experience; individuals doubted their judgments, their discomfort was caused by the pressure to conform. Asch reported that 75 percent of participants went along with the crowd rather than assert what they knew to be the right answer.

I am reminded of this classic study when I provide education and training on sexual harassment for campuses, because it illustrates how sexual harassment can confront victims with perceptions that are often invalidated by those around them. And the more the woman—and it is predominantly women who are victims—seeks validation for her view about the events that have occurred to her, the more hostile and rejecting her world becomes, until she feels she is failing in her most important life roles.

Like the participants in the Asch study, most victims of sexual harassment come to doubt what they see with their own eyes; they are encouraged to conform to their professor's and classmates' erroneous perspectives. Because they have lower social status in the college's hierarchy, they are perceived as being more conformist, as being easier to push around.

Based on my work as a private consultant, I have seen the need for an updated version of *Ivory Power*. Certainly there has been updated case law, necessitating the need for a second edition. But there has also been considerable work published concerning how to train campuses, how to set up policy statements and effective grievance procedures—information that needs to be shared with campuses across the country. Since the first edition of *Ivory Power*, there has been increased attention devoted to a topic only touched upon lightly a few years ago, namely, "consensual relationships" between faculty and students. And, events in the last few years at Antioch College and the University of Virginia that have stimulated discussion of peer sexual harassment also make a second edition of *Ivory Power* necessary.

For this second edition, I invited the contributors to the first edition to update their chapters, focusing on new research, case law, and theory. Several of these colleagues have revised their chapters for this edition. I also invited new contributors to offer their unique perspectives on academic sexual harassment. I am most grateful that all of these individuals wanted to be part of the second edition. They all told me of the necessity to keep the issues surrounding academic sexual harassment central, in the forefront of campus life.

For this second edition, I also invited colleagues to write forewords emphasizing their own perspectives on sexual harassment on campuses. Most notable of these forewords are the ones written by clergy—one a Methodist, one a Roman Catholic, who are dealing with sexual harassment with their parishoners, offering spiritual counseling for victims of sexual harassment and their families. Through the graciousness of Fr. John Provost, Pastor of St. John the Evangelist Church in Schenectady, New York, I have begun to facilitate a support group on sexual harassment for students and employees. This support group meets in a lounge in the parish offices, easily accessible for individuals to use the chapel before and/or after the support group meeting. Since the first edition of *Ivory Power*, I have learned how important a spiritual focus is for many women who are dealing with sexual harassment at school and at work. This new focus of my work has also helped me to work with family and friends of victims of sexual harassment. Sexual harassment has a radiating impact and can thus affect the learning and working experiences of all women and men in an organization. This radiating impact must be considered in the development of policy statements as well as in future research on the effects of sexual harassment, issues addressed in this volume.

I have been very gratified by the response to the first edition of *Ivory Power*. It was meant for students to read—and in fact has been used as a textbook for classes in women's studies, violence, and the psychology of gender. The book was also meant to be used by administrators and faculty—and it has been seen as a resource book for individuals wanting to make changes in their campus's policy and procedures. All of the contributors to the first edition were most honored in 1992 when *Ivory Power* received the Gustavus Myers Center Award an Outstanding Book on Human Rights in the United States. This award made it possible for more and more students, faculty, and administrators to take note of the book and the issue in general. This far exceeded my hopes for the book.

The reader will note a change in the title for the second edition—I wanted to put the words *Sexual Harassment* up front, to label the behaviors as they should be labeled. I also wanted to keep the literary phrase *Ivory Power*. I thought it best to name what sexual harassment is on college campuses: an an abuse of the power that accompanies the role of a professor. Thus, the new title for the second edition: *Sexual Harassment on College Campuses: Abusing the Ivory Power.*

All of the chapters in this edition focus on changing the way campuses deal with sexual harassment rather than on changing victims' perceptions of their experiences with their professors and classmates. This is really the next step in dealing with sexual harassment on college campuses: to value students and to empower them.

Michele A. Paludi
Schenectady, New York
1995

Forewords to the Second Edition

Anne Levy
Michigan State University

No one can sit across the desk from a student who is reporting a case of sexual harassment by a professor and be untouched by the experience. Such students' devastation is real and intense. The feelings of self-doubt, loss of self-esteem, and guilt overwhelm any sense that they are the ones who have been wronged or that they are the victims of a most insidious kind of power play. They want it to end. They want it never to have happened. Most of all, the students want solutions from the person they have turned to, having identified her or him as the only one, perhaps, that they can still trust in their academic setting. Unfortunately, in academia the processes for solving a sexual harassment problem, once it has occurred, can be protracted, complex, and fraught with roadblocks, and the results are usually inadequate and unsatisfying. The answer to the problem, as is clear then, lies not in reactive remedies but in proactive programs to alert the educational community to the lessons that this book teaches so pointedly.

Academia usually deals with problems of professorial sexual harassment either too trivially ("Just say no ") or in ways that can only be seen as revictimizing an already traumatized innocent. The process for trying to rid the institution of a problem professor, for example, consumes a student's time, energy, and psyche for weeks, months, and even years, often with little or no resulting concrete change. Participating in dismissal-for-cause procedures is a chilling and eye-opening experience when sexual harassment is the charge. A professor, whose very position demands and implies a commitment to justice, fair play, and nurturance of the human spirit, when faced with dismissal for harassing behavior, can display behavior as vicious as any hardened criminal defendant: maneuvering, manipulating, making irrational charges of bias, and using every possible tactic, ethical or not, to try to "shake" the complainant's resolve to see the process through. During what one might once naively have imagined as a dignified hearing before a faculty panel committed to learning the truth, a "win at all costs" mentality clearly moves in and takes hold. The victim is assaulted with questions that have been banned even in criminal rape trials. What was the student's sexual history? Didn't the student, in fact, seek out this kind of attention? Isn't it true that the student's father was an alcoholic or that her or his mother didn't give her children enough attention? Doesn't the student, in fact, have a vendetta against all men? What is her problem? Doesn't she get enough? All of this plays out before a panel of faculty members ill prepared for these courtroom-style tactics, who finally appear to give up trying to determine what is fair, acceptable, required, or appropriate and begrudgingly allow the assault to play out to its bitter end.

And bitter is the end, especially for the victims, who are left feeling empty, violated, and confused about why they bothered. In the best-case scenario, the faculty member may be gone (after years of appeals and perhaps court proceedings), but so is much of the students' lives. Years of therapy and reconstructing what may have been a fragile self-esteem in the first place probably await them. The faculty member probably moves on to harass at another institution. In the worst-case scenario, the faculty member is slapped on the hand and continues at the university, making it almost impossible for the victims to stay also. Fearing meetings in hallways, dreading what might be said about them, anticipating retribution from others, they likely will leave, perhaps giving up on an institution that appears to have failed them. It is an ugly picture, at best.

Discipline, dismissal, and the remedies of the law are very ineffective ways to deal with sexual harassment. For handling some hard-core harassers, they are the only solutions, and only on the infrequent occasions when they work, but for most members of the academic community, education about the problem is the key to real change. If faculty members have been as carefully chosen for their ethical makeup as anyone in such a sensitive position of trust should be, comprehension of the problems that harassing behavior causes should result in far more appropriate perspective, attitude, and behavior. It is axiomatic, in an ethical community, that power should not be converted to one's own ends. Everyone in the institution must be sensitized to the fact that even the most "consensual" appearing situation may be just such an abuse: the use for self-gratification of authority (intended for other purposes) made possible by the mystique of a position of power and intellectual superiority.

It is effective policies, procedures, and education that will solve the sexual harassment problem in education. Let those in academia know what is expected of them and what is the true nature of harassing behavior. Educate those in positions of trust to comprehend the responsibility that trust brings with it and the consequences of an abuse of that trust. Make it clear that sexual harassment can not be tolerated in any institution committed to high ideals, and that an environment where learning truly takes place on an equal plane for all requires more than a "business as usual" attitude toward professor-student interactions. Then, and only then, will an educational community be truly free of the problem of sexual harassment.

This is where this book finds its important niche. Understanding the phenomenon and how it operates is the first, vital step in solving the sexual harassment problem in academia. Putting together policies and procedures for rooting it out is the second. Written by those who are well respected in academia, this book is part of a much-needed effort from within the institutions of learning to get those steps taken. As the contributors to this book make abundantly clear, the problem belongs to us all. The solution, as is also very clear, will come only with a universal commitment to stop the abuse of power and trust in our own learning communities. No one can sit back and claim that the responsibility belongs to another. It belongs to everyone who claims a role in the academic world.

Reverend Richard Campbell
Scotia United Methodist Church
Scotia, New York

Women have been mistreated in our society for a long time. Until relatively recently, few appreciated how widespread was the abuse. A number of widely publicized incidents involving high-profile persons has cured our "innocence"! On my desk is a cartoon that vividly depicts the "education" of America. The cartoon portrays a courtroom. President Clinton is in the defendant's chair. The jury box contains six readily identified caricatures—Justice Clarence Thomas, Senator Edward Kennedy, boxing champ Mike Tyson, actor-director Woody Allen, singer Michael Jackson, and car mechanic Joey Buttafuco. All were accused in notorious cases of sexual harassment or abuse of women (except Michael Jackson, whose alleged victim was a boy). The jury could also have included Dr. "Willie" Smith, Senator Robert Packwood, and the naval officers associated with the "Tailhook" episode! Now we have been staggered by the case of celebrity O.J. Simpson, who had engaged in domestic abuse. Tragic as all these events have been, and as regrettable as is the suffering inflicted, these incidents have raised public consciousness of the problem.

As a clergy person, I must admit that the church has not been immune. Painful experience has led my own congregation to develop a sexual harassment policy and procedure for paid and volunteer staff. This is how I became acquainted with the editor of this volume, Dr. Michele Paludi. Dr. Paludi provided a very helpful workshop for the staff of our church as well as the counseling and nursery staff who use our church facility. Later, she also provided clergy workshops for both an all-Methodist group and an interfaith group. She has widely studied the problem, and her analysis has resulted in great insight. She shares her knowledge with an unusual combination of candor and caring. We are all indebted to her for her writing, academic teaching at Union College, and her workshop leadership.

My own denomination, the Troy Conference of the United Methodist Church, adopted in June 1994 a comprehensive set of guidelines for misconduct by clergy, bishops, youth workers, choir directors, Sunday School teachers, etc. Little more than a week prior to that, newspapers printed the results of a study done by the Center for Women in Government of the University of Albany (N.Y.). The lead sentence in one article stated: "The number of sexual harassment charges filed in the state and nation has skyrocketed in the last three years and the cost of sexual harassment to the nation's employers has nearly doubled" (*Daily Gazette*, Schenectady, N.Y., 25 May 1994, by reporter Jill Bryce).

The mistreatment of in our society is, thankfully, "a cause whose time has come." Thanks to people like Michele Paludi, we are becoming informed and beginning to take long-needed remedial action!

Stephen Arlington
Albany, New York

Sexual harassment is—very simply stated—wrong! It is as wrong in the workplace or social setting as it is on the college campus or anywhere else. As with virtually all emerging social issues, society is coming to recognize that sexual harassment violates the basic tenets and expectations of a fair and rational social order. Far more importantly, however, is the fact that sexual harassment devastates people! Good, solid, productive human beings are crippled in their work and personal lives by being subjected to wholly unnecessary sexual harassment. Our social system has come to accept that "accidents happen." While we expect the responsible party to compensate the victim, we do not punish people for genuinely accidental occurrences. Sexual harassment is not an accident! It is concerted and willful, designed and perpetrated solely for the purpose of inflicting harm. It has no other basis or purpose, and can be excused for no rational reason. Society has long condemned and punished the infliction of intentional physical harm. It is well time that society apply the full force of its collective condemnation to sexual harassment.

As a practicing attorney I have represented the victims of sexual harassment. I have seen firsthand the horrible destructive impact sexual harassment can have on real people. These are people just like you and me, doing their best to get along in their lives and work—trying, however suits them best, to gain the highest quality of life possible for themselves. When the specter of sexual harassment is visited upon them, it is hardly different for them from contracting a horrible disease or being the victim of a terrible accident. All of the individuals' previous expectations for what life should be are altered or destroyed. The self-confidence that provided the bulwark of their ability to function is undermined, often to the point of collapse. They see themselves no longer as viable human beings, but rather as someone who "must have done something wrong" to bring this all about. You need not be a trained psychologist to recognize these manifestations. They are glaring, obvious, and incredibly devastating.

Our legal system is just beginning to recognize the insidious and destructive effects of sexual harassment. As with most evolving legal issues, there is a wide disparity between the various legislative bodies and courts as to what can or even should be done about it. Much of the problem has proven to be one of definition. What in fact constitutes sexual harassment? However, simply because the question does not lend itself to a simple answer does not mean that it should be ignored. We may stumble and even fall as we move forward to deal with this issue, but we must continue to deal with it aggressively.

At the same time as we move forward to define and root out sexual harassment, care must be exercised to maintain general societal support for the effort. If every unwanted advance is promptly labeled "sexual harassment" regardless of degree or whether it was intentional or inadvertent, overall credibility and support will be quickly lost. Care must be exercised by the professionals dealing with sexual harassment issues on a daily basis to ensure that the definition of sexual harassment remains narrow enough to gain general acceptance in society. Regardless of how strongly a particular professional may feel about the actual scope of sexual harassment, effort must always be exercised to keep the definition within boundaries that can gain general acceptance. If the overall support of society is lost, it will become virtually impossible to move forward against sexual harassment in the courts and legislatures.

Sexual harassment is an important issue that we can, and hopefully will, deal with successfully as a maturing society. Works such as Michele A. Paludi's *Sexual Harassment on College Campuses: Abusing the Ivory Power* make a significant contribution to understanding the problem and the possible avenues of resolution. Without the willingness of people such as Dr. Paludi to concentrate their focus and effort on the methodology and systems necessary to resolve specific sexual harassment instances, the collective understanding and resolution of the problem will continue to evade us.

Fr. John Provost
St. John the Evangelist Church
Schenectady, New York

Most writings that concern themselves with sexual harassment are much more than a desire to cash in on a popular cause—and they are certainly much more than an effort to be politically correct when it comes to sexual correctness. I believe they are grounded in the challenging attempt to address what is obviously an ethical and moral responsibility. They speak to the very basic threads that form the fabric of our American society—namely freedom and responsibility.

We hold our freedoms as sacred and we abhor limitations on those freedoms. Yet freedom has a responsibility to other as well as self.

In November of 1994, former British Prime Minister Margaret Thatcher, now Baroness Thatcher of Kesteven and a member of the British House of Lords, delivered the concluding lecture in Michigan's Hillsdale College's Center for Constructive Alternatives seminar, "God and Man: Perspectives on Christianity in the 20th Century." Lady Thatcher, who served as Britain's first female prime minister from 1979 to 1990, gave a lengthy examination of how the Judaeo-Christian tradition has provided the moral foundations of America and other nations in the West and contrasted their experience with that of the former Soviet Union.

Lady Thatcher began by saying that history has taught us that freedom cannot long survive unless it is based on moral foundations. For over two centuries Americans have held fast to their belief in freedom for all—"a belief," Lady Thatcher says, "that springs from their spiritual heritage." Our Constitution, John Adams wrote in 1789, was designed only for a moral and religious people. It is wholly inadequate for the government of any other.

The faith of America's founders affirmed the sanctity of each individual. Every human life—man or woman, child or adult, commoner or aristocrat, rich or poor—was equal in the eyes of the Lord. It also affirmed the responsibility of each individul. This was not a faith that allowed people to do whatever they wished, regardless of the consequences. The Ten Commandments, the injunction of Moses, the Sermon on the Mount, and the Golden Rule made Americans feel precious—and also accountable—for the way in which they used their God-given talents. Thus they shared a deep sense of obligation to one another. And, as years passed, they not only formed strong communities but devised laws that would protect individual freedom—laws that would eventually be enshrined in the Declaration of Independence and the Constitution.

Lady Thatcher stated in 1994 "The most important problems we have to face today are problems, ultimately, having to do with the moral foundations of society. There are people who eagerly accept their own freedom but do not respect the freedom of others—they want freedom from responsibility."

Lady Thatcher continues, "But if they accept freedom for themselves, they must respect the freedom of others. If they expect to go about their business unhindered and to be protected from violence, they must not hinder the business of or do violence to others." They would do well to look at what has happened to societies without moral foundations. Accepting no laws but the laws of force, these societies have been ruled by totalitarian ideologies.

Those who refuse to respect the freedom of others ultimately do violence to others—whether it be the horrendous violence of April 1995 in a senseless and cowardly bombing of a Federal Building in Oklahoma City as supremacists struck at the heart of American value and virtue or in the more traditional violences that take the form of racism and sexism or in the much more subtle violences of intolerance, neglect, abuse and harassment.

Those who do respect the freedom of others ultimately affirm the value of others. These are the people described by Lady Thatcher as the responsible—the virtuous who share a sense of obligation to the other. They know the value of protecting individual freedom. This is one reason why I believe freedom and its roots in the moral foundations of our society must speak of virtue and value.

William J. Bennett's book, *The Book of Virtues*, spent ten weeks on the Best Seller list. In it he appeals to something special in the American people. He suggests a superior truth about the American character: "Americans do not so much care about differences in culture or even in color . . . as they care about character as it is expressed in behavior. The American challenge now is not to pay homage to every cultural variation and appease every ethnic sensitivity but rather to encourage universally accepted ideals of behavior: self-discipline, compassion, responsibility, friendship, worth, courage, perseverance, honesty, loyalty and truth." Bennett is concerned that we have lost a sense of these virtues the undergird our freedom.

Lance Morrow, writing in Time magazine, states that Americans need to be repersuaded about the virtue of virtue. What are the chief virtues now? All those that Bennett lists, no doubt. But those he lists seem so blurred today. Traditional societies evolve virtues. Experience over generations teaches them which virtues are necessary.

Morrow concludes his Time essay by saying that virtue is active, responsible and inner directed. The atmosphere of our present culture encourages petulant passivity and other-directedness. His thoughts echo those of Bennett who states "Some of the most important virtues (self-discipline, courage, responsibility) require self-abnegation—and nothing is further from the spirit of an age that regards self-abnegation as an offense against self-fulfillment, that pervasive American pseudo virtue that took root in the idiot 60s and killed all the healthy plants with it." Shades of Lady Thatcher!

To cite a more recent lesson in the importance of moral foundations, we should listen to Czech President Vaclav Havel, who observed "In everyone there is some longing for humanity's rightful dignity, for moral integrity, and for a sense that transcends the world of existence."

Sexual Harassment on College Campuses: Abusing the Ivory Power explores these important principles, virtues and lessons on campus. The entire campus community, administration, faculty, and students, have a moral and ethical responsibility to value one another. They are to protect and cherish each other's freedom for, bound as a community, they share a sense of obligation to one another. Michele Paludi permeates her writing with a sensitivity that encourages us to respect and support the person—both the victim and the perpetrator. She supports counseling for the families involved and urges people to go beyond the incident to find healing. The underlying theme is that lives can be rebuilt and people can be healed. Rather than shun the harassed or the victim, seeing them as all bad or a problem, we are asked to remember our responsibility to them and to cherish virtues that preserve freedoms. She asks us not to view sexual harassment only in terms of monetary damage but to see it as a loss to an individual's freedom. The reader is asked not to return violence with violence but to ensure that the ways in which sexual harassment is addressed still values people and is virtuous, respecting the sanctity and dignity of each individual.

We are encouraged to live life to the fullest based on the moral foundations of our American society. This is a particularly challenging task and this book is not an effort to tell us how to live. It is, instead, an invitation to live virtuously the freedom that is cherished and protected by those original moral foundations that formed our American society. As Sarah Crichton wrote about our society in 1993, "Real life is messy, rife with misunderstandings and contradictions. There's no eight-page guide on how to handle it. There are no panels of mediators out there to turn to unless it truly gets bad. Those who are growing up in environments where they don't have to figure out what the rules should be, but need only follow what's been prescribed, are being robbed of the most important lesson there is to learn. And that's how to live."

This book hopefully energizes us to live faithful to freedom based on America's moral foundation—for this freedom will allow women and men to work together, to be educated, learn and grow together, to trust one another and to understand one another.

Part I

Sexual Harassment

Legal, Methodological, and Conceptual Issues

Editor's Notes

Pretend you have just arrived at your campus for your first year in your doctoral program. Upon your arrival in the department, you are met by a senior professor in the same department who shows considerable interest in your research. You are flattered by his interest and agree to discuss your work over lunch in the faculty dining room. After a few lunches where the conversation is general and social rather than focused on professional issues, you find that he is touching you—rubbing, his knees against yours, placing his hand on your back and arms, and once patting you on the bottom. He asks you to meet him for early dinners off-campus. You decline, offering various excuses, and try to maintain a polite but distant tone in your conversations with him. One day he asks you to come into his office to discuss your obtaining a teaching fellowship to help offset your tuition. Once you are inside the office, he closes the door, moves toward you, and puts his arms around you. You try to push him away but he holds you tighter and tries to kiss you. There is a knock on the door, he releases you, and you open the door and hurry out of the office.

Is this sexual harassment? Why or why not?

If you believe this is sexual harassment, when did the harassment begin?

Does the professor have a responsibility (moral, legal, professional, or otherwise) to behave differently? Explain.

Do you have a responsibility to behave differently? Explain.

How did you answer these questions? Do you believe sexual harassment occurred between the faculty member and graduate student? Most professors and students to whom I show this scenario agree that sexual harassment occurred. When I ask the second question: When did the harassment began, I receive many answers. Most women report the harassment began at the beginning, when the faculty member started to ask the student out for lunch.

Most men, on the other hand, believe the sexual harassment began when the faculty member had the student cornered in his office. And when I ask individuals to pretend the graduate student is themselves, I obtain very few answers about what to do about the behavior that occurred. However, when I ask individuals to pretend the graduate student is someone other than themselves, I usually compile a very long list of suggested alternatives for behavior for both the professor and the graduate student.

The use of this scenario, adapted from Paludi and Barickman (1991), illustrates how much confusion exists because of individuals' lack of a clear, concise, widely accepted definition of academic sexual harassment. Definitions of sexual harassment are important because they educate the college campus and promote discussion and conscientious evaluation of experiences. Most students and faculty still cling to the myth that unless there has been a sexual assault, there hasn't been sexual harassment. Yet, as Barbara Watts discusses in chapter 1, on legal issues, sexual harassment includes behaviors far more pervasive than sexual assault. In fact, most women victims of sexual harassment experience behaviors that may never involve touching. As Barbara Watts and Louise Fitzgerald point out, there are two components of the legal definition of sexual harassment: *quid pro quo* and hostile environment.

Quid pro quo sexual harassment involves some direct sexual negotiation: getting a reward for complying with the sexual requests of a faculty member or being punished for failing to comply with the faculty member's sexual demands. Hostile environment sexual harassment involves an atmosphere that is created in the college classroom, faculty dining room, science laboratory, or dorm that is perceived by an individual to be hostile, offensive and intimidating.

Thus, sexual harassment takes many forms—from sexist remarks and covert physical contact (patting, brushing against their bodies) to blatant propositions and sexual assaults. Researchers have developed five categories to encompass the range of sexual harassment, as discussed by Louise Fitzgerald in chapter 2: *gender harassment, seductive behavior, sexual bribery, sexual coercion, and sexual imposition.* These levels of sexual harassment correlate with legal definitions of sexual harassment. *Gender harassment* consists of generalized sexist remarks and behavior designed not to elicit sexual cooperation but rather to convey insulting, degrading, or sexist attitudes about women. *Seductive behavior* is unwanted, inappropriate, and offensive sexual advances. *Sexual bribery* is the solicitation of sexual activity or other sex-linked behavior by promise of reward. *Sexual coercion* is the solicitation of sexual activity by threat of punishment, and *sexual imposition* includes gross sexual imposition, assault, and rape.

Sexual harassment is clearly prohibited within the college/university system as a form of sexual discrimination, under both Title IX of the 1972

Education Amendments (and, for employees, Title VII of the 1964 Civil Rights Act). Sexual harassment involves the confluence of authority (power) relations and sexuality (or sexism) in a culture stratified by sex. This power or authority is either formal or informal; it can be achieved or ascribed. Formal power is derived from a formal role (e.g., research supervisor, professor, graduate teaching assistant, mentor). Informal power is derived from men's sexual prerogative. Informal power thus suggests that men have a right to initiate sexual interactions or assert the primacy of women's gender role (and or race, class, age, and sexual orientation) over her role as student.

Professors are particularly powerful for certain student groups such as

a. Women of color, especially those with "token" status
b. Graduate students, whose future careers are often determined by their association with a particular faculty member
c. Students in small colleges or small academic departments, where the number of faculty available to students is quite small
d. Students in male-populated fields, such as engineering
e. Students who are economically disadvantaged and work part-time or full-time while attending classes

Thus, the structure of the academy interacts with psychological dynamics to increase women's vulnerability to all forms of sexual harassment. Professors' greatest power lies in the capacity to enhance or diminish students' self-esteem. This power can motivate students to learn course material or convince them to give up. The tone and content of the student-professor interaction is especially important. Is the student encouraged or put down? Do the faculty members use their knowledge to let students know how "stupid" they are or to challenge their thinking?. As Zalk, Paludi, and Dederick (1991) point out, This is *real power*.

Dziech and Weiner (1984) reported that 30 percent of undergraduate women suffer sexual harassment from at least one of their instructors during their four years of college. When definitions of sexual harassment include sexist remarks and other forms of "gender harassment," the incidence rate in undergraduate populations nears 70 percent. Research by Adams, Kottke, and Padgitt (1983) reported that 13 percent of the women students they surveyed said they had avoided taking a class or working with certain professors because of the risk of being subjected to sexual advances. A 1983 study conducted at Harvard University indicated that 15 percent of the graduate students and 12 percent of the undergraduate students who had been harassed by their professors changed their major or educational program because of the harassment. Wilson and Kraus (1983) reported that 9 percent of the female undergraduates in their study had been pinched, touched, or patted to the point of personal discomfort, while 17 percent of the women in the Adams et al. survey received verbal sexual advances, 14 pecent received sexual invitations, 6 percent had been subjected to physical advances, and 2 percent direct sexual bribes.

Bailey and Richards (1985) reported that of 246 women graduate students in their sample, 13 percent indicated they had been sexually harassed, 21 percent had not enrolled in a course to avoid such behavior and 16 percent indicated they had been directly assaulted. Bond (1988) reported that 75 percent of the 229 women members of Division 27 who responded to her survey experienced jokes with sexual themes during their graduate training, 69 percent were subjected to sexist comments demeaning to women, and 58 percent reported experiencing sexist remarks about their clothing, body, or sexual activities.

Research in progress by Paludi, DeFour, and Roberts (1994) suggests that the incidence of academic sexual harassment of ethnic minority women is even greater than that reported with white women. In chapter 3, Darlene DeFour suggests that ethnic minority women are more vulnerable to receiving sexual attention from professors. Ethnic minority women are subject to stereotypes about sex, viewed as mysterious, and less sure of themselves in the academy. Thus, although all women students are vulnerable to some degree, male faculty tend to select those who are most vulnerable and needy. As Tong (1984) commented, "sexual harassers tend to take advantage of those whom they perceive as most vulnerable, and whether we care to face it or not, Black women enflesh the vulnerability of their people's slave past" (165).

This form of interpersonal discrimination is also addressed in this volume by Bernice Lott. She describes empirical work as well as theoretical positions on ways women students, employees, and faculty on college campuses—are silenced by those in power in the academy. Viewing these distancing behaviors as a form of gender harassment and homophobia, Lott calls for campus task forces to include programs on feelings, cognitions, and actions involved in this type of sexist and homophobic behavior.

As each of the contributors to Part I discusses, sexual harassment is thus a major form of victimization of women in our system of higher education, even though it is still largely a "hidden issue" (as the Project on the Status and Education of Women called it in 1978). All of the contributors suggest that, rather than changing the level of analysis from the systemic to the individual, as is frequently done by researchers, it is important to pursue an organizational or institutional level of analysis to explain the prevalence of sexual harassment, and to recognize more explicitly the contexts within which harassment is more likely to occur, to avoid victim blame.

References

Adams, J., Kottke, J., and Padgitt, J. (1983). Sexual harassment of university students. *Journal of College Student Personnel, 24* 484–90.

Bailey, N., and Richards, M. (1985, August). *Tarnishing the ivory tower: Sexual harassment in graduate training programs in psychology.* Paper presented at the annual meeting of the American Psychological Association, Los Angeles.

Bond, M. (1988). Division 27 sexual harassment survey: Definition, impact, and environmental context. *Community Psychologist, 21,* 7–10.

Dziech, B., and Weiner, L. (1984). *The lecherous professor.* Boston: Beacon Press.

Paludi, M.A., and Barickman, R.B. (1991). *Academic and workplace sexual harassment: A manual of resources.* Albany: State University of New York Press.

Paludi, M.A., DeFour, D.C., and Roberts, R. (1994). *Academic sexual harassment of ethnic minority women.* Research in progress.

Tong, R. (1984). *Women, sex, and the law.* Totowa: Rowman and Allanheld.

Wilson, K., and Krauss, L. (1983). Sexual harassment in the university. *Journal of College Student Personnel, 24,* 219–24.

Zalk, S.R., Paludi, M.A., and Dederich, J. (1991). Ivory power revisited: Women's consensual relationships with male faculty. In M.A. Paludi and R.B. Barickman, *Academic and workplace sexual harassment: A manual of resources.* Albany: State University of New York Press.

1

Legal Issues

Barbara Watts

Two federal statutes apply to sexual harassment in higher education: Title VII of the Civil Rights Act of 1964[1] and Title IX of the Higher Education Amendments of 1972.[2] In recent years, several significant and encouraging developments have occurred in both case law and federal legislation applicable to sexual harassment. In 1993, the United States Supreme Court, decided *Harris v. Forklift Systems, Inc.,*[3] which clarified that a Title VII plaintiff claiming hostile or offensive work environment sexual harassment need not prove severe psychological damage to establish her right to recovery. Another Supreme Court case, *Franklin v. Gwinnett County Public Schools,*[4] established that a sexual harassment victim can recover money damages in a suit brought under Title IX. The Civil Rights Act of 1991[5] makes compensatory and punitive damages available to Title VII plaintiffs claiming intentional discrimination and accords them the right to a jury trial.

Lingering unresolved legal issues include the need for a clearer definition of the circumstances under which an institution can be held liable for co-worker harassment of employees and peer harassment of students. Also, some First Amendment issues have emerged in connection with claims of sexual harassment where the offensive conduct is exclusively verbal or involves displays of pornographic materials in the workplace.

In this chapter, the law under Title VII is discussed first and at some length. Many more harassment cases have been decided under Title VII, partly because it has been in effect longer and partly because, until recently, the incentives to pursue a private action were much better under Title VII than under Title IX.

THE UNIVERSITY AS EMPLOYER:
LIABILITY UNDER TITLE VII FOR SEXUAL HARASSMENT
OF FACULTY, ADMINISTRATORS AND STAFF

Title VII addresses the educational institution in its role as employer
and prohibits discrimination based upon sex in the terms, conditions, and
privileges of employment.

Several important federal cases interpret and define sexual harassment
as discrimination in employment. Though none of them was decided in the
context of an educational institution, the principles they stand for are
nevertheless relevant to harassment of a college or university employee.

Williams v. Saxbe,[6] decided in 1976, was the first federal court case in
which sexual harassment was found to be a form of illegal sex discrimination
under Title VII. Prior to that, even though Title VII had been in effect for
more than ten years, courts said that sexual harassment was merely disharmony
in a personal relationship (*Barnes v. Train*),[7] the result of personal urges of
individuals, not part of company policy (*Corne v. Bausch and Lomb, Inc.*).[8] The
courts justified their decisions, too, by suggesting that if women could sue
for amorous advances, ten times more federal judges would be necessary to
handle the upsurge in litigation (*Miller v. Bank of America,*[9] *Tomkins v. Public
Service Electric and Gas Co.*).[10]

In 1976, however, the District Court for the District of Columbia found
that Dianne Williams was the victim of sex discrimination based upon the
job-related punishment her Department of Justice supervisor inflicted after
she refused his sexual advances. This was the first in a line of cases accepting
the *quid pro quo* definition of sexual harassment.

In a *quid pro quo* case, the employer or the employer's agent expressly
or implicitly ties a "term, condition, or privilege of employment" to the
response of the employee to unwelcome sexual advances. The Equal Employment Opportunity Commission (EEOC), the governmental agency charged
with enforcement of Title VII, has published guidelines that define this type
of sexual harassment as

> unwelcome sexual advances, requests for sexual favors, and other verbal
> or physical conduct of a sexual nature . . . when (1) submission to such
> conduct is made either explicitly or implictly a term or condition of
> an individual's employment, or (2) submission to or rejection of such
> conduct by an individual is used as the basis for employment decisions
> affecting such individual.[11]

Failure to receive a promotion, failure to be assigned preferred working
hours, or retaliatory behavior, such as unjustifiably negative employment
evaluations or elimination of job duties, are an important part of the evidence

the employee must present to prove *quid pro quo* harassment. In *Barnes v. Costle*,[12] for example, the employee's job was eliminated after she refused her supervisor's sexual approaches.

An originally troublesome aspect of this type of case was the argument that an employer should not be liable if it knew nothing of the harassing behavior perpetrated, even by a supervisory employee. Fortunately, in 1986 the U.S. Supreme Court put this argument to rest. In *Meritor Savings Bank v. Vinson*,[13] discussed in further detail below, the Court strongly suggested that *quid pro quo* harassment of an employee by a supervisor results in automatic liability of the employer. This means that in *quid pro quo* cases, a victim can win her case without showing that her employer knew or should have known, or approved of the supervisor's unwelcome actions.

One element crucial to an employee's *quid pro quo* case is the loss of a tangible benefit of employment. Often, however, no such loss accompanies the harassing conduct. Another line of cases is therefore equally important to the definition of sexual harassment as unlawful sex discrimination by an employer under Title VII. *Bundy v. Jackson*[14] was the first case to hold that sexual harassment could exist without the loss of a tangible job benefit. This type of sexual harassment is called offensive or hostile environment harassment, defined by the EEOC guidelines as

> Sexual advances, requests for sexual favors, and other verbal or physical conduct of a sexual nature . . . when such conduct has the purpose or effect of unreasonably interfering with an individual's work performance or creating an intimidating, hostile, or offensive working environment.[15]

The EEOC guidelines recommend automatic liability for the employer in offensive environment harassment cases, but federal courts deciding offensive environment cases have not always followed the guidelines.

One important case, *Henson v. City of Dundee*,[16] said that an employee could not establish offensive environment harassment against her employer unless the employer knew or should have known of the intimidating, hostile, or offensive work environment. Other circuit courts found the reasoning in *Henson* persuasive (*Katz v. Dole*).[17] Adopting the EEOC position that the employer should be automatically liable were the D.C. Circuit Court in *Vinson v. Taylor*[18] and the District Court for Alaska (*Jeppsen v. Wunnike*).[19] When the United States Supreme Court agreed to hear an appeal of *Vinson v. Taylor*, advocates for both employees and employers hoped the Court would clarify the confusion about the standard of liability for an employer.

Reviewed under the name *Meritor Savings Bank v. Vinson*,[20] the case established important precedent for the proposition that an offensive work environment constitutes sexual harassment where the offensiveness is severe and pervasive.

Meritor did not, however, clearly resolve the important question of which theory of employer liability should be used in a hostile environment case. Writing for the majority, Chief Justice Rehnquist said that "general principles of agency" should apply.

He first explained that in a *quid pro quo* case involving a supervisor, the supervisor exercises authority given him by the employer when he makes or threatens to make decisions concerning the employment circumstances of the harassment victim. His actions are thus properly charged to the employer, resulting in automatic employer liability. Rehnquist went on to say that Title VII should not be read to hold employers to this same standard in offensive environment cases where the employer is typically unaware of the harassing conduct. It cannot be assumed that the harassing employee is acting with the authority of the employer when he engages in the harassing behavior that creates the hostile environment but is unrelated to tangible job benefits. The Court seemed to indicate that the employer should not be liable unless the victim could show that the harassing employee was acting in this role as agent of the employer.

Meritor was the first Supreme Court decision on sexual harassment and provided guidance to employers in three respects:

In-house grievance procedures. Although the automatic standard for offensive harassment was discarded, the Court did indicate that the employer is not "insulated" from liability by the mere existence of a procedure, a policy against discrimination, and the failure of the harassed employee to come forward. In his opinion, Rehnquist implied that if the employer's procedure properly informs employees that it will promptly investigate and resolve sexual harassment complaints, and if the procedures encourage victims to come forward, then an employer *might* avoid liability for offensive environment sexual harassment.

EEOC guidelines. The Court concluded unanimously that both *quid pro quo* and offensive environment harassment constitute illegal sex discrimination under Title VII, citing with approval the definitions in the EEOC guidelines. That the Court gave its blessing to these definitions increased their value to institutions preparing sexual harassment policy statements and to the lower courts in deciding other cases of sexual harassment, not only under Title VII, but also under state statutes addressing sexual harassment, or under Title IX.[21]

Evidence on the issue of welcomeness. There is an emphasis in the EEOC definitions of harassment on whether the behavior of the harasser is "welcome." The circuit court in the *Meritor* case had ruled that evidence of the victim's provocative dress and sexual fantasies was not relevant to the question of welcomeness. Unfortunately, the Supreme Court disagreed, stating expressly that in a hostile environment case, there must be an evaluation of the totality of the circumstances, including evidence concerning the victim's dress, speech, and actions. This aspect of the decision is reminiscent of a not-long-bygone day when victims of rape were accused of inviting attack by their behavior and dress. The Court's indication that the harasser and his employer may present such evidence has undoubtedly discouraged victims of harassment from coming forward.

The *Meritor* opinion left open a number of questions regarding hostile environment sexual harassment. In an effort to define with more specificity the circumstances under which a working environment was sufficiently replete with harassing behavior severe and pervasive enough to alter an employee's working conditions, federal appellate courts focused on the psychological harm to the employee victim; some of these courts held that unless the plaintiff's psychological well-being was seriously affected, no claim existed under Title VII.[22] Other courts rejected such a requirement.[23] This conflict in Title VII interpretation was resolved by the Supreme Court's 1993 decision in *Harris v. Forklift Systems, Inc.*[24] In an opinion written by Justice Sandra Day O'Connor, the Court held unanimously that tangible psychological harm is not a required element of a hostile environment sexual harassment claim under Title VII. The Court reiterated that, instead, to determine whether an environment is hostile requires looking at the totality of the circumstances.

> These may include the frequency of the discriminatory conduct; its severity; whether it is physically threatening or humiliating, or a mere offensive utterance, and whether it unreasonably interferes with an employee's work performance. . . . [P]sychological harm, like any other relevant factor, may be taken into account, [but] no single factor is required.[25]

Justice O'Connor observed that the purpose of Title VII, to establish workplace equality, is met only if "Title VII comes into play before the harassing conduct leads to a nervous breakdown."[26] She pointed out that a "discriminatorily abusive work environment, even one that does not seriously affect employees' psychological well-being, can and often will detract from employees' job performance, discourage employees from remaining on the job, or keep them from advancing in their careers."[27]

Another issue addressed by the *Harris* case was whether the conduct alleged to create the hostile environment should be judged from an "objective" or a "subjective" point of view. Using an objective standard requires a court to ask whether a reasonable person would find the environment abusive; the subjective standard inquires whether the victims reasonably or unreasonably— found the environment abusive.

The Ninth Circuit Court in *Ellison v. Brady*[28] had posited a "reasonable woman" standard that received considerable attention from legal experts.[29] The court's point was that conduct that men would find acceptable may be objectionable to women. The court's concern was that the reasonable-person standard seems to incorporate too much of male-oriented popular culture and stereotypically sexist attitudes into the determination of whether behavior is objectively welcome, or severe, or offensive. The law of sexual harassment addresses the elimination of sexist behaviors from employment settings. Asking whether a reasonable person would find the conduct harassing risks reinforcing the prevailing level of discrimination because the reasonable person in law has frequently assumed a stereotypically male point of view. "In evaluating the severity and pervasiveness of sexual harassment we should focus on the perspective of the victim,"[30] concluded the court.

The Supreme Court in *Harris* articulated an objective/subjective standard without commenting on the "reasonable woman" rational of the *Ellison* case. Under the standard articulated by Justice O'Connor, there are two relevant questions: Would a reasonable person find the environment hostile? and Did the victim subjectively find the environment hostile?

The *Harris* opinion does not define further the situations in which an employer may be held liable for the harassing behavior of its employees, because that issue was not presented by the facts of the case.

Title VII and the law of sexual harassment in the workplace apply to institutions of higher education.[31] Therefore, under *Meritor*, administrators and managers who have supervisory roles vis-à-vis other institutional employees expose their institutions to automatic liability if they engage in *quid pro quo* harassing activities. It is less clear that liability results where the administrator or manager is responsible for creating a hostile work environment, though if he were in some way acting as agent of the institution in his harassing activity, the institution would be liable.[32]

One area in which the Supreme Court's decisions provide little guidance is harassment by a co-worker. An employee would have a difficult time making a case of *quid pro quo* harassment, because a co-worker is not typically in a position of power, and therefore not in a position to offer the bargain in an expressed or implied way. In that more commonly encountered situation where the offensive work environment is created by a co-worker, no automatic institutional liability attaches; a court deciding such a case would probably look to the institution's knowledge of the existence of the harassing situation and find the institution liable for offensive environment harassment if the victim had complained of the harassment to a supervisor or if offensive behavior were pervasive and sustained over a period of time, such that the institution must have been aware of it. The institution, if it *is* aware of the harassing conduct, may be able to avoid liability by taking immediate action to eliminate the offensive conduct.[33] At the least, Rehnquist in *Meritor* gave clear instruction that colleges and universities as employers cannot avoid liability by ignoring the problem. The absence of clear, effective, and well-publicized procedures that encourage victims to report harassment, as well as grievance procedures for following up on reported instances of harassment, may lead to institutional liability.

As originally enacted, Title VII enabled a victim of sexual harassment to recover economic damages, such as back pay, lost wages, and benefits, and also to receive injunctive relief (i.e., a court order that the offensive behavior stop). One type of remedy that was not available was monetary damages for mental suffering and emotional upset. Title VII sexual harassment cases would often, therefore, combine an action under the federal statute with an action under state common law in the tort area, which would allow for these damages.

Since the Civil Rights Act of 1991, victims of sexual harassment have be allowed to recover both compensatory and punitive damages in cases in which discriminatory behavior is intentional.[34] Compensatory damages, which may be awarded for pain, suffering, and emotion upset, as well as future financial losses, plus punitive damages where they are awarded, are capped at different levels, depending on the size of the employer's operation.[35] The addition of compensatory damages to the list of remedies for Title VII plaintiffs appears to be a direct response to the plight of sexual harassment victims whose remedies for hostile environment sexual harassment were limited to an injunction and attorneys fees.[36]

The Civil Rights Act also permits a Title VII victim to demand a jury trial if she is asking for compensatory and punitive damages. Since the act was passed, one lingering issue has been its applicability to lawsuits filed before its effective date, 21 November 1991. In *Landgraff v. U.S.I. Film Products*,[37] the Supreme Court held, in a Title VII action for sexual harassment, that the provisions of the Civil Rights Act authorizing compensatory and punitive damages, and creating the right to a jury trial in such cases, do not cover a case pending on appeal on the act's effective date.

THE UNIVERSITY AS EMPLOYER: LIABILITY UNDER TITLE IX FOR SEXUAL HARASSMENT

Title IX as a remedy for discrimination of an employee of an institution of higher education has a mixed history. Several recent legal developments may bring Title IX to the forefront for employees who experience sexual harassment in colleges and universities.

Title IX of the Education Amendments of 1972[38] was passed to prohibit sex discrimination in higher education. Enforced by the Office for Civil Rights (OCR) of the U.S. Department of Education, Title IX states that "no person in the United States shall, on the basis of sex, be excluded from participation in, be denied the benefits of, or be subjected to discrimination under any educational program or activity receiving Federal financial assistance." The sanction threatened against an institution found in violation of Title IX is withdrawal of federal funds.

Under Title IX regulations, institutions receiving federal finds must establish a procedure through which victims of sex discrimination can complain, but the victim may also go directly to the OCR, if she prefers, with no obligation first to work through to completion the institutional process. The OCR may seek termination of the institution's federal funding if the complaint is valid and cannot be resolved informally.

In 1979, the Supreme Court held that an individual could also bring a private lawsuit directly against an educational institution for violation of Title IX (*Connon v. University of Chicago*).[39] In 1982, in *North Haven Board of Education v. Belt*,[40] the Court approved regulations promulgated under the Act that indicated that Title IX protects not only students, but also employees of educational institutions. Combined, these two cases should have enabled educational employees to sue their institutions directly for sex discrimination in employment, which would have included, presumably, sexual harassment. The OCR has no regulations[41] like the EEOC Title VII guidelines that define sexual harassment, but by that time *Alexander b. Yale*[42] had been decided, holding that the definition of sex discrimination under Title IX includes sexual harassment.

In 1984, however, the Court decided *Grove City College v. Belt*,[43] which had the effect of narrowing the interpretation of Title IX so that its prohibitions were deemed "program specific." In *Walters v. President and Fellows of Harvard College*,[44] the District Court for Massachusetts, following the *Grove City College* precedent, held that a custodial worker could not recover for sexual harassment under Title IX. Although Title IX does protect employees from sex discrimination, including sexual harassment, the position held by the employee was not directly enough related to the delivery of educational services and was not in a *specific* educational program or activity receiving federal funds.

The Civil Rights Restoration Act, passed in March 1988,[45] overruled the "program specific" requirements of *Grove City College*. Under this act, if any program of an educational institution receives federal funds, then the entire operation of the institution is subject to the requirements of Title IX.

A 1985 Supreme Court case interpreting a law with wording similar to Title IX, *Atascadero State Hospital v. Scanlon*,[46] construing the Rehabilitation Act of 1973, also limited the reach of Title IX.

In *Atascadero*, the Supreme Court held that a private suit could not be filed against a state institution unless the state expressly waived its immunity from suit granted by the Eleventh Amendment of the U.S. Constitution. Because of the similarity between the Rehabilitation Act and Title IX, this case was thought to prevent employees working at state-funded institutions of higher education from bringing suit against those institutions under Title IX for sex discrimination, including harassment. Given the significant number of state-funded institutions, this posed a real barrier to many institutional employees. Once again, Congress stepped in to counteract the narrowing of Title IX coverage by the Supreme Court. The Civil Rights Remedies Equalization Amendment[17] eliminated the states' Eleventh Amendment immunity as a defense to a plaintiff's suit under Title IX, thus reexposing state-funded institutions to liability for violations of Title IX.

Today, with help from Congress, a person suing under Title IX for harassment need no longer be concerned with the program-specific limitations of *Grove City College* or the Eleventh Amendment limitations of *Atascadero*.

Furthermore, following the Supreme Court's decision in *Franklin v. Gwinnett County Public Schoo.s*,[48] the remedies available to a Title IX plaintiff now include money damages. Prior to *Franklin*, the only remedy specified by Title IX was withdrawal of federal funding from the institution, which seemed inadequate compensation for an individual plaintiff. With monetary damages for emotional distress recoverable, individual incentives for pursuing private litigation under Title IX have increased. The winning Title IV plaintiff may be awarded monetary damages and attorneys fees, and may threaten an institution even more than a Title VII lawsuit because federal funding can be withdrawn from institutions under Title IX.

Yet to be decided definitively is whether the substantive standards that have evolved under Title VII sexual harassment litigation will be applied to cases decided under Title IX. In a case brought by a medical surgical resident against the University of Puerto Rico,[49] the first circuit court of appeals reviewed the legislative history of Title IX and previously decided cases and found that Congress intended substantive standards developed under Title VII to apply to Title IX employment cases. Although the Supreme Court has not been presented with an appropriate case for deciding this issue, it seems that the rationale that underlies the standards for determining when sexual harassment amounts to sex discrimination in an Title VII employment context is equally applicable to the same determination in the Title IX employment context.

In the final analysis, the many limitations that previously inhibited private complaints under Title IX have been overcome, and Title IX has become an effective companion to Title VII for combating sexual harassment of an employee of a college or university.

THE UNIVERSITY AS EDUCATOR: LIABILITY UNDER
TITLE IX FOR SEXUAL HARASSMENT OF STUDENTS

Although educational employees may bring suit under either Title VII, Title IX, or both, for students who experience sexual harassment, Title IX provides the only federal remedy. Few students have brought sexual harassment actions under Title IX, probably for reasons having to do both with the student circumstance and with the nature of the relief that until recently has been available. Students are transient members of the institutional community; they have little to gain personally by reform. Further, litigation takes a long time; it is not unusual for a student's case to be moot because she graduated before it was heard. Students are also inhibited by the perception that the institution will defend the accused harasser. Reprisals may come from peers; sexual harassment is somewhat like rape in that the victim may find herself stigmatized because she brought the charge.[50] Until *Franklin v. Gwinnett County Public Schools*, the relief available—the withdrawal of federal funds from the institutions—provided little satisfaction and no financial compensation to a student suffering the mental and emotional distress caused by sexual harassment.

Despite this discouraging picture, some few early Title IX cases articulate the law with respect to harassment of students. In *Alexander v. Yale*[51] the Second Circuit court of Appeals, affirming the lower courts' decision, approved the action of a student victim of *quid pro quo* harassment. The student alleged that she received a low grade in a course because she rejected her professor's proposition for an A in exchange for "sexual demands." The court cited a Title VII case, *Barnes v. Costle*,[52] for the principle that conditioning academic advancement on sexual demands is sex discrimination, just as is conditioning employment advancement on such demands.

The same court, however, dismissed claims by a male faculty member that he was unable to teach in the atmosphere of distrust created by faculty harassing women students. The court also dismissed the claim of a student that she suffered distress because of harassing activity directed toward another woman student.

None of the plaintiffs in *Alexander v. Yale* tried to make a claim of hostile environment sexual harassment, and the development of substantive standards for determining when hostile environment sexual harassment is sex discrimination of a student in violation of Title IX is still a challenge on the legal horizon. To date only a few lower courts have looked at this issue, none definitively.

In 1985, a Pennsylvania district court decided *Moire v. Temple University School of Medicine*,[53] a case in which a medical student did make such a claim. Although the court found that the student did not prove her particular case, it recognized that an "abusive" environment is sexual harassment under Title IX. The court accepted the EEOC Title VII guidelines as "equally applicable" to Title IX and said that "[h]arassment from abusive environment occurs where multiple incidents of offensive conduct lead to an environment violative of a victim's civil rights."[54]

By contrast, in 1989 a different Pennsylvania district court said that Title IX reaches *quid pro quo* harassment but not hostile environment harassment. The plaintiff urged the courts to adopt for Title IX purposes the hostile environment theory of harassment developed under Title VII, but the court refused to do so.[55] On appeal the case was affirmed, but on grounds unrelated to the substantive coverage the district court accorded Title IX. The circuit court recognized the importance of the issue presented, but expressly refused to decide "whether the evidence of a hostile environment is sufficient to sustain a claim of sexual discrimination in education in violation of Title IX."

The Supreme Court all but put this issue to rest in *Franklin v. Gwinnett County Public Schools.* There, the Court cited the *Meritor* case and analogized a student's relationship to a teacher to an employee's relationship to her supervisor. The Court said:

> [W]hen a supervisor sexually harasses a subordinate because of the subordinate's sex, that supervisor 'discriminates' on the basis of sex, *Meritor Saving Bank v. Vinson* [citation omitted]. We believe the same rule should apply when a teacher sexually harasses and abuses a student.[56]

Having cited *Meritor*, a Title VII hostile environment case, with approval in this Title IX case, the Supreme Court appears to signal that the case law developed under Title VII is an appropriate guide as courts develop sexual harassment definitional standards under Title IX. Several student sexual harassment cases have been decided under Title IX since the *Franklin* decision; they have all been brought against secondary schools, and the results have been mixed. It is becoming increasingly important for the OCR to issue guidelines on sexual harassment to provide guidance to institutions seeking to comply with the requirements of Title IX and to bring some consistency to the court decisions addressing the issue.[57]

As courts develop the standard of liability of the educational institution for offensive environment harassment, the special nature of the enterprise should be considered. A student expects her college or university to provide an environment that promotes learning, or at least one that does not hinder it. The student is relatively powerless in almost every relationship she experiences with faculty, teaching assistants, and administrators. Because sexual harassment occurs "in the context of relationship of unequal power," the student is especially vulnerable. Given the damaging effect harassment can have on the educational environment, it would not be unreasonable for courts to hold institutions of higher education to a more demanding standard of liability in a case where the victim of harassment is a student, rather than an employee. Thus, while in *Meritor* the Court stopped short of holding the employer automatically liable to an employee in a Title VII offensive environment case, it might be argued that automatic liability of the institution is appropriate in a Title IX offensive environment case where the victim was a student harassed by a member of the faculty or staff in a position to influence that student's future.

There are few legal guideposts where a student is sexually harassed by another student. However, Rehnquist's comments in *Meritor* concerning policies and procedures may enlighten the area somewhat. While institutional liability would not be automatic, no college or university can safely ignore any complaint of harassment, whether by faculty, staff, or fellow students. If the institution knows of the harassment and does nothing, the possibility of liability increases. Strong policies and effective grievance procedures, both well publicized to encourage students to report instances or patterns of harassment, are crucial.

Two remaining issues arise that institutions must address to deal effectively with the sexual harassment of students.

It is unrealistic and unfair, and probably counter to Rehnquist's admonishments about effective procedures that encourage victims to come forward, to expect the student victim to represent herself in the grievance proceedings or to hire a private attorney to represent her and prosecute the case. On the other hand, if the institution vigorously prosecutes those accused of harassment through the in-house grievance channels and makes a good argument on behalf of the victim against the accused, might not the student victim use that very same argument against the institution in a federal lawsuit under Title IX? The answer is yes, though the institution should be able to avoid liability by showing that, as soon as it learned of the harassment, it investigated and punished the offending individual.

The second issue concerns whether "welcomeness" is a defense to offensive environment harassment and whether consent on the part of the student victim is a defense to *quid pro quo* harassment. As mentioned above, the *Meritor* opinion instructs lower courts hearing charges of sexual harassment to permit evidence of the victim's behavior and dress to determine whether, given the totality of the circumstances, an offensive environment existed.

Courts should seriously question whether a student by her behavior and dress expresses any degree of "welcomeness" to the sexually oriented harassing behavior of a faculty member or administrator. Likewise there is serious doubt that a student in a *quid pro quo* situation "consents" to the sexual demands in any manner. Even though in both situations the student's behavior might not be physically coerced, the unequal power of the student and the faculty member make it unlikely that her behavior is voluntary, in the sense of being freely agreed to.

STATE LAWS AND THE EQUAL PROTECTION CLAUSE

State laws and the equal protection clause (Fourteenth Amendment, U.S. Constitution) should also be mentioned as providing alternative theories for relief of victims of sexual harassment, although they have become less important since the Civil Rights Act of 1991 and *Franklin v. Gwinnett County Public Schools*[58] have opened the door to monetary damages for individual plaintiffs under Title VII and Title IX, respectively. State tort law still provides employee and student victims with an alternative claim for monetary damages for the mental suffering and emotional distress associated with sexual harassment. Two examples of cases are *Howard University v. Best*[59] and *Micari v. Mann*.[60] Success with this theory depends on the common law of each state concerning damages for intentional infliction of emotional distress.[61]

There are also cases that recognize sexual harassment as discrimination prohibited by the equal protection clause. The Court of Appeals for the Seventh Circuit in *Bohen v. City of East Chicago*[62] approved the use of the equal protection clause, and said that the victim needed to prove only intentional discriminatory treatment, not that the harassment altered the terms or conditions of employment.

FIRST AMENDMENT ISSUES

Emerging issues in sexual harassment for plaintiffs may include meeting the First Amendment as a defense to harassing behavior that consists solely of harassing statements or posted pornography. The Supreme Court in *R.A.V. v. St. Paul*[63] suggests that constitutional issues arise when institutions attempt to prohibit harassing speech. Where a claim of harassment is based only on verbal harassment, the First Amendment rights of the speaker may come into play. The opinion in *R.A.V. v. St. Paul*, written by Justice Antonin Scalia, does note that Title VII's prohibition of discriminatory behavior is not called into question by the *R.A.V.* decision.[64]

Notes

1. 42 U.S.C. 2000e et. seq. (1982).

2. 20 U.S.C. 1681 (1982).

3. 114 S. Ct. 367 (1993).

4. 112 S. Ct. 1028 (1992).

5. 42 U.S.C. (Supp. 1992).

6. 413 F. Supp. 654 (D.D.C. 1976), rev'd on other grounds as *Williams v. Bell*, 587 F.2d 1240 (D.C. Cir. 1978).

7. 13 F.E.P. Cases 123, (D.D.C. 1974), rev'd as *Barnes v. Costle*, 561 F.2d 983 (D.C. Cir. 1977) (ultimately finding discrimination).

8. 390 F. Supp. 161 (D. Ariz. 1975), vacated without opinion, 562 F.2d 211 (9th Cir. 1977).

9. 418 F. Supp. 233 (N.D.Gl. 1976) rev'd on other grounds, 600 F.2d 211 (9th Cir. 1979).

10. 422 F. Supp. 553 (D.N.J. 1976) rev'd, 568 F.2d 1044 (3d Cir. 1977) (ultimately finding actionable harassment).

11. 29 C.F.R. 1604.11 (1986).

12. 561 F.2d 983 (D.C. Cir. 1981).

13. 477 U.S. 57 (1986).

14. 641 F.2d 934 (D.C. Cir 1981).

15. 29 C.F.R. 1604.11 (1986).

16. 682 F.2d 897 (11th Cir. 1982).

17. 709 F.2d 251 (4th Cir. 1983).

18. 753 F.2d 141 (D.C. Cir. 1985), rev'd and remanded as *Meritor Savings Bank, FSB v. Vinson*, 477 U.S. 57 (1986).

19. 611 F. Supp. 78 (D.C. Alaska 1985).

20. 477 U.S. 57 (1986).

21. 477 U.S. 57 (1986).

22. *Rabidue v. Osceola Refining Co.* (805 F.2d 611 (6th Cir. 1986), cert. denied, 481 U.S. 1047 (1987).

23. *Ellison v. Brady*, 924 F.2d 872 (9th Cir. 1991).

24. 114 5. Ct. 367 (1993).

25. 114 5. Ct. 367, 371 (1993).

26. 114 5. Ct. 367, 370 (1993).

27. 114 5. Ct. 367, 370–71 (1993).

28. 924 F.2d 872 (9th Cir. 1991).

29. See, e. g. Ehrenreich, *Pluralist Myths and Powerless Men: The Ideology of Reasonableness in Sexual Harassment Law*, 99 Yale L. J. 1177 (1990); Estridge, *Sex at Work*, 43 Stan. L.Rev. 813 (1991).

30. 924 F.2d 872, (9th Cir. 1991).

31. Added by amendment in 1972.

32. See *Karibian v. Columbia University*, 14 F.3d 773 (2d Cir. 1994).

33. EEOC guidelines 29 C.F. R. §1604.11 (1)(d).

34. 42 U.S.C. §1981a. (b)(1) (Supp. 1992). Punitive damages are not recoverable against a government agency, the definition of which could be broad enough to include a state-supported institution of higher education.

35. 42 U.S.C. §1981a. (b)(3) (Supp. 1992).

36. 1 *Lex K. Lawson, Employment Discrimination: Special Pamphlet The Civil Rights Act of 1991*, 14 (1992).

37. 114 S. Ct. 1483 (1994).

38. 20 U.S.C. 1681 (1982).

39. 441 U.S. 677 (1978).

40. 456 U.S. 512 (1982).

41. The OCR has a policy memorandum defining sexual harassment, which it issued in 1981.

42. 631 F.2d 178 (2nd Cir. 1980), aff'g 459 F. Supp. 1 (D. Conn. 1977).

43. 465 U.S. 555 (1984).

44. 601 F. Supp. 867 (D. Mass. 1985).

45. 20 U.S.C. §1687 (2)(A) (1988).

46. 473 U.S. 234 (1985).

47. 42 U.S.C. §2000 d-7 (1988).

48. 112 S. Ct. 1028 (1992).

49. *Lipsett v. University of Puerto Rico*, 864 F.2d 881 (1st Cir. 1988).

50. R. Schneider, *Sexual Harassment and Higher Education*, 65 Tex. L. Rev. 525 (1987).

51.   631 F.2d 178 (2nd Cir. 1980), aff'g 459 F. Supp. 1 (D. Conn. 1977).

52.   561 F.2d 983 (D.C. Cir. 1977).

53.   613 F. Supp. 1360 (E.D. Pa. 1985).

54.   613 F. Supp 1360, (E.D. Pa. 1985).

55.   *Bougher v. University of Pittsburgh*, 882 F.2d 74 (3rd Cir. 1989) aff'g 713 F. Supp 139 (W.D.Pa.).

56.   112 S. Ct. 1028, 1033 (1992).

57.   Carrie N. Baker, *Comment: Proposed Title IX Guidelines on Sex-Based harassment of Students*, 43 Emory L.J. 272 (1994).

58.   112 S. Ct. 1028 (1992).

59.   484 A.2d 958 (D.C. Appl. 1984).

60.   481 N.Y.S. 2d 967 (Supp. 1984).

61.   Some states have adopted statutes that require schools to establish policies and procedures to address sexual harassment. (See, e.g. Minn. *Stat. Ann.* §127.46 (West Supp.1993) and *Cal. Ed. Code* §212.5 (West Supp.1993).

62.   799 F.2d 1180 (1986).

63.   112 S. Ct. 2538 (1992).

64.   R. Schneider, *The Law of Sexual Harassment: Some Brief Observations*, 4 Md. J. Contemp. Legal Iss. (1993).

2

Sexual Harassment:
The Definition and Measurement of a Construct

Louise F. Fitzgerald

One of the most persistent and troubling problems in the sexual harassment literature has been the lack of a widely agreed upon definition of the concept, one that is both broad enough to comprehend the variety of experiences to which the construct refers, and yet specific enough to be of practical use. As MacKinnon (1979) notes "It is not surprising . . . that women would not complain of an experience for which there has been no name. Until 1976, lacking a term to express it, sexual harassment was literally unspeakable, which made a generalized, shared and social definition of it inaccessible" (27). She notes that, Working Women United Institute appears to have been the first to use the term, in connection with the case of Carmita Wood, one of the first women to seek unemployment compensation after leaving a job due to the sexual advances of her superior (*In re Carmita Wood* 1975). It was also advanced at about the same time by the Cambridge-based Alliance Against Sexual Coercion (1976) and by Brodsky (1976). Over a decade later, a decade marked by an explosion of interest, research, and litigation, MacKinnon's "generalized, shared and social definition" remains inaccessible.

Separate from this problem, but related to it, is the lack of a generally agreed upon *operational* definition, one that can be used in research and theory-building in this area. Although many studies have been conducted, each has tended to develop its own methodology, a practice yielding conflicting estimates of incidence rates and behaviors. This not only leads to disarray in the literature, but also has the unfortunate "real world" effect of diminishing the credibility of such reports within the legal system and the opportunity for social science to contribute to social change in this important area of women's rights.

The present chapter begins by analyzing the most influential of the various sexual harassment definitions that have been proposed, both those that are *a priori* (theoretical) in nature, and those that have been developed empirically, particularly through investigation of what various groups of people perceive sexual harassment to be under different circumstances and in different contexts. We then move to a consideration of *operational definitions*, that is, to the instruments that have been developed to measure sexual harassment, and conclude with a discussion of theoretical and practical issues in the definition and measurement of harassment in higher education as well as the workplace.

DEFINITIONS

A Priori Definitions

Although likely based to some degree on previously, informally observed phenomena, most definitions of sexual harassment are *a priori* in nature; that is, rather than being explicitly data-based, they are derived from theoretical propositions concerning the nature of the construct. Such *a priori* definitions take one of two forms, the first (type 1) of which consists of a general statement describing the *nature* of the behavior and (sometimes) the status relationship of the persons involved. Such statements generally do not, however, define or list any particular behaviors or classes of behavior. The second type (type 2) takes a quite different, and in some ways opposite, form, consisting of a list of specific actions, with no formal explication of the theoretical framework from which such a list is derived, with the general exception that the behavior is usually described as unwanted by the recipient. It is sometimes the case that the first type of definition is followed by examples, and the second occasionally the basis of some later generalization; thus we appear to have instances of what is generally comprehended by the terms *deductive* and *inductive*. However, a closer examination reveals both forms to be examples of deductive reasoning, with the distinction being that the original theory statement is sometimes explicit and sometimes not. (Since the list of behaviors found in type 2 definitions are not preceded by or based on any data collection activity, it his logically necessary that they derive from the writer's theoretical perspective, however implicit that may be.)

Definitions of the first type include all legal and regulatory constructions, as well as other, more explicitly theoretical statements. For example, the Equal Employment Opportunity Commission (1980) states in its Interim Interpretive Guidelines on Sex Discrimination:

> Unwelcome sexual advances, requests for sexual favors, and other verbal or physical conduct of a sexual nature constitute sexual harassment when

(1) submission to such conduct is made either explicitly or implicitly a term or condition of an individual's employment, (2) submission to or rejection of such conduct by an individual is used as the basis for employment decisions affecting such individual, or (3) such conduct has the purpose or effect of substantially interfering with an individual's work performance or creating an intimidating, hostile, or offensive working environment." (33)

Similarly, the National Advisory Council on Women's Educational Programs developed the following working definition of sexual harassment in an educational context:

Academic sexual harassment is the use of authority to emphasize the sexuality or sexual identity of the student in a manner which prevents or impairs that student's full enjoyment of educational benefits, climate, or opportunities. (Till 1980, 7)

Probably the most influential nonregulatory definition (and one by which all others were, to some degree, influenced) is MacKinnon's: "Sexual harassment . . . refers to the unwanted imposition of sexual requirements in the context of a relationship of unequal power. Central to the concept is the use of power derived from one social sphere to lever benefits or impose deprivations in another. . . . When one is sexual, the other material, the cumulative sanction is particularly potent" (MacKinnon 1979, p.1). A conceptually similar definition is offered by Benson (1979): "Sexual harassment is broader than sexual coercion . . . (and) can only be understood as the confluence of authority relations *and* sexual interest in a society stratified by gender" (quoted in Till 1980). And LaFontaine and Tredeau (1986) suggest "sexual harassment is defined as any action occurring within the workplace whereby women are treated as objects of the male sexual prerogative. Furthermore, given that women are invariably oppressed by these actions, all such treatment is seen to constitute harassment, irregardless of whether the victim labels it as problematic" (435). Farley (1978) asserts: "Sexual harassment is . . . unsolicited nonreciprocal male behavior that asserts a woman's sex role over her function as worker" (14). These statements constitute the most well known and influential examples of the first type of a priori definitions described above. Type 2 definitions, on the other hand, take quite a different form, being much more concrete and "point-at-able" in nature. Betts and Newman (1982), for example, state "A good definition of sexual harassment . . . includes the following behaviors:

1.   Verbal harassment or abuse;
2.   Subtle pressure for sexual activity;

3. Unnecessary patting or pinching;
4. Constant brushing against another person's body;
5. Demanding sexual favors accompanied by implied or overt threats concerning an individual's employment status;
6. Demanding sexual favors accompanied by implied or overt promise of preferential treatment with regard to an individual's employment status (48).

Similarly, the Working Women United Institute (WWUI 1978) notes: "Sexual harassment can be any or all of the following: verbal sexual suggestions or jokes, constant leering or ogling, 'accidentally' brushing against your body, a 'friendly' pat, squeeze, pinch or arm around you, catching you alone for a quick kiss, the explicit proposition backed by threat of losing your job, and forced sexual relations" (1). Finally, the Project on the Status and Education of Women (1978) stated that sexual harassment may take the form of "verbal harassment or abuse, subtle pressure for sexual activity, sexist remarks about a woman's clothing, body, or sexual activities, unnecessary touching, patting, or pinching, leering or ogling of a woman's body, demanding sexual favors accompanied by implied or overt threats concerning one's job, grades, letters of recommendation, etc., physical assault" (2).

Empirical Definitions

A more inductive, data-based definitional strategy, one generally employed more by researchers than by legal theorists, regulatory agencies, or women's political or professional organizations, is to ask women directly if they have ever been harassed, and if so, to describe their experiences. These qualitative data are then content-analyzed, and a classification scheme developed, the categories of which serve as the general elements of the definition. (Ideally, such a system would then be validated with data from an independent sample, using raters trained in the classification scheme. To date, however, this has not occurred.) The most complete effort of this sort is that of Till (1980), who classified the responses of a national sample of college women into five general categories, covering a wide spectrum of behaviors from sexist comments to rape. The first of these categories, or types, was labeled *generalized sexist remarks and behavior*—similar in appearance to racial harassment, such behavior is designed not necessarily to elicit sexual cooperation, but rather to convey insulting, degrading, or sexist attitudes about women. Category 2 consists of *inappropriate and offensive, but essentially sanction-free sexual advances.* Although such behavior is unwanted and offensive, there is no penalty attached to the woman's negative response. The third category includes *solicitation of sexual activity or other sex-related behavior by promise of reward,* while the fourth covers *coercion of sexual activity by threat of punishment.* (It is these "contingency," or *quid pro quo*, situations that appear to be what most people mean when they refer to sexual harassment.) Finally, Till reports instances of *sexual crimes and misdemeanors*, including rape and sexual assault. He notes in his discussion that "categories are not sharply delineated, although they are arranged in a roughly hierarchical continuum. Many of the reported incidents involve several categories, as when a student is promised something in exchange for sexual favors and simultaneously threatened about noncooperation" (8). Despite such classificatory difficulties, Till's work has been extremely influential and provides the basis for much of the research described below and in other chapters of this book. A slightly different, but conceptually related, definitional strategy has been to present a series of behaviors, varying in severity, type, and context, and ask subjects whether or not, in their opinion, the situation constituted sexual harassment. Such a strategy thus shifts the definitional locus (i.e., from victim to "observer") and attempts to develop the construct through consensual validation. Gutek, Morasch, and Cohen (1983) reported one of the earliest and most influential studies of this type. In this study, subjects (218 undergraduate psychology majors) were presented with a series of vignettes portraying "sociosexual behavior" in a workplace setting. The vignettes systematically varied the sex of the initiator, the status of the initiator (supervisor, coworker, subordinate), and his/her behavior (sexually suggestive touching was depicted in some vignettes and accompanied by either a personal or a work-related comment). A typical vignette read, "Jane is walking down the hall at work. Mr. Davidson, Jane's boss, walks up from behind. As Mr. Davidson passes Jane, he pats her on the fanny and says 'Hurry up, you'll never get everything done today' " (35). Subjects rated the incident on nineteen Likert-type items that were factor-analyzed to produce five dimensions: The quality of the relationship between the two, (e.g., the extent to which they were friends, liked each other); the qualitative aspects of the incident itself (was it friendly, insulting, welcome, and so forth); the appropriateness of the initiator's behavior; the probability of the incident; and, finally, the probability of such an incident's occurring with the roles reversed. In general, women viewed the incidents much more negatively, particularly when they involved touching combined with a work-related comment (as in the example above). In addition, the women assessed the general quality of the relationship between the participants somewhat more negatively ($p < .08$). The relationship was also viewed more negatively by the subjects when the initiator was male, or of higher status. This was particularly true if a high-status initiator was portrayed as touching and making work-related comments.

The results reported in this study identified many of the important variables that have since been shown to influence perceptions of sexual harassment: sex of rater, status of initiator, explicitness of behavior, and degree of connection to work situation. The finding of gender differences in perceptions of sexually harassing behaviors is the most robust of all that have been examined to date, having been reported in almost every investigation so far completed. (See, for example, Collins and Blodgett 1981; Ormerod 1987; Padgitt and Padgitt 1986; and Powell 1986. For one of the few exceptions, see Terpstra and Baker 1986.) Not surprisingly, women are consistently more likely to view such behaviors as harassment (Kenig and Ryan 1986; Ormerod 1987), as offensive (Padgitt and Padgitt 1986), or both. While various attempts have been made to "explain" such differences—for instance, in terms of gender role (Powell 1986) or organizational variables (Konrad and Gutek 1986)—they have been relatively unsuccessful and are probably unnecessary. As Powell (1986) points out, "women as a group have consistently been demonstrated to experience more unwanted sexual attention than men . . . further explanation may be unnecessary and inappropriate" (18).

A similarly consistent finding has been that behaviors initiated by supervisors or others with a substantial power advantage are more likely to be judged as harassment. In her investigation of perceptions of sexual harassment on a college campus, Ormerod (1987) reported that several forms of sexual behavior were rated more severely when the faculty member was portrayed as having some formal responsibility for evaluating a student. This parallels Gutek, Morasch, and Cohen's (1983) report that subjects viewed incidents more negatively when they were initiated by a supervisor.

A variably closely related to initiator status is the degree of coercion represented by the behavior. Subjects overwhelmingly agree that requests for sex linked to threats of retaliation for noncompliance constitute sexual harassment; to a slightly lesser degree, the same is true of behaviors that link sex to promises of reward. For example, 94 percent of the men and 98 percent of the women in Konrad and Gutek's (1986) sample agreed that "Being asked to have sexual relations with the understanding that it would hurt your job situation if you refused or help if you accepted" was sexual harassment. In Adams, Kottke, and Padgitt's (1983) sample of college students, sexual bribery was defined as harassment by over 97 percent off the men and 99 percent of the women. Eliciting sexual cooperation by threats (either direct or subtle) received the highest sexual harassment ratings from the students and faculty in Ormerod's (1987) sample (6.95 and 6.92, respectively, on a 7-point scale). Thus, both *a priori* and empirical definitions clearly agree that such *quid pro quo* behaviors constitute sexual harassment of the most basic, unambiguous sort.

At the opposite end of the spectrum lie the more ambiguous behaviors and those that are more sexist (as opposed to sexual) in nature. Behaviors drawn from Till's gender-harassment category received the lowest sexual harassment ratings from Ormerod's sample, while only 30 percent of the male (but 47 percent of the female) students surveyed by Adams, Kottke, and Padgitt.

(1983) defined sexist comments as sexual harassment. Similarly, Padgitt and Padgitt (1986) found that their original data (perceptions of eight sexually harassing behaviors) did not form a Guttman scale, using standard criteria for scalability and reproducibility. They noted that three items seemed to account for many of the inconsistent answers: sexist comments, body language (such as leering at the woman's body or standing too close) and invitations (e.g., for dates) in which sexual expectations are not stated. When these items were removed, the five remaining behaviors demonstrated sufficient pattern to approximate a reasonable Guttman scale for both male and female subjects.

Review of these and similar studies would seem to suggest that the more coercive *quid pro quo* behaviors are always seen as harassment, whereas *gender harassment* and *seductive behavior* (the first and second categories in Till's 1980 typology) elicit much less agreement. Although this is generally the case, it is also true that contextual variables moderate such perceptions in even the most seemingly clear-cut cases. A study by Reilly et al. (1982) makes this point. These researchers utilized a "factorial survey" methodology (Rossi and Anderson 1982) as a means of assessing what factors are of importance in judgments of sexual harassment. Briefly, this methodology involves presenting respondents with a series of brief stories or vignettes that vary along the various dimensions of interest. Using a computer program to generate vignettes of faulty-student interaction, several factors were systematically varied, including (a) the instructor's status (graduate student or professor), age, and marital status; (b) the class standing of the female student; (c) the setting of the interaction; (d) the nature of any past relationship between the instructor and student; (e) behavior of the student; (f) verbal behavior of the instruction; (g) physical behavior of the instructor; and (h) presence or absence of threat or coercion. The authors offer the following illustrative vignette: "Andrea G., a senior, after being asked had declined to go out with Donald L., a 30-year old professor. While at the library they ran into each other and started talking. She asked about her grades. He said that he looked forward to working with her while he playfully poked her in the ribs" (103). The subjects (faculty and undergraduate students) read each vignette and then judged, on a ninepoint scale, the extent to which the incident did or did not constitute an instance of sexual harassment. These ratings were then analyzed using multiple regression. Table 2.1 summarizes the relevant results and presents unstandardized regression coefficients that provide an estimate of how much overall impact, on the average, any particular factor had on the dependent variable. For example, if the woman was portrayed as saying she would "do anything" for a grade, or brushing up against the instructor as they talked, the average rating of the vignette decreased by almost 1 point (-0.93) on the 9-point scale, whereas if the faculty member admired the student's hair, or suggested dinner and a movie, the rating was correspondingly increased (0.94 and 0.97, respectfully).

TABLE 2.1

Factors That Affect Perceptions of Whether a Particular Student
Interaction Constitutes Sexual Harassment (Reilly et al. 1982)

Factors that Lowered Rating Regression	Regression Coefficient[a]
1. Nature of Past Relationship	
— They were close friends	−0.27
— They had gone out several times	−0.41
— They had been dating regularly.	−0.99
2. Female Student Action	
— She said she would do anything for a grade.	−0.93
— She used suggestive language.	−0.86
— She touched his arm.	−0.49
— She brushed up against him.	−0.93

Factors That Raised Rating

1. Nature of Past Relationship	
— She had previously declined a date.	0.21
2. Female Student Action	
— She said she was concerned about her grades.	0.27
3. Instructor Verbal Behavior	
— He asked about her courses.	0.28
— He remarked on her progress in class.	0.40
— He said he looked forward to working together.	0.71
— He said he wanted to speak more privately.	0.84
— He admired her hair.	0.94
— He commented on her personalaity.	0.67
— He said she reminded him of an old girlfriend.	0.98
— He suggested dinner and a movie.	0.97
— He asked her home.	1.33
— He told a dirty joke.	0.99
— He said she would be good in bed.	1.98
4. Instructor Action	
— He straightened her hair.	0.72
— He held her hand.	0.43
— He put his hand on her shoulder.	0.47
— He moved closer to her.	0.59
— He poked her in the ribs.	0.63
— He squeezed her waist.	1.13
— He fondled and kissed her.	1.82
— He attempted sex.	3.13
— He forced her down.	3.16

[a] All results are significant at or beyond the .05 level of probability.

What seems clear from table 2.1 is that any prior social relationship between the pair or any "suggestive" behavior on the part of the student predictably lowered the rating, while faculty suggestive or coercive behavior had the opposite effect. Predictably, faculty coercive (*quid pro quo*) behaviors or forceful ones (e.g., attempted sex, forced her down, and so forth) had the most powerful effect on subject responses. No student behavior, however seductive, had an equivalent effect. Unfortunately, this study reports only main effects and does not evaluate any possible interaction effect of various combinations of variables. This presents a difficulty, as the various factors undoubtedly combine in ways that affect the meaning assigned to a particular interaction. For example, "he touched her hair" and "suggested dinner and a movie" projects a different image when the two people "have been dating regularly" than when they had merely "talked on occasion." Despite this shortcoming, the Reilly et al. (1982) research remains one of the most sophisticated attempts to date to develop an empirical definition of sexual harassment (see Rossi and Weber-Burdin 1983 for a discussion and integration of both studies).

A somewhat different approach to this problem was taken by Terpstra and Baker (1986). Rather than vary the contextual components of interactions, these researchers used a standard stimulus list and examined the effect on perceptions of individual differences in subjects' attitudes, attributes, and behaviors (gender, attitudes toward women, religiosity, self esteem, and locus of control). The results of this study are complex and somewhat difficult to interpret, consisting as they do of a series of interaction effects, such as "non-religious subjects with liberal attitudes toward women perceived a relatively high number of incidents as harassment, whereas religious liberal subjects perceived fewer examples as harassment. The opposite relationship was found for subjects with conservative attitudes toward women" (468). Discussing the complexity of their results, these authors offer a model of perceptions of sexual harassment that includes individual difference variables with respect to the perceiver (e.g., sex, age, attitudes), situational variables (including characteristics of the offender), the actual behavior exhibited, and variables involved in the cognitive appraisal process (e.g., causal attributions).

MEASUREMENT

Not surprisingly, a satisfactory operational definition of harassment has proven even more difficult to achieve than a linguistic one. Although numerous surveys and studies have appeared, each has typically constructed its own data collection instrument, a situation that has resulted in much confusion in the literature.

In their discussion of the progression of research in new fields, Edwards and Cronbach (1952) describe the initial phase as one of *survey* research, in which investigators attempt to identify and isolate variables of importance. This stage is typically followed by that of *technique* research, where the focus is on operationalizing the variables in a reliable manner, a process that is necessary before research can proceed to the more advanced *experimental* and *applied* stages. Even the most cursory review of the sexual harassment literature makes clear that the field is only now beginning to make the transition from survey to technique investigations.

As Edwards and Cronbach (1952) suggest, initial efforts were open-ended in nature, as investigators attempted to isolate and define the variables of interest. Thus, Crull (1979) reported on the experiences of 92 women, self-identified as victims of sexual harassment, and identified types of behaviors and experiences that appeared to typify the phenomenon, while Till (1980) classified responses to his open-ended survey of harassment in higher education into five types or levels, each of progressively greater severity. Similarly, Benson and Thompson (1982) presented their subjects (senior women at the University of California-Berkeley) with the definition of sexual harassment developed by the Working Women United Institute (WWUI 1978) and then asked them, among other things, whether they had ever been sexually harassed, and if so, to describe the incident. Responses were classified into seven categories, ranging from body language and undue attention to sexual bribery. Somewhat more structured approaches included that of Wilson and Kraus (1983), who presented their subjects with the seven types of harassment identified by the Project on the Status and Education of Women (1978) and asked them to report the numbers of professors who had engaged in each. Adams, Kottke, and Padgitt (1983) took a similar approach, albeit with a slightly different list, while Maihoff and Forrest (1983) asked subjects about only four behaviors, three of which were extremely severe. Finally, in an extensive examination of harassment at the University of Rhode Island, Lott, Reilly, and Howard (1982) asked respondents not only about sexual insults (both verbal and nonverbal), threats or bribery, or sexual assault that they themselves had experienced, but also if they had ever heard of such incidents happening to others, and present figures for both types of data.

The investigations reviewed to this point have all (with the exception of Crull 1979) taken place within the university environment; examinations of the workplace, however, reveal similar methodologies. In the largest investigation undertaken to date, the U.S. Merit Systems Production Board asked a stratified probability sample of the federal workforce whether they had experienced any of seven sexually harassing behaviors during the previous twenty-four months. At about the same time, in a large-scale study of the private sector, Gutek (1985) used a structured interview conducted by telephone to elicit information about six behaviors (sexual comments, sexual looks or gestures, sexual and nonsexual touching, and coerced dating and sexual relations).

As a review of these studies makes clear, the objective measurement of sexual harassment remains at a somewhat rudimentary level. As important as these investigations are, they contain several problems from a measurement perspective, suggesting that researchers have seriously neglected (or thought unnecessary) the *technique* research requirement outlined by Edwards and Cronbach (1952). These problems center on the very basic issues of reliability and validity, the *sine qua non* of any data collection technique. To examine the latter first, let us consider for a moment the issue of validity. Of the three facets of validity generally contemplated by measurement theorists, content validity is probably the most relevant here. According to commonly accepted definitions, content validity requires, at a minimum, an adequate specification of the domain of interest, and the generation of a set of items that adequately sample this domain. Each facet of the domain should be represented and appropriately weighed, and care must be taken to construct the items in such a way that they are interpreted similarly by all respondents. This last consideration brings us to the concept of reliability—that is, whether or not the instrument consistently measures what it is supposed to measure, both across subjects, and within subjects across time.

In reviewing the studies considered so far, it is apparent that these issues have not been sufficiently addressed. With respect to stability, no study reports a test-retest correlation coefficient (nor an internal consistency coefficient, for that matter, although that is a separate issue). We have no assurance that the subjects' responses are stable—that is, that they would answer the same way if asked again. Equally important, there are logical grounds upon which to suspect that the subjects may not have interpreted the items in the same manner. For example, some studies have utilized the term *sexual harassment* and asked women whether or not they have been harassed (e.g., Till 1980); others label their intentions in cover letters or survey titles and then present women with a list of behaviors to consider (U.S. Merit Systems Protection Board [USMSPB] 1981); finally, some do not use the term *harassment*, but ask women to determine whether the touching was meant to be sexual, or the comments were meant to be insulting (e.g., Gutek 1985). Such procedures introduce a large element of error into the measurement. It has been widely demonstrated that substantial individual differences exist in the perceptions of what constitutes sexual harassment (see, for example, Ormerod 1987), therefore, asking respondents whether they have been harassed, or labeling behaviors "harassment" and asking whether a respondent has experienced them, introduces systematic as well as random error into the procedure (random because of idiosyncratic definitions of harassment; systematic because most women have been socialized to accept many forms of sexual exploitation under the guise of joking or compliments, thus systematically reducing their rate of response). A conceptually similar problem is introduced when a researcher asks a subject to make a subjective determination of the intent of a behavior (e.g., Was it meant to be insulting?) before they can say whether or not they have experienced it. Although this may be feasible when examining person perception or attribution, it is likely not appropriate for collecting incidence data. The likely result, again, is a lowering of true incidence rates, given that women are less likely than men to label a behavior as sexual and are socialized not to recognize many sexually insulting behaviors as being just that.

Finally, it appears that investigators have not paid sufficient attention to the concept of content validity. Many studies give no rationale for the behaviors they have chosen to include, while others include a statement to the effect that these items were chosen because they had been used in previous research. Examination of the studies suggest that several (e.g., Maihoff and Forrest 1983) tap a rather narrow spectrum of behavior, while others (e.g., Reilly et al. 1982; USMSPB 1981) list what might be considered the major facets of the domain but do nnt include multiple items to measure each facet, suggesting that they may not have been adequately sampled and measured.

It was in an effort to address these considerations and others of a similar nature that the Sexual Experiences Questionnaire (SEQ) was constructed. First reported in Fitzgerald and Shullman (1985) and elaborated in a more extensive study by Fitzgerald, Shullman, et al. (1988), the SEQ represents, to our knowledge, the only inventory of sexual harassment that attempts to meet standard psychometric criteria. To define the domain of interest, we began with Till's (1980) five levels of sexual harassment, identified by him through content analysis of responses to his national open-ended survey of college women. This classification has the advantage of being derived from a broadly based sample and of appearing to encompass all types of sexual harassment that had previously been identified in the literature (MacKinnon's [1979] distinction between *quid pro quo* situations, where a distinct reward or punishment is contingent on sexual cooperation, and *conditions of work*, a somewhat more subtle situation where the woman is the target of sexually charged behavior but no explicit demand is made; and Franklin et al.'s [1981] concept of *gender harassment*). Once this theoretical framework had been identified, the first step in instrument development was the generation of an item pool; thus, items were identified from the literature or written to measure the five general areas:

1.   *Gender harassment.* Generalized sexist remarks and behavior designed not necessarily to elicit sexual cooperation, but to convey insulting, degrading, or sexist attitudes about women.
2.   *Seductive behavior.* Inappropriate and offensive sexual advances. Although such behavior is unwanted and offensive, there is no

penalty explicitly attached to the woman's negative response; nor does this category include sexual bribery.

3. *Sexual bribery.* Solicitation of sexual activity or other sex-linked behavior (e.g., dating) by promise of rewards.

4. *Sexual coercion.* Coercion of sexual activity, or other sex-linked behavior by threat of punishment.

5. *Sexual imposition.*[1] Sexual imposition (e.g., attempts to fondle, touch, kiss, or grab) or sexual assault.

All items were written strictly in behavioral terms, and took the form "Have you ever been in a situation where a professor or instructor . . . [e.g., made crudely sexual remarks, either publicly in class, or to you privately?]." The words *sexual harassment* did not appear anywhere on the instrument until the final item ("Have you ever been sexually harassed by a professor or instructor?"). Every attempt was made to avoid ambiguity in terminology and to develop a full range of items measuring each area. The five scales and representative items from each appear in table 2.2. The items were piloted on 468 students (both female and male, graduate and undergraduate) enrolled at a medium-size state university in the Midwest, who were instructed to respond to the items in terms of their clarity, wording, ambiguity, and so forth, and to suggest additional items where necessary. The instrument was then revised with their feedback, and scoring options developed.

For each item, the instructions direct the respondents to circle the response most closely describing their own experiences. The options include (1) Never; (2) Once; and (3) More Than Once. If the subject circles (2) or (3), she is further instructed to indicate whether the person involved was a man or a woman (or both, if it happened more than once) by circling M, F, or B. Since the SEQ is designed primarily to identify the frequency of various types of harassment, it is scored simply by counting the number of subjects who endorse the *Once* or *More Than Once* response options for each item. (This distinction was introduced to control for the possible tendency of subjects who had experienced a low-level or nontraumatic harassment behavior on a single occasion to dismiss that experience because "it only happened once." The distinction is, however, typically not used in scoring.) Initial psychometric analysis using Cronbach's coefficient *alpha* yielded an internal consistency coefficient of .92 for the entire 28-item inventory on a new sample of 1,395 university students (again, both famale and male, graduate and undergraduate) enrolled at the same university where the pilot was conducted. Test-retest stability on a small subsample of graduate students ($N = 46$) yielded a stability coefficient of .86 over a two-week period. Corrected split-half reliability coefficients for the five "scales" of the SEQ ranged from .62 to .86, and averaged .75, reasonable for scales of this length.

TABLE 2.2

Definitions of and Representative Items from the Five Levels of the SEQ

Level 1: Gender Harassment

Definition: Generalized sexist remarks and behavior.
Sample item: "Have you ever been in a situation where a professor or instructor habitually told suggestive stories or offensive jokes?"

Level 2: Seductive Behavior

Definition: Inappropriate and offensive, but essentially sanction-free sexual advances.
Sample item: "Have you ever been in a situation where a professor or instructor made unwanted attempts to draw you into a discussion of personal or sexual matters (e.g., attempted to discuss or comment on your sex life)?"

Level 3: Sexual Bribery

Definition: Solicitation of sexual activity or other sex-linked behavior by promise of rewards.
Sample item: "Have you ever felt that you were being subtly bribed with some sort of *reward* (e.g., good grades, preferential treatment) to engage in sexual behavior with a professor or instructor?"

Level 4: Sexual Coercion

Definition: Coercion of sexual activity by threat of punishment.
Sample item: "Have you ever been *directly* threatened or pressured to engage in sexual activity by threats of punishment or retaliation?"

Level 5: Sexual Imposition

Definition: Gross sexual imposition or assault.
Sample item: "Have you ever been in a situation where a professor or instruction made *forceful* attempts to touch, fondle, kiss, or grab you?"

As described above, content validity was built into the SEQ through basing item construction on Till's (1980) empirically derived categories. In addition, an attempt was made to evaluate the criterion-related validity of the inventory. Thus, the final item ("I have been sexually harassed") was treated as a criterion, and correlated with each of the other items. With the exception of two items measuring sexual bribery (that showed very little variance) and one item measuring gender harassment, all items were significantly positively correlated with the criterion item. In addition, if the five areas of harassment are considered as levels, we would expect the average item-criterion correlations to increase systematically from level 1 to level 5. With one exception, the correlations conformed to theoretical expectation, ranging from $r = .15$ for level 1 (gender harassment) to $r = .37$ for level 4 (sexual coercion). The coefficient for level 5 (sexual imposition) was lower than expected, most likely because several items showed very little variance.

With respect to construct validity, three relevant investigations have been completed. First, Fitzgerald and Shullman (1985) factor-analyzed the original SEQ as well as a second version designed for employed women, the SEQ2. Their results failed to confirm the hypothesized five-level structure; rather, a three-factor solution, in which bribery and coercion collapse into one factor, seduction and sexual imposition group together as another, and gender harassment stands along as a separate factor, appeared to more accurately account for the data. This structure was further supported through a complete link cluster analysis of the original SEQ that yielded three clusters conforming to the original three factors.

However, as Fitzgerald, et al. (1988) point out, such solutions must be considered tentative, due to the unstable nature of the correlations computed on the items showing very little variance. Thus, although the SEQ may yield a three-factor solution in all samples tested to date, this does not clearly speak to the dimensionality of the construct itself, but speaks to the methodological constraints inherent in attempts to measure critical but relatively low frequency behaviors. This interpretation is supported by Fitzgerald (1987). Using ratings of the SEQ items developed by Ormerod (1987) to develop a complete inter-item correlation matrix, with data from all subjects on all items, a five-factor solution was reported that conformed quite closely to the five levels suggested by Till (1980).

Finally, Ormerod's (1987) data itself provides support for the construct validity of the SEQ. Briefly, Ormerod presented faculty members and students at two West Coast universities with items from the SEQ and requested them to rate the items on a seven-point, Likert-type scale, anchored at one pole by "Definitely is not harassment" and at the other by "Definitely is harassment." If a mean rating for each level is developed by averaging over the items within each level, and these mean ratings examined, they arrange themselves according to theoretical expectation, ranging from a mean score of 4.37 for level 1 to 6.40 for level 5.

In summary, then, although more research is obviously necessary, it appears that the SEQ (and its companion instrument for working women, the SEQ2) possess acceptable psychometric characteristics of reliability and validity for research use at this time.

ANALYSIS, INTEGRATION, AND RECOMMENDATIONS

In reviewing the definitions described above, it becomes apparent that none of those so far articulated are completely satisfactory; similarly, although progress has been made toward the development of adequate measurement devices, several problems, both theoretical and practical, remain to be solved. This section of the chapter will address these issues in an attempt to integrate the literature and recommend directions for future research in the area.

Definitions

As outlined above, the discussion of definitions began witH the basic distinction between those that are *a priori* in nature and those that have been developed in a more empirical manner. (The measurement-minded reader will note the resemblance to the *rational* and *empirical* models of test construction.) Although each is informative, neither is completely satisfactory; for example, while many behaviors are clearly harassing no matter what relational context which they occur in, this is not always the case. Thus, simple "lists" of behaviors cannot serve as adequate definitions of harassment, and are generally less useful than formulations in which the *principles* or *elements* of harassment (e.g., power, authority, sexuality, gender stratification, lack of consent, and so forth) are articulated. Without such statements of essential elements and the necessary relations among them, there is no basis for identifying and classifying novel instances of behavior as harassment.

Similarly, although social consensus is important (and a worthwhile subject for investigation in its own right), it cannot serve as the sole definitional basis for the construct. The reasons for this are twofold: First, the perceptions of observers, influenced as they are by various demographic and attitudinal factors, likely differ in important ways from those of the recipient of the behaviors in question. MacKinnon (1987) makes this point when she notes that the laws against sexual harassment mark the first time in legal history that injuries to women have been defined *by* women, and from their point of view. Thus, a woman's experience of harassment is definitionally valid whatever the perceptions of observers may be; her perception of an interaction as harassing is definitionally sufficient. It is not, however, necessary. As LaFontaine and Tredeau (1987) point out, "given that women are invariably oppressed by (sexual harassment) all such treatment is seen to constitute harassment, *irregardless of whether the victim labels it as problematic*" (435, emphasis added). It is this premise that gives rise to the assertion that perceptions alone (whether those of observers or victims) are not adequate for a valid definition. Women are, after all, socialized to accept many nonconsensual or even offensive sexual interactions as being nonremarkable, a fact of life. One has only to peruse the literature on acquaintance or marital rape to see that this is so. That it is also true of sexual harassment can be seen from the data reported by Fitzgerald, et al. (1988), in which women students indicated experiencing many behaviors clearly qualifying as harassment (e.g., propositions, fondling), yet often did not label those as such. This still widespread acceptance of what LaFontaine and Tredeau (1987) label the "male sexual prerogative" is at the heart of the assertion that victim perceptions are sufficient but not necessary for a definition of harassment.

It would appear that, before a definition can be attempted, it is necessary to outline the premises upon which it is to be based. First, to paraphrase Benson (1979), sexual harassment involves the confluence of authority (power) relations and sexuality (or sexism) in a society stratified by gender. Second, it is important to remember that power or authority can be either *formal* or *informal* in nature; that is, it can be either achieved or ascribed. Formal, or achieved, power is derived from a formal role, such as supervisor, employer, or professor. Informal power, on the other hand, arises from the male sexual prerogative, which implies that men have the unfettered right to initiate sexual interactions or to assert the primacy of woman's gender role over her role as worker or student. It is this prerogative, a sort of psychological *droit de seigneuer*, that accounts for the mystification that often leads women to misperceive and mislabel their experiences of harassment. Based on these premises, the following definition is suggested:

> Sexual harassment consists of the sexualization of an instrumental relationship through the introduction or imposition of sexist or sexual remarks, requests or requirements, in the context of a formal power differential. Harassment can also occur where no such formal differential exists, if the behavior is unwanted by or offensive to the woman. Instances of harassment can be classified into the following general categories: gender harassment, seductive behavior, solicitation of sexual activity by promise of reward or threat of punishment, and sexual imposition or assault.

Such a linguistic definition appears to have several advantages. It combines both a rational and an empirical component, thus providing both the theoretical elements necessary to define a given interaction as harassment, as well as a framework within which to classify such interactions. The nature and elements of harassment are drawn from theory, whereas the classificatory framework is essentially data-based. Finally, the concept of intent is not addressed; rather, it is the power differential and/or the woman's reaction that are considered to be the critical variables. Thus, when a formal power differential exists, all sexist or sexual behavior is seen as harassment, since the woman is not considered to be in a position to object, resist, or give fully free consent; when no such differential exists, it is the recipient's experience and perception of the behavior as offensive that constitutes the defining factor.

One of the more controversial implications of such a definition is that, within this framework, so-called consensual relationships between persons of formally different statuses (e.g., professor/student) would be, strictly speaking, impossible. This leads to a difficult and very complicated issue. On the one hand, Hoffman (1986) argues eloquently against the position suggested above, at least in the educational setting. Beginning with MacKinnon's (1979) statement that "women wish to chooses whether, when, where, and with whom to have sexual relationships, as one important part of exercising control over their lives" (25), she argues that an absolute prohibition against faculty-student amorous relationships assumes that "the relatively powerless group—students—is incapable of empowerment and, in seeking to prevent its victimization, reinforce(s) and perpetuate(s) its powerlessness and vulnerability" (113). Arguing the opposing view, Mead (1980) suggested some years ago that society should institute taboos proscribing sex among people who work together, to ensure that women are not victimized by sexual advances from the men with whom they work.

The present definition does not address this problem explicitly, but does clearly imply that truly consensual relationships are probably not possible within the context of unequal power, and thus may be generally inappropriate (a point with which Hoffman [1986] agrees). As noted elsewhere, "while not always unethical, such relationships are almost always unwise" (Fitzgerald, Gold, et al. 1988).

Measurement

Operational definitions are, to some degree, more easily addressed directly than linguistic ones. Given that a sufficiently articulated framework exists, it becomes a merely technical (as opposed to philosophical) problem to generate a reasonably adequate measurement device, to test it, refine it, and so forth. Possibly because such a framework has only recently become available, and further complicated by the fact that research has proceeded in two parallel but different domains (academic and the workplace), it is only lately that such efforts have been undertaken. The SEQ represents a promising beginning, but much more remains to be done. In addition to the need for more validity studies on this instrument, and the development of other, alternative devices, several additional problems require attention, possibly the most pressing of which is to insure sampling adequacy.

One of the more salient criticisms of current research is that women who have been harassed, or who are sensitive to the issue of harassment, are most likely to return surveys on this topic, thus possibly inflating estimates of the phenomenon. Although the collection of data from intact groups (e.g., classrooms, professional meetings) avoids this problem, it also risks rendering the obtained data setting-specific, or, in the latter case, nonrandom. Many studies of sexual harassment report unacceptably low response rates (for example, Till received only 259 responses to the 8,000 calls for information he sent out, and our own return rate for mail-out questionnaires has averaged only about 30 percent, compared to the nearly 100 percent we obtained from intact classes [Fitzgerald, et al. 1988]). Although appropriate (but expensive) follow-up techniques can raise this to a more acceptable level, and some studies have had success with these (USMSPB 1981), it is unlikely that mail surveys will ever approximate the desired precision. A more promising approach may be that of Gutek (1985), who utilized standardized telephone interviews to achieve a random sample of the Los Angeles workforce, with only a 23 percent refusal rate. It is imperative that adequate samples be obtained if such data are to be useful within either a scientific or a practical context.

A more basic issue may simply be the acceptability of self-report data in this extremely sensitive area. There is still, unfortunately, a tendency to disbelieve women's reports of sexually exploitive experiences. That this is so can be seen from policy statements (such as that of one university) that have more extensive discussions of the penalties for false accusations of harassment than for harassment itself! MacKinnon (1987) addresses this issue when she notes, "In 1982 the EEOC held that if a victim was sexually harassed without a corroborating witness, proof was inadequate as a matter of law. . . . To say a woman's word is no proof amounts to saying a woman's word is worthless. Usually all the man has is his denial. In 1983, the EEOC found sexual harassment on a woman's word alone. It said it was enough, without distinguishing or overruling the prior case. Perhaps they recognized that women don't choose to be harassed in front of witnesses" (113). She could just as easily have said that men don't choose to harass in front of witnesses.

It is possible that this is a legal issue, more than it is a scientific one. After all, the great majority of data in many fields of psychology is based on self-report, and, given the usual qualifiers concerning response bias and response set, is none the less acceptable for that. Still, if the data are to be useful as a basis for social policy and legal change, the issue must be attended to. Possibly the best way of doing so is to address the sampling issues raised above. After all, if 40 to 70 percent of a rigorously selected random sample of women endorse items indicating that they have been sexually harassed, it is only the most unreconstructed misogynist that could respond (as a student once did, after a two-hour lecture on harassment), "How do you know they're not just making it all up?"

CONCLUSIONS AND RECOMMENDATIONS

Although the measurement of sexual harassment is still in its infancy, it seems possible to make some recommendations based on what has been learned so far. First, instruments attempting to measure harassment must demonstrate, at a minimum, the same characteristics of reliability that are required of any other psychometric technique. Second, at least some validity data should be reported. Evidence of content validity is probably the most appropriate at this time, as well as the most practical, given the criterion problem. Third, researchers should avoid the term _sexual harassment_ in the title and body of their instrument, as well as in their instructions or cover letter. To do otherwise introduces an unknown amount of error into the data. Fourth, it appears that asking respondents about the _intent_ of a behavior they have experienced (was it meant to be playful, complimentary, insulting, etc.) is useful for examining attributions or perceptions; it is, however, quite problematic when collecting incidence data. Similarly, asking respondents if they know of anyone who has been harassed or has experienced a certain behavior is a useful way to document awareness of the problem. Such data should not, however, be used to support inferences about incidence rates, if only because multiple respondents may report the same incident. This is particularly true as episodes of sexual harassment received wider publicity and media coverage. Finally, the traditional techniques for sampling and criteria for response rates should be adhered to.

As Boring once said of psychology, sexual harassment has a long past but a short history. The phrase itself is barely a decade old, its definition is still a matter of controversy, and its measurement is only a beginning. The present chapter has attempted to summarize what is known concerning these issues and to contribute to the dialogue by developing a rational-empirical definition and recommending guidelines for research.

Notes

1. Till's original system used the term _sexual crimes and misdemeanors_ for this category. We used the more inclusive term to enable reference to less-severe behaviors.

References

Adams, J.W., Kottke, J.L., and Padgitt, J.S. (1983). Sexual harassment of university students. _Journal of College Student Personnel, 24_, 484–90.

Alliance Against Sexual Coercion (1976). _Fighting against sexual harassment: An advocacy handbook._ Cambridge, MA: Alliance Against Sexual Coercion.

Benson, D.J., and Thompson, G.E. (1982). Sexual harassment on a university campus: The confluence of authority relations, sexual interest and gender stratification. _Social Problems, 29_, 236–51.

Betts, N.D., and Newman, G.C. (1982). Defining the issue: Sexual harassment in college and university life. *Contemporary Education, 54,* 48–52.

Brodsky, C.M. (1976). *The harassed worker.* Lexington, MA: Lexington Books.

Collins, E.G., and Blodgett, T.B. (1981). Sexual harassment. Some see it . . . some won't. *Harvard Business Review, 59,* 46–95.

Crull, P. (1979). *The impact of sexual harassment on the job: A profile of the experiences of 92 women.* Working Women's Research Series, Report No. 3.

Edwards, A.L., and Cronbach, L.J. (1952). Experimental design for research in psychotherapy. *Journal of Clinical Psychology, 8,* 51–59.

Equal Employment Opportunity Commission. (1980). Guidelines on discrimination because of sex. *Federal Register, 45,* 74676–77.

Farley, L. (1978). *Sexual shakedown: The sexual harassment of women on the job.* New York: McGraw-Hill.

Fitzgerald, L.F. (1987, August). *Sexual harassment: The structure of a social phenomenon.* Paper presented to the Annual Meeting of the American Psychological Association, New York.

Fitzgerald, L.F., and Shullman, S.L. (1985). *The development and validation of an objectively scored measure of sexual harassment.* Paper presented to the annual meeting of the American Psychological Association, Los Angeles.

Fitzgerald, L.F., Shullman, S.L., Bailey, N., Richards, M,, Swecker, J., Gold, Y., Ormerod, A.J., and Weitzman, L. (1988). The incidence and dimensions of sexual harassment in academia and the workplace. *Journal of Vocational Behavior, 32,* 152–75.

Fitzgerald, L.F., Weitzman, L.M., Gold, Y., and Ormerod, A.J. (1988). Academic harassment: Sex and denial in scholarly garb. *Psychology of Women Quarterly, 12,* 329–40.

Franklin, P., Moglin, H., Zatling-Boring, P., and Angress, R. (1981). *Sexual and gender harassment in the academy.* New York: Modern Language Association.

In re Carmita Wood. (1975). App. No. 207, 958. New York State Department of Labor, Unemployment Appeals Board (6 October 1975).

Gutek, B.A. (1985). *Sex and the workplace.* San Francisco: Jossey-Bass.

Gutek, B.A., Morasch, B., and Cohen, A.G. (1983). Interpreting social-sexual behavior in a work setting. *Journal of Vocational Behavior, 22,* 30–48.

Hoffman, F.L. (1986). Sexual harassment in academia: Feminist theory and institutional practice. *Harvard Educational Review, 56*, 105–21.

Kenig, S., and Ryan, J. (1986). Sex differences in levels of tolerance and attribution of blame for sexual harassment on a university campus. *Sex Roles, 15*, 535–49.

Konrad, A.M., and Gutek, B.A. (1986). Impact of work experiences on attitudes toward sexual harassment. *Administrative Science Quarterly, 31*, 422–38.

LaFontaine, E., and Tredeau, L. (1986). The frequency, sources, and correlates of sexual harassment among women in traditional male occupations. *Sex Roles, 15*, 433–32.

Lott, B., Reilly, M.E., and Howard, D.R. (1982). Sexual assault and harassment: A campus community case study. *Signs: A Journal of Women in Culture and Society, 8*, 296–319.

MacKinnon, C.A. (1979). *Sexual harassment of working women.* New Haven: Yale.

———. (1987). *Feminism unmodified.* Cambridge: Harvard University Press.

Maihoff, N., and Forrest, L. (1983). Sexual harassment in higher education: An assessment study. *Journal of the NAWDAC, 46*, 3–8.

Mead, M. (1980). A proposal: We need taboos on sex at work. In D.A. Neugarten and J. Shafritz (Eds.), *Sexuality in organizations.* Oak Park, IL: Moore.

Ormerod, A.J. (1987, August). *Perceptions of sexual harassment.* Paper presented to the annual meeting of the American Psychological Association, New York.

Padgitt, S.C., and Padgitt, J.S. (1986). Cognitive structure of sexual harassment: Implications for university policy. *Journal of College Student Personnel, 27*, 34–39.

Powell, G.N. (1986). Effects of sex role identity and sex on definitions of sexual harassment. *Sex Roles, 14*, 9–19.

Project on the Status and Education of Women. (1978). *Sexual harassment: A hidden issue.* Washington, DC: Association of American Colleges.

Reilly, T., Sandra, S., Dull, V., and Bartlett, K. (1982). The factorial survey technique: An approach to defining sexual harassment on campus. *Journal of Social Issues, 38*, 99–110.

Rossi, P.H., and Anderson, A.B. (1982). The factorial survey approach: An introduction. In P. Rossi and S. Nock (Eds.), *Measuring social judgements: The factorial survey approach*. Beverly Hills, CA: Sage.

Rossi, P.H., and Weber-Berdin, E. (1983). Sexual harassment on campus. *Social Science Research, 12*, 131–58.

Terpstra, D.E., and Baker, D.D. (1986). A framework for the study of sexual harassment. *Basic and Applied Social Psychology, 7*, 17–34.

Till, F. (1980). *Sexual harassment: A report on the sexual harassment of students*. Washington, DC: National Advisory Council on Women's Educational Programs.

Weber-Burdin, E., and Rossi, P.H. (1982). Defining sexual harassment on campus: A replication and extension. *Journal of Social Issues, 38*, 111–120.

Wilson, K.R., and Kraus, L.A. (1983). Sexual harassment in the university. *Journal of College Student Personnel, 24*, 219–24.

Working Women's Institute. (1978). *Responses of fair employment practices agencies to sexual harassment complaints: A report and recommendations*. Research Series Report, No. 2. New York: Working Women's Institute.

U.S. Merit Systems Protection Board. (1981). *Sexual harassment in the federal workplace: Is it a problem?* Washington, DC: U.S. Government Printing Office.

3

The Interface of Racism and Sexism on College Campuses

Darlene C. DeFour

In each of the chapters in this volume there is a plea to the academy to establish a new taboo with respect to sexual and gender harassment. The academy needs to offer models that define the academy in modes that do not have a masculine bias. There is also a need to develop models that are less Eurocentric. An example of this can be seen in what are considered to be appropriate standards for research and publication. Sue (1983) pointed out the difficulty in getting work published using within-group designs when people of color are the study participants. It is considered "bad" design if the people of color are not compared to white participants. The same demand is not required in studies with white samples. Thus, the experience of the white samples is considered the norm.

The necessity for models that are less Eurocentric can also be seen in the sexual harassment literature. Researchers have indicated the high rate of the different levels of sexual harassment that have plagued women in academic settings. These studies have paid some attention to the women's stage of career development when reporting incidence rates. In all or most of the studies, the investigators were careful to report whether they were studying under-graduates, graduates, or professional women (e.g., Bond 1988; Dziech and Weiner 1984; Gutek and Morasch 1982). However, in the majority of the studies the researchers have failed to look at the impact of sexual harassment on women of color. In most of the studies the researchers have not asked the respondents to indicate their race or ethnicity (DeFour 1988). As a result of this omission, we do not have a knowledge of the level of victimization of women of color in the academy. Thus, not only have there been androcentric and Eurocentric biases in the academy, there has also been a Eurocentric bias in the sexual harassment literature in regard to women of color.

In this chapter I will talk about types of power and how they intersect with the levels of harassment. I would first like to provide a general definition of power. "Power, specifically social or interpersonal power, refers to the ability to achieve ends through influence" (Huston 1983, 170). Social psychologists have studied power and it bases extensively (e.g., French and Raven 1959; Raven 1965; Raven, Centers, and Rodrigues 1975). French and Raven (1959) identified six types of power: (a) reward power, (b) coercive power, (c) referent power, (d) legitimate powers (e) expert power, and (f) informational power.

Reward power involves the ability to give positive reinforcement to influence behavior. Coercive power involves the use of threats to remove a reward or threats of punishment to influence behavior. Under "referent power" individuals comply with requests because they like or admire the powerholder. Legitimate power is based on the authority that the powerholder derives as a result of in a particular social role. Expert power is that of an individual who is perceived to have superior knowledge or skill in an area. Persons can exert "informational power" when they have access to information that other individuals want or need.

I would now like to illustrate how I think that the types of power can manifest themselves within the following levels of harassment: gender harassment, seductive behavior, sexual bribery, sexual coercion, and sexual assault.

Gender harassment. Women of color have reported being victims of gender harassment that also has racist overtones (see Demby 1990). For example, a student in an American literature course wants to do her paper on Maya Angelou's work. She is told by her instructor that this is not an author who can be studied in his course. He doesn't consider Maya Angelou's work to be "important." In this example, both legitimate and expert power are being exerted. On the one hand he is indicating that in his role as professor he has the right to set up what is acceptable in his course (legitimate power). His standard excludes the work of women of color. In addition, the instructor could also be perceived as having expert power. "He has a Ph.D. in this field; he should know." Statements such as "It is my experience that Asian women usually do not do well in this course" fall into this category of harassment. All of these remarks are both sexist and racist and can seriously affect women of color's sense of competency and self-worth.

Seductive behavior. Unwanted inappropriate and offensive sexual advances can also have both racist and sexist components. Here both referent power and reward power could be at its base. An untenured Hispanic faculty member has an appointment with her department chair in his office to request travel funds. When she enters the room the lights are dim. There is soft music playing in the background. The chair that she is asked to sit in reclines. He indicates that there is an excellent chance that she will receive the travel funds she is seeking. He goes on to discuss how bright and attractive" she is. He states that although minorities in the past haven't done well in the department, she will. He will see to it. Here reward and legitimate power are being used. There is a suggestion that her cooperation will lead to concrete resources (reward power). The chairperson is also using the power of his role (legitimate power).

Sexual bribery. Obviously one power base that underlies sexual bribery is reward power. An example of this would be a male faculty member who offers rewards such as authorship on papers, work on grants, or fellowships appointments to students in return for sexual favors, dates, etc. The flip side to this is the use of coercive power that underlies *sexual coercion.* For instance, a student is told that she will not be granted authorship or recognition for work she has performed. Another example is receiving threats of the withdrawal of fellowship money and sponsorship if she will not date him. Coercion is also being used when a woman is told that her professional reputation will be damaged if she does not comply with the wishes of a male who is well known in her field. Referent power can also be the basis of both sexual bribery and sexual coercion, as when a woman complies with her harasser because she admires him. This is illustrated when an undergraduate is given special attention by her professor and he later makes sexual advances toward her. In a later section of this paper I will discuss why women of color may be vulnerable to sexual bribery and sexual coercion.

Sexual Imposition. Behaviors involved in sexual imposition include gross sexual imposition, assault, and rape (Fitzgerald, Shullman, et al. 1988). Others have described coercive power as the power base that underlies rape (e.g., Anderson-Barboza 1983). As Anderson-Barboza stated, "*Coercion,* a power type fundamental to understanding rape, reflects the means by which a rape victim is forced to succumb to her violator's sexual demands. . . . It deprives the victim of virtually all freedom of choice" (8). A full professor sexually assaults his undergraduate research assistant. The professor does not view this attack as rape because he believes that Hispanic women always desire sex. This is an example of sexual imposition with racist overtones.

RACISM AND SEXISM REVISITED

The failure to examine incidence rates of sexual harassment among women of color is alarming when one realizes that these women may be particularly vulnerable to this form of victimization. As suggested by Harrigan in Betz and Fitzgerald (1987):

The victim is a woman who is financially vulnerable and the perpetrator . . . is necessarily a male supervisor or employer who wield power over her. (231)

From the examples presented earlier in this paper, there are at least two types of factors that may serve to make women of color more vulnerable to harassment: economic factors, and images and stereotypes that are held about women of color.

Economic Factors

As pointed out in the quote by Harrigan, women who fall prey to harassment are often financially vulnerable. Women of color frequently hold positions that result in their economic vulnerability. As undergraduates they are often dependent upon financial aid to fund their education. Their family's income can not provide economic support (National Board of Graduate Education 1976). As graduate students, they have loans and fellowships more often than research assistantships (Blackwell 1981). Furthermore, female faculty members are more often concentrated in "gypsy scholar" positions. These are typically one-year contracts. In some cases the appointments are only one semester or one quarter. And faculty members who are in tenure-track jobs are often untenured. A large number of women of color in academic settings are outside of the classroom. They are secretaries, administrative staff, cooks, and housekeepers. These are all jobs where the women are supervised (very often by men).

The financial vulnerability of women of color is further illustrated when one examines the 1980 U.S. Census Bureau figures of annual salaries (National Committee on Pay Equity, 1988). The annual salaries are as follows: Asian women $12,432; white women $11,213; Black women $10,429; Native American women $10,052; and Hispanic women $9,725. These salaries are 60.0 percent, 55.1 percent, 51.3 percent, 49.4 percent, 47.8 percent, respectively, of the average salary for white males.

Images of Women of Color

The images and perceptions of women of color also increase their vulnerability to harassment. These images portray the women either as weak, and thus unlikely to fight back if harassed; or as very sexual and thus desiring sexual attention. Hispanic women have been described as hot-blooded, ill-tempered, religious, overweight, lazy, always pregnant, loudmouthed, and deferent to men. Native American women are perceived as poor, sad, un-educated, isolated, and devoted to male elders. Asian women have been described as small, docile, and submissive. However, they are also viewed by some as the exotic sexpot who will cater to the whims of any man (Kumagai 1978/1988). Black women have been perceived as domineering, having low morals, highly sexed, heads of households, and "loose." As pointed out by Tong (1934):

Sexual harassers tend to take advantage of those whom they perceive as most vulnerable, and whether we care to face it or not, black women enflesh the vulnerability of their people's slave past. (165)

IMPLICATIONS FOR RESEARCH AND PROGRAM PLANNING

When doing work on women of color we must be careful of the types of research models that we use. Sue (1983) outlined two research models that negatively conceptualize the experiences of people of color. We must be careful not to use (a) inferiority models that imply women of color are socially and intellectually inferior to white women as the result of biology and heredity; or (b) deficit models, which also assume that women of color are inferior but attribute their inferiority to external factors such as prejudice, discrimination, and social and economic conditions. Sue points to the need for research that is bicultural or multicultural when examining ethnic minority issues. Bicultural research is thought to have the following properties, implicit values, or orientation:

1. It attempts to conceptualize the influences of different cultures that interact with and are influenced by one another.
2 It tends to emphasize understanding ethnic minority groups on their own terms.
3 It is concerned about within-group variations and individual differences.

For example, results of recent research have indicated that Black women might use a sociocultural model to explain harassment, rather than the natural/biological or organizational explanatory models (Hunter College Women's Career Development Research Collective 1988). According to the sociocultural model of harassment, men harass in order to assert their personal power as men. Women who attribute sexual harassment to the sociocultural viewpoint report that victims of harassment should notify a therapist, women's studies coordinator and faculty, women's center, and support groups for women who have been victimized (Hunter College Women's Career Development Research Collective 1988). In regards to Black women, one must view the use of this strategy in the context of the history of African Americans in this country. These women have seen that the legal system has not always worked for them in the past. As a result of this, they may just want social support for dealing with the psychological pain involved in the victimization process (Hunter College Women's Career Development Research Collective 1988). In addition, different explanatory models of harassment may hold depending on whether the harasser is white or Black. As indicated by Tong (1984):

In those cases where their harassers are white men, black women generally observe that their harassers use sex as an excuse not only to control their *individual* bodies but also to exercise power over all of them as a *class* of persons: as women (sexism) or blacks (racism) or as disadvantaged blacks (classism). . . . That black women's reports of sexual harassment by white male superordinates "reflect a sense of impunity that resounds of slavery and colonization" is, in this connection highly significant. (165)

This is not to say that harassment is to be condoned depending on the race/ethnicity of the harasser. This is also not to imply that Black women feel less violated when the harasser is a Black male. The implication is that when racism, sexism, and classism combine, a qualitively different type of sexual harassment is the result (Tong, 1984). College campuses must recognize this issue when handling complaints of harassment, when designing prevention and intervention strategies, and when creating sexual harassment panels.

Historically research on gender and sexual harassment has excluded women of color. In the current paper I have outlined how types of power intersect with the various levels of harassment, and why women of color may be particularly vulnerable to harassment, as well as suggested a research model that could be used to study harassment among women of color.

References

Anderson-Barboza, L. (1983). *Women's perception of power and their vulnerability to coerced sexual experiences.* Unpublished doctoral dissertation, Columbia University, New York.

Betz, N., and Fitzgerald, L.F. (1987). *The career psychology of women.* New York: Academic Press.

Blackwell, J.E. (1981). *Mainstreamin outsiders: The production of black professionals.* Bayside, General Hall.

Bond, M. &1988). Division 27 sexual harassment survey: Definition, impact, and environmental context. Community Psychologist, 21, 7–10.

DeFour, D.C. (1988, July). Interface of racism and sexism in the academy. In M.A. Paludi (Chair), *Ivory power: Victimization of women in the Academy,* Symposium conducted at the 4th World Congress of Victimology, Tuscany, Italy.

Demby, L. (1990). In her own voice: A woman student's experience with sexual harassment. In M.A. Paludi (Ed.), *Ivory power: Sexual harassment on campus.* Albany: State University of New York Press.

Dziech, B., and Weiner, L. (1984). *The lecherous professor: Sexual harassment on campus.* Boston: Beacon Press.

Fitzgerald, L.F., Shullman, S., Bailey, N., Richards, M., Swecker, J. Gold, Y., Ormerod, M., and Weitzman, L. (1988). The incidence and dimensions of sexual harassment in academia and the workplace. *Journal of Vocational Behavior, 32,* 152–75.

French, J., and Raven, B. (1959). The basis of social power. In D. Cartwright (Ed.), *Studies in social power.* Ann Arbor: University of Michigan Press.

Gutek, B., and Morasch, B. (1982). Sex ratios, sex-role spillover and sexual harassment of women at work. *Journal of Social Issue, 38,* 55–74.

Hunter College Women's Career Development Research Collective. (1988, March). *Women's attitudes and attributions about sexual harassment.* Paper presented at the 13th Annual Meeting of the Association for Women in Psychology, Bethesda, MD.

Huston, T. (1983). Power. In H. Kelley et al. (Eds.), *Close relationships.* New York: W.H. Freeman.

Kumagai, G.L. (1978/1988). The Asian woman in America. In P.S. Rothenberg (Ed.), *Racism and sexism: An integrated study.* New York: St. Martin's Press. (Reprinted from *Explorations in Ethnic Studies, 1* [1978].)

National Board on Graduate Education. (1976). *Minority participation in graduate education.* Washington, DC: National Academy of Science.

National Committee on Pay Equity. (1988). The wage gap: Myths and facts. In P.S. Rothenberg (Ed.), *Racism and sexism: An integrated study.* New York: St. Martin's Press.

Raven, B.H. (1965). Social influence in power. In I.D. Steiner and M. Fishbein (Eds.), *Current studies in social psychology.* New York: Holt.

Raven, B.H., Centers, R., and Rodrigues, A. (1975). The basis of conjugal power. In R.S. Cromwell and D.H. Olsen (Eds.), *Power in families.* New York: Wiley.

Sue, S. (1983). Ethnic minority issues in psychology *American Psychologist, 38,* 583–92.

Tong, R. (1894). *Women, sex, and the law.* Totowa: Rowman & Allanheld.

4

The Perils and Promise of Studying Sexist Discrimination in Face-to-Face Situations

Bernice Lott

The objective of the research program discussed in this paper is a systematic investigation of sexist discrimination in face-to-face situations. My focus is on interpersonal discrimination, as distinct from institutional discrimination, with the former operationalized as distancing behavior. The central question addressed is what men *do* in the presence of women, not what they say they feel or believe about women.

From a social psychological/behavior oriented model of sexism in which prejudice, stereotypes, and discrimination are conceptually and operationally distinguished, I have derived predictions about men's behavior in the presence of women. The results of two studies (Lott 1987b, 1989) support the general proposition that men tend to distance themselves from women, and data from a third study (Lott, Lott, and Fernald 1988) illuminate individual differences in such distancing behavior. This program of research is intended (in the long run) (1) to identify some of the conditions under which the probability of distancing responses to women by men will be increased (or decreased); (2) to relate individual differences in men's distancing behavior to other measures of sexism and to background variables; and (3) to examine such behavior in a wide range of samples in a variety of situations.

I have proposed that a social psychological analysis of interpersonal sexism should include three theoretically related but independently measurable components: prejudice, stereotypes, and discrimination. Translating these concepts into the language of general behavior theory (in the liberalized S-R tradition; cf. Lott and Lott 1985) these components of sexism are distinguishable as follows: (1) *negative attitudes* toward women—hostility, dislike, misogyny—or, in more familiar terms, *prejudice*; (2) a set of *beliefs* about women that reinforce, complement, or justify the prejudice and involve an assumption of inferiority; these are the *stereotypes*—well-learned, widely shared, socially validated generalizations about women's nature or attributes; and (3) *overt behaviors* that achieve separation from women through exclusion, avoidance, or distancing—behaviors that define *discrimination* in face-to-face situations.

If we were to place overt acts of face-to-face discrimination against women on a continuum, we would likely begin with sexist jokes or putdowns, catcalls, leers, unwanted sexual attention of any kind and end with sexual assault, battering, and murder. Such a continuum includes behaviors that typically define sexual harassment as well as acts of devaluation, exclusion, and violence. While some of these specific behaviors clearly entail moving toward women and not away from them, it can be argued that their end result is to put a woman "in her place," to objectify her, and to thereby distance the actor from her.

The ample documentation of sexism in our society suggests that negative attitudes, beliefs, and behaviors directed toward women are acquired (primarily by men) under a wide array of differing circumstances. We know, of course, that men also learn positive attitudes, beliefs, and approach behaviors to women as a consequence of our association with nurturance and sexual pleasure. Because of the widespread reinforcement of sexism in our society, however, it is expected that sexist responses to women will predominate in relatively neutral situations.

Most psychological investigations of sexism have been concerned with beliefs or attitudes, and a large literature supports the conclusion that stereotyped beliefs and prejudice against women are common among men in our society (cf. Lott 1987a). Yet, with the exception of harassment and assault, the overt behaviors of men toward women in face-to-face situations have rarely been the focus of study. As noted by Geffner and Gross (1984) "there have been . . . very few experiments investigating discriminatory behavior in actual interactions between men and women" (974).

The research program described in this paper is directly concerned with the behaviors of men that are instrumental in avoiding or distancing themselves from women in relatively neutral face-to-face situations. This program is thus an attempt to validate empirically the personal experiences reported anecdotally by many women—that men tend to ignore and turn away from us in situations in which there is minimal expectation of sexual, nurturant, or other specifically positive consequences. Thus, for example, in describing the experiences of women administrators in universities, Mary Rowe (1973) has noted the frequency with which a woman found her name "mysteriously missing" from lists.

> Hers are the announcements and invitations which fail to come . . . , the pages which were not typed. . . . It is her work which by mistake

was not properly acknowledged, not reviewed, not responded to, not published, her opinion which is not asked for. (4)

Rowe referred to such behaviors as "the minutiae of sexism." I have never talked to a woman anywhere who did not report similar experiences of sexist "minutiae" in work or social situations.

In its focus on empirical tests of this significant realm of women's experience, the research reported here can be regarded as part of a feminist/behaviorist agenda in social psychology that extends areas of research to consider new questions stimulated by the study of women's lives (Lott 1985). In addition, this research moves beyond the existing psychological literature on sexism by focusing on overt behavior (not self-reported feelings or beliefs). As noted recently by Skinner (1987),

> There can scarcely be anything more familiar than human behavior. . . . We are always in the presence of at least one behaving person. Nor can there be anything more important. . . . Nevertheless it . . . has seldom been thought of as a subject matter in its own right, but rather has been viewed as the mere expression or symptom of more important happenings inside the behaving person. (780)

DISTANCING BEHAVIOR

The use of interpersonal distancing as a dependent measure of attitudes was common in an earlier literature (cf. Lott and Lott 1976) and dates back to the classic work of Bogardus (1925), who developed the "Social Distance Scale" to assess prejudice toward ethnic/racial groups. In a review of the literature, Evans and Howard (1973) concluded that "The preponderance of data suggest that persons who are friendly with each other or wish to communicate a positive affect will tend to interact at smaller interpersonal distances than those who are not friendly" (336f). A sizable literature supports this conclusion. For example, it has been reported (Allgeier and Byrne 1973) that college students in a laboratory situation placed themselves farther away from a disliked than from a liked confederate; that a sample of college men (but not women) approached more-likable persons than closer to less-likable persons (Wittig and Skolnick 1978); and that a sample of nonhandicapped college students avoided sitting next to a person in a wheelchair when there was an acceptable pretext for doing so (Snyder et al. 1979). Studies in which distancing is treated as an independent variable, and its consequences for observers are assessed, have generally found that positive and negative attitudes toward persons are communicated by smaller and larger distances, respectively (e.g., Mehrabian 1968).

That distancing behavior indicates a negative interpersonal response seems to be well supported by the literature. But are such responses made by men to women more often than to other men and more often than by women to either women or men? Such a proposition is supported by a variety of investigations using measures that have ranged from direct physical distance to the contents of dreams. In one study, for example (Barefoot, Hoople, and McClay 1972), male students were observed drinking from water fountains when either a male or female confederate sat some distance away. Only when the confederate was a woman did a greater percentage of men drink farther away than closer to the confederate. In a different kind of investigation, college students were randomly assigned to work in pairs on a drawing task with a nine-year-old child, either a girl or a boy. The investigators (Hoffman et al. 1984) found that while the women participants did not respond differently to boys and girls on any of the dependent measures, the college men spoke significantly less to girls than to boys. Suggestive data have also been reported by Hall (1984) on the contents of dreams studied across the world. Men, he found, in 29 of 35 samples, dream less frequently about women than about men, while women dream equally of both. "The sex difference occurs in groups on every continent; in a diversity of cultures . . . ; in all age groups; in dreams collected in the laboratory, in the classroom, and in the field by many different investigators over a period of 30 years" (1115).

From another group of studies has come evidence that in certain situations men tend to approach women at closer distances than they approach men, particularly situations in which such approach behavior indicates the "invasion of the personal space" of another person. Nancy Henley (1977) has argued that persons in high-status positions are more likely to encroach on the personal space of persons in subordinate positions than vice versa, and a review of research by Brenda Major (1981) led her to conclude that "men are overwhelmingly more likely to touch women than women are to touch men" (21). More recent reviewers, however, have questioned the earlier conclusions. For example, Hall (1987) concluded from her study of the literature on gender differences in nonverbal communication that the "evidence relating status to distance does not give much support to the assumption that low-status individuals are accorded smaller interpersonal distances" (190). And Stier and Hall (1984), who reviewed over forty observational studies, reported no overall tendency for men to touch women more than vice versa.

There is certainly good reason to expect that under appropriate conditions men will respond to women with a variety of approach behaviors. Such conditions are likely to be defined by contextual factors that signal the probability if obtaining nurturant, sexual, or other goals, including status enhancement. But under circumstances where no specific gain from approach is likely, men are more apt to avoid, withdraw, and separate themselves from women than from men, or than women are from same- or other-gender persons.

The research described in this paper focuses on behavior that is instrumental in achieving separation, withdrawal, or distance from others. Most of us, I believe, would agree that we make judgments about persons' feelings toward one another by observing their behavior and, in particular, whether it is of an approach or avoidance nature. How accurately such behaviors reflect attitudes and beliefs is an important question, but *the overt behavior itself has primary social significance*. Regardless of what it may tell us about feelings and beliefs, interpersonal distancing tells us something about face-to-face discrimination, per se. When one person avoids, withdraws, or distances from another, this behavior directly and clearly denotes separation or exclusion. Separation may also function as a necessary antecedent to aggression. Rachel Hare-Mustin and Jeanne Marecek (1987) have recently suggested, for example, that "distancing permits hostility and abuse toward women, as seen in pornographic images and sexual and physical abuse."

A LABORATORY DEMONSTRATION AND PRIME-TIME TV

Two completed studies have tested and found support for the general hypothesis that men tend to separate or distance themselves more from women than from men while women do not behave differently on this dimension toward same- and other-gender persons. In the first study (Lott 1987b), men's and women's behavior toward same-gender and other-gender partners with whom they had no prior acquaintance was compared in dyads brought to a laboratory to participate in a domino contest (to be judged on originality and complexity). Each pair was instructed to work together for ten minutes to build a structure with dominos (as they used to do "when you were children"). In this task-focused situation, self-report paper-and-pencil measures did not reveal bias against other-gender partners in feelings or beliefs on the part of either women or men. However, the observations of trained observers who watched the pairs behind a one-way-vision window indicated that men more frequently made negative statements and turned away from their partners when these were women than when these were men, and less frequently followed the advice of women partners than that of men partners. For the women, on the other hand, their partner's gender made no difference with respect to any of the measured behaviors. An additional finding was that the domino structures built by mixed-gender pairs were significantly more often closer to the man than to the woman, providing a concrete, physical illustration of the tendency of men to distance themselves from women.

In this study, no differences would have been found between men's responses to women and to other men had the data been restricted to self-reports of feelings and beliefs. Self-report measures did not reveal prejudice or stereotypes. Only observation of behavior revealed significant interactions between gender of actor and gender of partner, specifically, reliable differences in the way men responded to women partners and men partners, but no such differences in the behavior of women. These findings underscore the theoretical and practical necessity of separating the overt behavioral component of sexism (discrimination) from both the affective (negative attitudes) and the cognitive (stereotyped beliefs).

In the second study (Lott 1989), the behavior of men and women toward same- and other-gender persons was observed on the television screen, as performed by characters in episodes of weekly dramatic or comedy shows. If sexism is a dominant feature of our present society, an assumption supported by a wide array of data, one would expect to find it reflected in the mass media that communicate to us so much about our culture's ideology. With respect to television, in particular, it has been amply demonstrated that this medium, both in programming and in advertising, reinforces and perpetuates gender stereotypes (e.g., Singer, Singer, and Zuckerman 1981). According to Liebert, Sprafkin, and Davidson (1982), for example:

> Content analyses invariably show that [men] enjoy highly prestigious positions [while] most TV women are assigned marital, romantic, and family roles. . . . In terms of how they behave, TV males are portrayed as more powerful, dominant, aggressive, stable, persistent, rational, and intelligent than females. Females are portrayed as more attractive, altruistic, sociable, warm, sympathetic, happy, rule abiding, peaceful, and youthful than males. (163)

There is clear documentation for the conclusion that the television shows we watch carry a relatively consistent message that conforms to our society's stereotypes about gender. But do the characters behave in ways that also illustrate the discrimination component of sexism? Do men, in other words, tend to be shown distancing themselves from women?

To answer this question, ten prime-time TV programs found to be most popular with a sample of eighth-graders were observed by a group of trained college students. Men and women TV characters were observed interacting with same- and other-gender persons, and the frequency of distancing behaviors (as well as positive approach and aggressive approach behaviors) was recorded. Observers were preassigned on a random basis to watch four programs and, for each, the gender of the character to be observed was also preassigned. During the first segment of a TV program, each observer chose a character of the preassigned gender, who was then monitored in interaction with other persons during the second 10- to 12-minute segment. As predicted, men TV characters were observed more frequently to distance themselves from women than from men. Distancing responses by women TV characters, on the other hand, were not related to the gender of the person they were with. It was also found that women characters appeared less often in the TV programs than men, and that when they did appear they were significantly more likely to be shown interacting with men than with other women.

In this study, TV characters were observed across a wide variety of situations, and the finding of greater distancing by men from women was a general one, cutting across programs, specific circumstances, contexts, relationships, age and ethnic groups, geographic and environmental locations. The data obtained not only span diverse situations and conditions, but also come from a large number of independent observers who watched different characters on different shows. When the observations of women and men were analyzed separately, each sample of observers yielded the same findings in support of the hypothesis. The use of many participants observing a wide array of situations follows a model of research proposed by Egon Brunswik (1956). According to this model, the sampling of both observed stimuli and observers enables research to be done in natural situations where standard controls are not possible or desirable.

SOME NEGATIVE REACTIONS TO THIS RESEARCH

I thought the findings obtained from these studies were exciting and was, of course, interested in publishing them. As a well-seasoned contributor to professional journals, I anticipated that I would get my share of suggestions, criticisms, questions, and both frustrating and helpful feedback from reviewers and editors. But I didn't expect a response to this work that was different in kind from reactions to previously submitted work. I will not identify the journals from which this feedback came, but I would like to share some of the comments that do not deal with issues of method, analysis, organization, or detail. These I appreciated and found generally constructive; it is with comments of a different sort that I had difficulty since they seemed to reflect an anxiety about both my conceptual analysis and the empirical findings.

To begin with, I found that my original tile for these studies, "Women As Aversive Stimuli for Men," made some reviewers uncomfortable. When one reader called the title "provocative" (in the negative sense), I decided to change it. Several reviewers quarreled not with my designs or analyses but with my concepts, one saying that it is "ambiguous to call sexism . . . a psychological phenomenon," another arguing that women's lower pay, for example, is less a matter of discrimination than of men's "economic self interest."

Some reviewers simply refused to accept my definition of discrimination in face-to-face situations as distancing behavior, illustrated by the behavior observed by men toward women in the domino and TV studies. One reviewer suggested that men may actually feel more at ease with women since they can dominate them; and another suggested that TV "writers [may] believe that female characters are less interesting to viewers," and that this might be a better explanation of the observed paucity of interactions among women characters.

One editor, in commenting on the TV study, argued that some of the observers might "for some unconscious reason [have] preferred to watch male subjects behaving in a stereotypic fashion toward female targets [and] might well have selected a subset of characters who in fact confirmed the avoidant pattern, overlooking male characters who behaved differently." I wrote to this editor and told him that I considered this comment a "classic" and that I was looking forward to sharing it. This same editor did not believe that the findings of the TV study went beyond those obtained in the domino task study. "Certainly," he wrote, "the two studies together would have been an impressive package. In that the other paper is already forthcoming in the literature, the novelty of this contribution is somewhat attenuated." You can imagine the laugh I got out of that when I recalled that the first paper of this "impressive package" was turned down by the very same journal.

The comments I found most disturbing were those that accused me of going too far. One critic objected to my saying that the finding that women TV characters were shown significantly less often in the company of other women than in the company of men illustrates the general proposition that in our society women's value derives primarily from association with men. Another said that it was an overgeneralization to assert, as I had, that the dominant response of men to women in our society reflects prejudice and stereotypes. And one reader wrote the following:

> I do not subscribe to the view that psychology can be or should be value-neutral, but I find the conceptual framework offered . . . to be so heavily value-loaded that I wonder whether any data could disconfirm it.

The conceptual framework referred to by this reviewer is the same one I presented at the start of this paper.

Fortunately, some reactions were positive. Reports of both studies have been published in the *Psychology of Women Quarterly*, and the domino task paper received a distinguished publication award in 1987 from the Association for Women in Psychology.

PROPOSED NEXT STEPS

What are my next steps in this program of research? First, since most of the literature on sexist discrimination is concerned with its institutional forms—in the educational, political, legal, and workforce systems, a thorough and careful review of the psychological literature dealing with face-to-face interaction between women and men is needed. Methodological and conceptual problems need to be identified and conclusions drawn from the empirical findings.

The general hypothesis that men (but not women) are more likely to distance themselves from other-gender than from same-gender persons must be tested under varied and relatively natural conditions. These conditions should satisfy the criteria of not presenting cues that are likely to evoke expectations of possible sexual pleasure, nurturance, or other specific positive outcomes, nor expectations that distancing (discrimination) will be disapproved. Both demand characteristics and cues likely to evoke competing behavior (such as "helping") must be minimized.

Some studies will vary the conditions under which distancing behavior will be observed. For example, it is hypothesized that distancing responses by men to women will be less probable in situations in which the behavior will be observed by persons known to favor gender equality in opportunities, and more probable in situations in which the behavior will be observed by persons known to strongly support the status quo. It is also hypothesized that distancing responses by men to women will be less probable in situations in which face-to-face interaction is between persons of equal social or work status and more probable in face-to-face situations in which the man is of higher status. (Women's distancing behavior to men under these conditions will also be observed.)

It is likely that the extent to which men distance themselves from women will be related to their expectation of positive or aversive consequences for doing so. The most probable antecedent conditions for these expectations are one's own past experiences and the observation of the behavior of others and the consequences received by others. In a series of proposed studies, therefore, samples of adults and children will be exposed to conditions such as the following: They will observe a high-status adult man interact with persons of both genders and consistently (or inconsistently) ignore/turn away from (or positively approach) women more than men (or men more than women); they will observe a highly liked peer of the same or different gender who has been the source of prior reward, interact with individuals of both genders and consistently distance (or not distance, or positively approach) girls/women (or boys/men). In each case the effects of the experimental conditions will be tested under new conditions. These studies will require the use of confederates (in live and/or videotaped scenes) and will necessitate careful debriefing of participants, a process through which information can be shared about the nature of sexism and the acquisition and maintenance of discriminatory behavior.

In an effort to identify other variables related to individual differences in men's distancing responses to women, measures of such behavior will be correlated with demographic/background variables and with other (affective and cognitive) measures of sexism, such as attitudes toward women, tolerance for sexual harassment, or a belief that gender relations are adversarial. For each of these variables, reliable and valid measures are available, thus enabling connections to be made among a wide range of phenomena.

My colleagues and I have developed a simulated measure of distancing behavior in the form of a Picture Choice Task that requires a participant to choose from pairs of photographs of middle-aged adults the one who is preferred for a particular interaction. Participants respond to a series of 24 cards, each of which contains the photographs of two adults previously judged by a sample of raters as being of moderate and relatively equal attractiveness. Each card presents a question beginning with "Who would you choose" and the participant is asked to choose from the two photographs the person who is preferred. Eight different sets of three cards present eight different service interactions (e.g., "Who would you choose as your real estate agent?"). For each different service interaction (relatively nonstereotyped by gender) there are three different cards, one showing the photographs of two women, one showing two men, and one card showing a woman and a man. Thus, 8 of the 24 cards, a choice is requested between persons of different gender. There are 22 sets of 24 cards containing the photographs of 48 different persons in completely randomized orders.

In a study of a heterogeneous sample of 262 adult respondents (Lott, Lott, and Fernald 1988), the number of men chosen over women has been related to gender and age of the chooser, and to scores on two widely used measures of beliefs developed by Burt (1980)—Adversarial Sex Beliefs, and Sex Role Stereotyping. As predicted, men, whether over 30 or younger than 30, chose women significantly below chance level, while women over 30 made other-gender and same-gender choices that did not differ from chance. Women under 30, however, chose women over men reliably more than chance. An examination of mean differences in belief scores among groups of persons whose scores on the picture choice task were low, medium, and high revealed that men who were more likely to turn away from women in hypothetical situations were also more likely to adhere to stereotyped beliefs about sex roles and to view relationships between women and men as adversarial; this same pattern of individual differences was found among women.

Other studies are planned that will test relationships among behavioral measures of distancing, a simulated measure like the picture choice task, demographic variables, and other self-reported affective and cognitive responses such as attitudes toward women (Spence and Helmreich 1972) and tolerance for sexual harassment (Lott, Reilly, and Howard 1982).

IMPLICATIONS FOR THE REAL
WORLD AND SOCIAL POLICY

If the data from this research program continue to support the conclusion that sexist behavior (discrimination) in face-to-face situations is independent of what men say they feel or believe about women, then programs directed toward the reduction of sexism must provide for the separate assessment of actions, feelings, and cognitions and include strategies appropriate for each domain. Variables found to relate significantly to the increased (and decreased) probability of distancing responses to women will help us to understand how such behavior is learned and maintained, and will assist us in teaching what we know to others.

Porter and Geis (1981) have reported a similar lack of congruence among expressed beliefs and sexist behavior. They had participants in one study look at slides of five-person groups and make judgments about the group leader. The person sitting at the head of the table was seen as the group leader in same-gender groups, and in mixed-gender groups when the person at the head of the table was a man. But when a woman was seated at the head of the table in a mixed-gender group, participants tended not to name her as the group leader. In other words, as concluded by the investigators, "The only condition in which seeing was not believing was the one showing a woman in the leadership position in a mixed sex group" (58). What is most relevant to the present discussion is that this kind of sexist discrimination was not revealed by self-reports of belief in aspects of feminist ideology.

Taking a step-by-step approach to a major social problem (sexism), like the one described in this paper, permits us to concentrate on "small wins" and may temper the tendency to feel overwhelmed by the problem's enormity and complexity. As Karl Weick (1984) has argued, contributing to the difficulty of solving social problems is the fact that "people define these problems in ways that overwhelm their ability to do anything about them. Changing the scale of a problem can change the quality of resources directed at it" (48). If we redefine a social problem as a series of small tasks that can be accomplished, then a social problem becomes amenable to change by less than superhuman effort.

It is toward this social objective that the research program I have described is directed. Separating overt behavior from attitudes and beliefs is theoretically sound and empirically necessary, and it also increases the probability that we will understand more clearly and simply the conditions that influence the occurence of sexist discrimination in face-to-face situations. This, in turn, should help us to make thoughtful and realistic suggestions about ways to improve social life.

Notes

This chapter is a revised version of a paper read at the national conference of the Association for Women in Psychology, March 1988, Bethesda, Maryland.

POSTSCRIPT

In addition to the study utilizing the picture choice test mentioned in this chapter, another investigation, by Renee Saris, Ingrid Johnston, and me, provides more information about interpersonal sexist discrimination. In this investigation an equal number of adult women and men sitting alone were approached randomly at four different train stations by a college student, either female or male. The 240 participants were diverse in age and ethnicity. Persons who agreed to answer questions filled out two simulated distance measures and a measure of attitudes toward egalitarian sex roles. One of the distance measures is a seating measure, devised by us, that presents seven hypothetical situations, each involving a row of seats in which four are empty while the second and fifth seats are occupied. In three situations one of the seats is occupied by a woman and one by a man. A second measure, the Movie Choice Measure, also devised by us, contains seven items in which the respondent is presented with a choice between two movies of different types. Each movie choice involves placing oneself in a row of three seats, the first of which is already occupied. For three times, the choice is between a movie where a woman is already seated and where a man is already seated.

For women respondents, as predicted, gender of the persons already seated in the hypothetical situations did not influence where they chose to sit. Men's choices, on the other hand, were influenced by the gender of the persons seated. Most men were in the extreme categories, that is, they had chosen to sit near a man rather than near a woman above the median (three or more times) or below the median (one or zero times). When the women and men were compared on just the proportions in the median score category, the difference between these proportions (.41 for women, .25 for men) was found to be statistically significant. The results of this study suggest that men are less likely to react neutrally to women than they are to men, even in relatively sex-neutral situations, with some tending to distance and others to approach.

Another, more qualitative study, by Therese Doyan and Randi Cohan, explored the experience of distancing by men reported by a sample of 92 adult women, half of whom were over 35 and half of whom were women of color. The purpose of this study was to test the generality of our distancing hypothesis across categories of age, ethnicity, and income. Preliminary analyses of the data indicate that neither age nor ethnicity of the woman makes a difference in the numbers of women who report being turned away from by men or in the frequency of this experience.

References

Allgeier, A.R., and Byrne, D. (1973). Attraction toward the opposite sex as a determinant of physical proximity. *Journal of Social Psychology, 90*, 213–19.

Barefoot, J.C., Hoople, H., and McClay, D. (1972). Avoidance of an act which would violate personal space. *Psychonomic Science, 28*, 205–6.

Bogardus, E. (1925). Measuring social distance. *Journal of Applied Sociology, 9*, 299–308.

Brunswik, E. (1956). *Perception and the retresentative design of psychological experiments* (2nd ed.). Berkeley: University of California Press.

Burt, M.R. (1980). Cultural myths and supports for rape. *Journal of Pesonality and Social Psychology, 38*, 217–30.

Evans, G.W., and Howard, R.B. (1973). Personal space. *Psychological Bulletin, 80*, 334–44.

Geffner, R., and Gross, M.M. (1984). Sex-role behavior and obedience to authority: A field study. *Sex Roles, 10*, 973–85.

Hall, C.S. (1984). "A ubiquitous sex difference in dreams" revisited. *Journal of Personality and Social Psychology, 46*, 1109–17.

Hall, J.A. (1987). On explaining gender differences: The case of nonverbal communication. In P. Shaver and C. Hendrick (Eds.), *Sex and gender* (177–200). New York: Sage.

Hare-Mustin, R.T., and Marecek, J. (1987, August). *Gender and the meaning of difference*. Paper read at the meeting of the American Psychological Association, New York.

Henley, N.M. (1977). *Body politics: Power, sex, and non-verbal communication*. Englewood Cliffs, NJ: Prentice-Hall.

Hoffman, C.D., Tsuneyoshi, S.E., Ebina, M., and Fite, H. (1984). A comparison of adult males' and females' interactions with girls and boys. *Sex Roles, 11*, 799–811.

Liebert, R.M., Sprafkin, J.N., and Davidson, E.S. (1982). *The early window: Effects of television on children and youth* (2nd ed.). New York: Pergamon.

Lott, A.J., and Lott, B. (1976). The role of reward in the formation of positive interpersonal attitudes. In T.L. Huston (Ed.), *Foundations of interpersonal attraction.* New York: Academic Press.

Lott, B. (1985). The potential enrichment of social/personality psychology through feminist research, and vice versa. *American Psychologist, 40,* 155–64.

———. (1987a). *Women's lives: Themes and variations in gender learning.* Pacific Grove, CA: Brooks/Cole.

———. (1987b). Sexist discrimination as distancing behavior: I. A laboratory demonstration. *Psychology of Women Quarterly, 11,* 47–58.

———. (1989). Sexist discrimination as distancing behavior: II. Prime time television. *Psychology of Women Quarterly, 13,* 341–345.

Lott, B., and Lott, A.J. (1985). Learning theory in contemporary social psychology. In G. Lindzey and E. Aronson (Eds.), *The handbook of social psychology* (3rd ed., vol. 2, 109–36). New York: Random House.

Lott, B., Lott, A.J., and Fernald, J. (1988). *individual differences in distancing responses to women on a photo choice task.* Unpublished paper, Department of Psychology, University of Rhode Island, Kingston.

Lott, B., Reilly, M.E., and Howard, D.R. (1982). Sexual assault and harassment: A campus community case study. *Signs, 8,* 296–319.

Mehrabian, A. (1968). Inference of attitudes from the posture, orientation, and distance of a communicator. *Journal of Consulting and Clinical Psychology, 32,* 296–308.

Porter, N., and Geis, F. (1981). Women and nonverbal leadership cues: When seeing is not believing. In C. Mayo and N.M. Henley (Eds.), *Gender and nonverbal behavior* (39–61). New York: Springer-Veriag.

Rowe, M.P. (1973). *The progress of women in educational institutions: The Saturn's rings phenomenon.* Unpublished paper, Office of the President and Chancellor of MIT, Cambridge.

Singer, D.G., Singer, J.L., and Zuckerman, D.M. (1981). *Teaching television: How to use TV to your child's advantage.* New York: Dial.

Skinner, B.F. (1987). Whatever happened to psychology as the science of behavior? *American Psychologist, 42,* 780–86.

Snyder, M.L., Kleck, R.G., Strenta, A., and Mentzer, S.J. (1979). Avoidance of the handicapped: An attributional ambiguity analysis. *Journal of Personality and Social Psychology, 37,* 2297–2306.

Spence, J.T., and Helmreich, R.L. (1972). The Attitudes toward Women Scale. *JSAJ Catalog Sel. Doc. Psychology, 2,* 66.

Stier, D.S., and Hall, J.A. (1984). Gender differences in touch: An empirical and theoretical review. *Journal of Personality and Social Psychology, 47,* 440–59.

Weick, K.E. (1984). Small wins: Redefining the scale of social problems. *American Psychologist, 39,* 40–49.

Wittig, M.A., and Skolnick, P. (1978). Status versus warmth as determinants of sex differences in personal space. *Sex Roles, 4,* 493–503.

Part II

Abuse of the Power
of the Professoriate

Faculty Who Harass and "Consensual Relationships"

Editor's Notes

One way student victims of sexual harassment are asked to change their perceptions of their experiences concerns focusing attention on the motives of the harasser. Most individuals believe that sexual harassers are pathological and abnormal and can easily be spotted. Louise Fitzgerald reported, following her study of men on college/university faculties, that "the stereotype that there is a 'typical' harasser who can be identified by his blatant and obvious mistreatment of many women is a serious oversimplification of a complex issue and contributes to the misunderstanding of this issue." Harassers are found in all types of occupations, at all organizational levels, among business and professional individuals as well as among college professors. Fitzgerald also noted that although "it is difficult and painful to confront the reality that harassment can be perpetrated by individuals who are familiar to us, who have traditional family lives, and who appear to be caring and sensitive individuals, it is indeed a reality and cannot be ignored." Research has thus suggested that there is no typical harasser.

Individuals who harass typically do not label their behavior as sexual harassment, despite the fact that they report that they frequently engage in initiating personal relationships with individuals. They deny the inherent power difference between themselves and their students as well as the psychological power conferred by this difference, which is as salient as the power derived from evaluation.

John Pryor (1987) reported that the man who is likely to initiate severe sexually harassing behavior appears to be one who emphasizes male social and sexual dominance, and who demonstrates insensitivity to other individuals' perspectives. In addition, men are less likely than women to define sexual harassment as including jokes, teasing remarks of a sexual nature, and unwanted suggestive looks or gestures. Men typically view sexual harassment as a personal, not an organizational, issue. Men were also significantly more likely than women to agree with the following statements, taken from my "Attitudes toward Victim Blame and Victim Responsibility" survey:

Women often claim sexual harassment to protect their reputations.

Many women claim sexual harassment if they have consented to sexual relations but have changed their minds afterwards.

Sexually experienced women are not really damaged by sexual harassment.

It would do some women good to be sexually harassed.

Women put themselves in situations in which they are likely to be sexually harassed because they have an unconscious wish to be harassed.

In most cases when a woman is sexually harassed, she deserved it.

Bernice Lott (see this volume) and her colleagues have also found empirical support for a widely accepted assumption among researchers in sexual harassment: that sexual harassment is part of a larger and more general dimension of misogyny, or hostility toward women, expressed in extreme stereoytpes of women, including the mythical images of sexual harassment—that sexual harassment is a form of seduction, that women secretly need/want to be forced into sex.

In some of my new research on why men sexually harass women, I have focused not on men's attitudes toward women but instead on men's attitudes toward other men, competition, and power. Many of the men with whom I have discussed sexual harassment in my research often act out of extreme competitiveness and concern with ego or out of fear of losing their positions of power. They don't want to appear weak or less masculine in the eyes of other men, so they will engage in such behaviors as scoping of women, pinching women, making implied or overt threats, demanding sexual favors from women, or spying on women. Women are the game to impress other men. Similar to Peggy Sanday's findings concerning fraternity men's involvement in date rapes, I am finding that when men are being encouraged to be obsessionally competitive and concerned with dominance, it is likely that they will eventually use violent means to achieve dominance. They are also likely to be verbally abusive and intimidating in their body language. Deindividuation is quite common among men who scope women students as they walk into and out of their classrooms or laboratories. These men discontinue self-evaluation and adopt group norms and attitudes. Under these circumstances, group members behave more aggressively than they would as individuals.

The element of aggression that is so deeply embedded in the masculine gender role is present in sexual harassment. For many men, aggression is one of the major ways of proving their masculinity, especially among those men who feel some sense of powerlessness in their lives. The-male-as-dominant or male-as-aggressor is a theme so central to many men's self-concept that it literally carries over into their interpersonal communications, especially with women co-workers. Sexualizing a professional relationship might be the one area where the average man can still prove his masculinity when few other areas allow him to prove himself to be in control or the dominant one in a relationship. Thus, similar to what Diana Russell has stated with respect to men who rape, sexual harassment is not so much a deviant act as an overconforming act.

Margaret Mead (1978) once argued that a new taboo is needed on campus that demands that faculty make new norms, not rely on masculine-biased definitions of success, career development, and sexuality. What is also needed is an ethic of care—and the restructuring of academic institutions so that caring can become a central and active value. These sentiments suggest changes in the present institutional structures that dominate the college and university system.

One important change needs to be in the mentor-protégé relationship where women are protégés and men are mentors (Haring-Hidore and Paludi 1991). Women have reported needing very different kinds of information from mentors than men do. For example, women report wanting their mentoring relationship to include psychosocial aspects, such as receiving advice (mostly from women) on personal problems, receiving information on dealing with role strain involved in combining a career and family life, and being assisted with personal development (Paludi and DeFour 1992). Women place considerable emphasis on working with mentors who combine personal and professional roles and who are likely to affirm them as professionals as well as encourage and support their profesional goals. Women indicate that this affirmation and encouragement typically comes from women faculty.

However, many mentoring relationships involve men as mentors and women as protégés. This common arrangement by which men are in positions of power within mentoring relationships (as mentors) and women are in more vulnerable positions (as protégés) suggests the possibility of sexuality and sex as significant and complex factors within such relationships. More women than men experience problems in mentoring relationships, such as not being included in faculty members' professional networks and not being encouraged in their field of study. This finding is consistent with findings of Brooks and Haring-Hidore (1987). Further, women are typically isolated from informal collegial contacts; they consequently receive less encouragement for their successes and are avoided by their male mentors. Clow and Paludi (1985) reported that male mentors are reluctant to mentor women because they believe that women are not as dedicated to their careers as men are. Male mentors indicate that they perceive women who are apprenticed to them as requiring help, remedial assistance. Thus, women are described as "needing" mentoring. This raises a paradox in the mentoring literature (LaFrance 1987): As women continue to get the mentoring they *need*, they will be perceived as *needing* the mentoring they get. Women's achievements may thus be explained by external, unstable causal factors, such as help from a senior man.

Mentors are seen as essential because they generate power. The introduction of sexuality and sex into mentoring relationships can have negative implications for achievement for women protégés. Women who are suspected of having "slept their way to the top" are castigated by others, sometimes unfairly when the accusation is false. Women who have sex with their mentors may be unjustly deprived of their achievements if the achievements did not depend on an unfair advantage gained by a sexual mentoring relationship. Whether it is fair or not, achievements made in sexual mentoring relationships may never boost protégés' careers and may, in fact, detract from their careers because of the stigma attached by others (Haring-Hidore and Paludi 1991).

The chapters in this section deal with this overconforming to the masculine gender role in our culture. Sue Rosenberg Zalk has stated:

> The bottom line in the relationship between faculty member and student is POWER. The faculty member has it and the student does not. As intertwined as the faculty student roles may be, and as much as one must exist for the other to exist, they are not equal collaborators. The student does not negotiate—indeed, has nothing to negotiate with.

Zalk notes that this power imbalance is ignored by men faculty. And it is to this issue that Jan Salisbury and Fredda Jaffee turn in their work in training faculty harassers about verbal and nonverbal gestures of power and how faculty must decenter from their own perspective to understand how students perceive them.

M. Cynara Stites offers her perspective on the costs of such faculty-student "consensual relationships" for women undergraduate and graduate students. Stites also notes how including consensual relationships as part of the definition of academic sexual harassment has been met with considerable resistance. There are a few campuses (e.g., University of Iowa, Harvard University, Temple University) that prohibit sexual relationships between faculty and students over whom the professor has some authority (i.e., advising, supervising, grading, teaching). A few other campuses (e.g., University of Minnesota, University of Connecticut, New York University Law School, Massachusetts Institute of Technology) have "discouragement policies, in which "consensual relations" are not strictly prohibited but are discouraged.

More recently, the University of Virginia called for a total ban on all sexual relationships between faculty and students, regardless of the professor's role vis-à-vis the student. However, the faculty senate approved a prohibition-only policy rather than the total-ban policy. Thus, this campus prohibits sexual relations between a faculty member and a student when the faculty member has some organizational power over the student. The case can be made, however, that a faculty member does not have to be the student's professor in order for that faculty member to be powerful and to potentially abuse that power over the student. All faculty members have an ethical and professional responsibility to provide a learning environment that is respectful of students and fosters the academic performance and intellectual development of students.

The fact that a student is an adult can in no way remove the obligation of a faculty member or college/university administrator to refrain from engaging in sexual harassment, and the student's adulthood is in no way a proxy for consenting to a relationship. The stories women students tell about their "consensual relationships" do not parallel romances or typical stories about sexual affairs; they instead resemble stories depicting patterns of manipulation and victimization, responses identical to those of women students who are sexually harassed in nonconsensual relationships.

Is there such a thing as a women student's informed consent in a sexual relationship with a male faculty member? In answering this question, Stites asks us to think about power relations in the campus setting that are stratfied by sex.

References

Brooks, L., and Haring-Hidore, M. (1987). Mentoring in academe: A comparison of mentors' and protégés perceived problems. *International Journal of Mentoring, 1,* 3–9.

Clow, C., and Paludi, M.A. (1985). *Mentoring: An intergenerational perspective.* Unpublished data, Kent State University.

Haring-Hidore, M., and Paludi, M.A. (1991). Power, politics, and sexuality in mentor-protégés relationships: Implications for women's achievement. In S. Klein (Ed.), *Sex and sexuality in education.* Albany: State University of New York Press.

LaFrance, M. (1987, July). *The paradox of mentoring.* Paper presented at the Interdisciplinary Congress on Women, Dublin, Ireland.

Mead, M. (1978). A proposal: We need new taboos on sex at work. Reported in B. Dziech and L. Weiner (1984). *The lecherous professor.* Boston: Beacon Press.

Paludi, M.A., and DeFour, D.C. (1992). The Mentoring Experiences Questionnaire. *Mentoring International*, 6, 19–23.

Pryor, J. (1987). Sexual harassment proclivities in men. *Sex Roles*, *17*, 269–90.

5

Men in the Academy:
A Psychological Profile of Harassers

Sue Rosenberg Zalk

What prompts a faculty member to sexualize his relationship with a student and cross over the parameters of his professional role by simultaneously engaging in an incompatible role?

This chapter explores some of the psychological dynamics of male faculty who relate sexually to female students and the structural context of the academy within which they operate.[1] "Relate sexually" is being used to refer to sexual overtures (e.g., aggressive demands or subtle seductions), respectivity to students' sexual invitations, and behavior designed to achieve sexual intimacy with a student or to establish a special, exclusive bond built on flirtatious relating. Gender harassers whose behaviors are not directed toward sexual intimacy are excluded. Gender harassment is so pervasive that it would require a lengthy, almost endless analysis of the "hows, whys, and wherefores" of misogyny.

There is remarkably little literature which specifically addresses the psychological dynamics of male teachers who sexually harass students. Dziech and Weiner (1984) entitle a chapter of their book "The Lecherous Professor: A Portrait of the Artist." Many of their observations and analyses are referred to later in this chapter. Using an anonymous questionnaire, Fitzgerald, Weitzman, et al. (1988) asked male professors their thoughts about sexual encounters with students. The rationales for condoning the behavior varied somewhat in angle, but they all had one common feature—*denial of power.*

Short of these pieces, however, the literature is sparse. The reasons for the blank pages are obvious. How does one collect data that sheds light on the psychological dynamics of these men? Professors who sexually harass women students are understandably reticent to volunteer as participants for such a study. They do not, as a rule, declare themselves publicly. There are no lists from which to solicit participants or clinics or self-help groups for harassers. In short, these men do not judge their behavior to be in any way symptomatic of a personal problem. They do not apply the label *sexual harasser* to themselves.

A number of researchers have collected demographic data on faculty sexual harassers from faculty as well as students who were subject to incidences of sexual harassment. Professors who sexually harass students cross all ages, professorial ranks, disciplines, and family situations (e.g., Fitzgerald, Weitzman, et al 1988; Sandler 1981). Similar findings have been reported in research on sexual harassment in the workplace, and Tangri, Burt, and Johnson (1982) suggest that the behavior is so multi-determined that it may approximate a random event. If this is so, what, if anything, is to be learned by studying the sexual harasser?

It is clear that we cannot understand sexual harassment without placing it within the context of misogyny and sexist oppression. As such, although individuals commit the act of harassment, can it be understood as in individual dynamic? Can we understand why some male professors harass women students by studying these men? Is sexual harassment indicative of a maladjustment of the harasser or of society? While one can argue either position (assuming one accepts the premise that it is evidence of a pathology), the two may not be so easy to separate. These men are products of, and mirror, a sexist culture. But one cannot stop here, for *that culture also reflects the psychology of men.*

Sexual harassment is a symptom—both of the individual and of society. It is one among countless expressions of gender stratification. In most societies men have more power than women and they use that power difference to maintain it. Power provides many licenses, including the right to exploit the less powerful. Sexual harassment conforms to role expectations and operates within cultural guidelines.

Placing sexual harassment within the context of sexual oppression paves the way for an analysis of the academy and its role in promoting harassment. Nonetheless, not all male professors sexually harass female students. There is valuable psychological and social information embedded in the dynamics of sexual harassment.

An analogy to misogyny elucidates this point. The fact that misogyny is rampant in most societies and that these societies provide for and promote its expression does not explain why men hate women. Concluding that men hate women because they *can* is nonsensical. Just as hating women is not simply an expression of many individuals' idiosyncratic psychological histories existing in a societal vacuum, neither is sexual harassment the acting out of isolated individuals' emotional irritants.

Not all men sexually harass women, but such harassment is pervasive enough in most societies to indicate that the social structure nurtures a male psychology that finds gratification in this behavior. It is instilled in the psychological development of these males and is sufficiently pervasive to reflect a pattern of shared experience. The study of men who sexually harass women will enlighten our understanding of male psychological development, gender dynamics, and the ways in which cultural definitions and roles shape the repetition of patterns through psychological needs.

Behaviors, even emotions, do not exist in a vacuum. As such, an understanding of the professor who engages in a sexual liaison with a student requires an understanding of the context with which these events occur.

THE ACADEMY: A MODEL PATRIARCHY

The academy is, in many ways, a microcosm of the larger society. The differences that do exist, however, seem striking for their exaggeration of roles-roles created and legitimized by an institutional design that fosters power and status inequities ripe for exploitation.

The formal academy was instituted to educate men for the betterment of society (which was to be achieved by providing educational resources to an elite few whose social status targeted them as the future leaders). Men teaching men. Women were intruders, and their presence was strongly resisted. But that is history. Today, most academic institutions educate women as well as men. However, the academy is still a male domain, dominated by men (e.g., there are more male professors, males hold higher professorial ranks and more top administrative positions). Women's very presence in the academy represents their movement out of traditional spheres and into male turf and is resisted.[2]

Academic institutions are structured hierarchically. Students are at the bottom of the hierarchy,[3] "officers" (e.g., presidents, provosts, deans) are at the top. In the middle sit the faculty—with their own hierarchical markers. There is little mobility between these categorical ranks and some within them. Students usually remain students until they leave the institution, and few faculty are promoted to college president. The professor's recognition comes from peers, where "he" must be a "man among men," receive acknowledgment from "his" peers for the quality of "his" work, and, as a result, move into leadership positions and reap the rewards.

College professors are admired. Many people are in awe of us. They think we know more than we do and they think we are smarter than we are. But our professional contributions are generally acknowledged by a narrowly defined group of colleagues. Our incomes are limited and our power is elusive. Few of us become advisors to political leaders, and our achievements and status grant us few social " perks."

But there are many benefits to being an academician. In many ways the role of professor in the academy is a unique work situation. Tenure, once achieved, means job security (barring some outrageous, illegal or indefensible unethical behavior) and the pressure to "prove" oneself is no longer tied to continued employment. The job is somewhat unstructured and flexible. Although fulfilling professorial obligations responsibly can be demanding and time consuming, the range of demonstrable commitment is wide and there is considerable freedom in organizing one's time. In the United States, professors are given tremendous autonomy. The status of the role and a commitment to academic freedom make administrators, deans, chairs, and colleagues most reticent to judge a professor's competence or style in carrying out the role.

Not surprisingly, there are also few guidelines for faculty-student relations. Faculty can commit a minimum amount of time to students' individual needs or exceed professional expectations; they can meet students in their offices or outside of institutional grounds; they can cultivate friendships, share personal histories, feelings, and nonacademic activities, or remain strictly business and focus only on the specific academic issues at hand.

This autonomy gives the professor an exaggerated sense of self-importance and contributes to arrogance (Dziech and Weiner 1984). It readily lends itself to feeling "licensed." Exactly what the license legitimates is a reflection of the psychological dynamics of the professor operating in this particular context. It also contributes to an aura that shrouds the professor in the eyes of many.

Students, the *raison d'être* of the academy and the complement to the professor, enter this setting and must adapt to it—it will not accommodate to them. Although students are at the bottom of the hierarchy (and, sadly, treated as such), they are not support staff or employees. Theoretically, the organization exists to serve them. The product of their work is theirs. Its assessment is a measure of personal achievement. And students are definitionally nonpermanent. They do, and are supposed to, move out and on.

Students attend college to advance themselves intellectually and, as a result, in the social order. The professor is the vehicle for doing this—even in the more progressive institutions. So the roles of professor and student are intertwined—although it is not an equal partnership. However, the "contract" does not operationalize roles. The scipts are not clearly delineated, and the professorial role, in relationship to the student, is vague and somewhat confusing. The "job description" outlines professional obligations but hints at roles that nurture the intellectual and emotional maturity of the individual—a task that encourages, perhaps requires, more personal relating. The student also struggles with her or his script in the complementary scenario.

Whatever form their relationship takes, students are another source of recognition for the professor. The professor "knows" what the student wants to "know," is looked upon by the student as an authority, as smart, as having "proved" him- or herself in a way students have yet to realize. The professor is often admired, and students frequently believe they will never be as clever, no matter how much they learn.

Who among us would not be flattered by such idealization? This admiration is not the same, however, as recognition by one's colleagues. One need not compete by the standards set by peers to attain it. The recognition lacks status, but it is most gratifying. It feeds one's sense of self-worth, importance, superiority—in short, one's ego. Students are a powerful, sometimes pervasive, source for the gratification of emotional needs—needs that can dominate and motivate behavior.

POWER AND FACULTY-STUDENT ROLES

It is not just the distorted aggrandizement by the students, or the greater store of knowledge attributed to the professor that "feels good" and is emotionally gratifying. These can be problematic, and they are fragile. They are not guaranteed (they have to be cultivated), and many students do not get hooked by them.

The bottom line in the relationship between faculty member and student is POWER. The faculty member has it and the student does not. As intertwined as the faculty-student roles might be, and as much as one must exist for the other to exist, they are not equal collaborators. The student does not negotiate—indeed, has nothing to negotiate with. There are no exceptions to this.

All the power lies with the faculty member—some of it is real, concrete, and some of it is imagined or elusive. Professors give grades, write recommendations for graduate schools, jobs, and awards and the like, and can predispose colleagues' attitudes toward students. But it goes beyond this.

Knowledge and wisdom are power. While superior knowledge, and thus presumably greater wisdom, are often ascribed to faculty members by society at large, the students' adolescent idealism exaggerates its extent. The knowledge and experience ascribed to age add to this source of power. The extension of the power of knowledge is often made into the realm of values, and students often accept, uncritically, as true or right what the professor espouses.

It is easy to see how this imbalance of power exacerbates the vulnerability of all students. One can also understand what a heady experience it is for the student who is singled out as "special" by a professor.

There is another dimension to the professor's power that is more elusive. The professor's purpose does not stop at feeding information and facts. Professors are expected to nurture a student's capacity to think analytically, to reason logically, to harness creativity, in short, to mature intellectually and esthetically. This implies that tne professor's power extends over the minds of his students. Whether or not this is true, many professors believe it. The more humble refer to it as "tapping and nurturing potential"; the more grandiose think in terms of unformed minds to be "shaped." Dziech and Weiner (1984) refer to this dynamic as it operates in the context of sexual harassment as the Galatea/Pygmalion myth: The professor believes that female students are drawn to male faculty "as necessary and desirable guides to maturity" and the students are portrayed as needing their touch for intellectual and sexual vitality. So the faculty member's aura of power far exceeds his official assessment of students' performance.

Finally, the professor's greatest power lies in the capacity to enhance or diminish students' self-esteem. This power can motivate students to master material or convince them to give up. It is not simply a grade, but the feedback and the tone and content of the interaction. Is the student encouraged or put down? Does the faculty member use his/her knowledge to let students know how "stupid" they are or to challenge their thinking? This is *real* power.

What about the professor? Isn't all this power enough? How is it some use this power to sexually exploit female students? Faculty members are well aware of the imbalance of power, although they commonly deny the relevance of power in their sexual encounters with students (Fitzgerald, Weitzman, et al. 1988). Nonetheless, they have chosen this relationship for the unequal balance of power. They feel safer, by far, holding all the high cards than in relationships of greater equality.

The above blueprint describes the setting in which the sexual harassment of students occurs. It is necessary background for a fuller understanding of the psychology of harassment. Not only is the environment conducive to sexual harassment, it can stimulate, as opposed to inhibit, intense, unresolved conflicts and provides the setting for acting them out. These conflicts are more likely to surface, the terrain nurtures them, and the props are available to perform the script.

PROFESSORIAL STYLE: ASSUMED ROLES AND "SEDUCTION" SCRIPTS

Professors have styles of relating to and interacting with students. They execute the role of professor in very different ways. These roles are generally quite apparent, and students recognize them from a distance. Dziech and Weiner (1984) cite five "classical" professorial roles assumed by male faculty who sexually harass female students. Their discussion of how these roles serve to facilitate sexual exploitation is valuable, particularly for community educational endeavors. Additionally, attention to the subtle dynamics of the faculty-student script each role elicits reveals the required, and potentially exploitable, power differential that forms their common foundation.

A brief description of the five professorial roles described by Dziech and Weiner follows.

1. *The Counselor-Helper* takes the role of nurturer and caretaker. By encouraging students' confidences, he uncovers vulnerabilities and information that are useful in deciding on the seduction script. The student is flattered by his concern and active interest in her life.

2. *The Confidant* treats students as friends and equals. He readily shares personal information with them while inviting them to do the same. Feeling trusted and valued, the student finds herself unwittingly engaged in an emotional intimacy that she sees no way out of. He may also create feelings of obligation by doing favors for the student.

3. *The Intellectual Seducer* impresses students by flaunting his knowledge. He might use his class for eliciting personal information about students that enables him to select his target or determine his approach. Students are often coerced into revealing personal information about themselves under the guise of intellectual, content-relevant course experiences.

4. *The Opportunist* uses physical settings and circumstances or infrequently occurring opportunities to mask premeditated or intentional behavior. This might involve inappropriate touching while obstensibly providing instruction (e.g., "guiding" a student through a movement exercise) or changing the environment in order to minimize the inhibitory effects of the institution (e.g., field trips, conferences).

5. *The Power Broker* uses his professorial "right" to determine grades, write recommendations, and so forth, in order to obtain sexual "favors" from students. It might take the form of promises of rewards or threats of punishment. It might be overt, the "trade" directly communicated, or it might be hinted at and subtle.

Dziech and Weiner present these five roles as typical *Modi operandi* of the faculty "seducer." They are plays, varying in degree of elaboration and camouflage, for achieving sexual intimacy with students. But most of us in the academy can recognize similarities between our own styles with students and some of these roles and can probably slot most of our colleagues into one or the other category. Introspection will reveal the emotional needs the role reflects and gratifies.

Professors motivated to establish sexual liaisons with students use these roles as seduction ploys. Whether the role taken is consciously deceptive and premeditated or integral to the self-image, successfully assuming and/or identifying with it and the "strokes" it provides is not sufficiently affirming, gratifying, or meaningful to these men. It does not provide an adequate defense against underlying emotional conflicts, and the professor lacks the emotional maturity to settle within the limits of the symbolic meaning the role holds. Like the child who cannot resist the forbidden when no one is watching, they act out because the environment does not provide controls and they have not sufficiently internalized control. While the more mature individual diverts needs rooted in early disappointments into appropriate adult endeavors (e.g., professional achievements), the sexual harasser lacks adequate defenses and coping strategies and must "play out" the conflict.

Power Dynamics and Professorial Style. Dziech and Weiner's "seduction" role classification is particularly useful in the ways it highlights the common theme of power and control. The faculty member controls the circumstances and orchestrates the opening scenario. The imbalance of power is easily apparent in four of the five scripts. The Counselor-Helper, Intellectual Seducer, Opportunist, and Power Broker roles require, by definition, a power difference. The power element is more elusive in the Confident role—but it is there. Because the power dynamic of this style is so easily missed, it is useful to look more closely at how the Confident operates.

The professor's confidences are a "gift" he bestows. Its very value rests on the power and prestige of his position. His confidences and pretense of friendship between equals is manipulative. It is the power of his position that is used to "set her up," that exaggerates the appeal of her assigned role and that eventually renders her its victim.

Although students initially feel flattered and privileged by the attention the Confidant offers, they also feel uneasy. Their histories in relationships, with family, peers, bosses, and teachers, provide neither guidelines for participating in this new friendship nor hints about the rules of the game. The desire to measure up, the uncertainty about what is expected and considered "correct" behavior, and concern about the costs of mistakes all create anxiety. The incongruities—indeed, the outright contradictions—inherent in the double identity required for, and the premise underlying, their relationship (i.e., equality between unequals) creates dissonance and heightens the student's vigilance in "reading" and following the professor's lead. As the relationship escalates, the student often feels increasingly burdened by the demands of the relationship, in over her head, and powerless to exit. How, after all, do you tell a professor who has trusted you, made himself vulnerable to you, and valued your friendship that you are too busy to find time to talk with him? It is the power and control his position grants that nurtures this scenario, holds her captive, and renders escape routes risky.

PROFILES OF SEXUAL HARASSERS IN THE ACADEMY: ATTITUDES AND BEHAVIOR

The five roles commonly assumed by male professors in the service of obtaining sexual intimacy with students depict how diverse behavioral styles lend themselves to sexual exploitation and provide a context for illuminating the common underlying theme of power and control, elements the professor depends on to achieve his aim.

A professor's proclivity for a particular role is a function of the behavioral repertoire most accessible to him, his self-image, and the projected image he finds most comfortable or desirable. It reveals little about the underlying dynamics that motivate him to use this role to establish sexual liaisons with students. They are vehicles for exploitation, not reasons. However, within a particular role, there are a range of "attitudinal stances" reflected in the professor's behavior. These attitudinal stances dictate the parameters and requirements, define the arena, and establish the tone of the relationship. In short, they guide his actions.

These attitudinal stances are different from the professorial roles described above. They operate within a role. They are the attitudes with which the role is approached, the attitude the professor has about the sexual liaison. Attitudinal stances are analogous to personality traits. The "attitudes" (like "personality" attributions) are inferred from one's "stance" (behaviors) within specific contexts. The context, here, is relating sexually to students.

Attitudinal stances are likely to suggest some of the motivational dynamics underlying the harasser's behavior: how he feels about himself and how he views women. The attitude with which the harasser approaches his behavior may suggest how ego-syntonic the harassment is (i.e., the degree to which the harasser experiences conflict and guilt around his behavior), the rationale he adopts to justify or understand his behavior, and even the psychological meaning hidden in the harassment.

In order to shed further light on the psychodynamics of male faculty who sexually harass female students, we have identified four familiar themes or dimensions useful in developing profiles of these men.[4] Each is a continuum between two poles, and it is likely that most harassers can be ranked on all four dimensions. They are not independent dimensions, and one's position on one of them will often suggest a trend on another. The dimensions are characterized by, and labeled for, behavioral patterns representing the extremes of each pole. The dimensions are these:

1. *The Public versus the Private Harasser.* (Dziech and Weiner 1984). This dimension assesses the professor's behavior of sexually relating to

students along a continuum from open, "public" displays to hidden, secretive advances and encounters.

2. *The Seducer/Demander versus the Receptive Non-Initiator.* This dimension can be viewed as an "active-passive" continuum and refers to the degree to which the professor actively pursues sexual encounters with students.

3. *The Untouchable versus the Risk Taker.* This dimension refers to the degree of "entitlement" and invulnerability/vulnerability with which the professor engages in sexual liaisons with students.

4. *The Infatuated versus the Sexual Conqueror.* This dimension contrasts professors along the continuum of affection and care felt toward their student lover—how "special" she is to him.

While the two poles of each dimension appear to be opposites and to reflect different underlying needs, this is not always the case. For example, although the opinionated person is operating from a different psychological constellation than one who never has an opinion, both may be motivated by a fear of being wrong, of being exposed as "stupid." The different expressions of the same feeling reflect developmental experiences and superego constraints. If a feeling is judged unacceptable and creates anxiety, the expression may, on the surface, appear antithetical to its meaning. Another example, relevant to these dimensions, is the behavioral expression of hostility toward women. Thus, the need to denigrate women might be couched in gratuitous behavior, flattery, and the bestowing of favors. Although this seems to suggest a fondness for the person, it may well be a vehicle for rendering the woman submissive, dependent and obliged.

An analysis of the psychological dynamics portrayed in these four attitudinal dimensions sheds light on the emotional constellation of the male faculty harasser and the way in which the structure of the academy nurtures this behavior.

The Public versus the Private Harasser

Dziech and Weiner (1984) present a most vivid behavioral depiction of the first attitudinal dimension. The Public Harasser "performs" in public. He prefers an audience. His posturing toward women is flagrant (e.g., touching) and patronizing. He is quick with sexist and glib comments. This is the professor who spends a lot of time with students, often hanging out at student pubs and the like. He is available, approachable, and informal.

The Private Harasser conforms to the stereotype of the academic, somewhat elite scholar. He is formal, aloof, and conservative in appearance. His presentation usually makes him the last to be suspected and, as such, perhaps the most dangerous (Dziech and Weiner 1984). While avoiding notoriety, he uses his position to gain private access to women students. Students are caught off guard and disoriented by his sexual advances.

While both the Public and the Private Harasser obtain gratification from being able to use and abuse their power without censure, there are different dynamics operating for the two men. The public behavior is "showing off." It is a call for attention, an advertisement about one's manhood. It is a competitive gesture directed toward other males. His desired audience may be colleagues, but it is equally likely to be male students. Taking liberties with women is an adolescent symbol of manhood, and the Public Harasser is crudely attempting to let other men know he is "one of the boys."[5] Accordingly, he prefers to be surrounded by attractive, popular students (male and female) and courts the attention of women students who, in his opinion, are highly desired by other males. The women victimized by his behavior are, in and of themselves, unimportant and interchangeable. Like stage props, they are required but not central, except as evidence of manhood. Motivated to mask feelings of inadequacy, the Public Harasser is undaunted by the fact that his more perceptive colleagues are unimpressed. If he is at all aware, he chalks it up to their jealousy or divides the faculty into teams: those who are "in"/"with it" and those who are not. He, of course, is in the "in" crowd. The readiness of the system to tolerate his behavior permits him to maintain his illusion, while his blatant display has sufficient risks to add excitement to the role. Risk highlights his assertion about being a "real" man. Since the audience for this performance is men, the Public Harasser is actually less invested in engaging in sexual relations with students than his behavior suggests, in contrast to the Private Harasser (Dziech and Weiner 1984).

The Private Harasser is a man with a "secret." Although it might appear on the surface that his behavior is motivated simply by the desire for sexual encounters, the dynamics are considerably more complex. The secrecy is not simply prudence, an attitude reserved for his sexual behavior. It is noticeably characteristic of the way he presents himself in all professional arenas. The Private Harasser is intensely invested in his public image. Indeed, the rigidity with which he adheres to this image suggests how excessive this investment is and its importance in maintaining an intact self-concept. Why, then, would a man who is so protective of his image risk destroying it? Clinical observations suggest several possibilities.

The very secretiveness of the Private Harasser's activities is, in and of itself, exciting and gratifying. He takes pleasure in the deception. While the Public Harasser gets gratification from what people know about him, the Private Harasser finds it in what they do not know. Just as his lectern separates him from his students, his very demeanor is a shield from the eyes of others. He guards all his secrets, not so much because he is ashamed of them (he may or may not be) but because there is power in the secret—the power of getting away with something and never being suspected, the power of deception. Needless to say, there is disdain for those deceived.

There is another aspect to the secret worth noting. It is part of a more elaborate fantasy life, and the fantasy is an important source of emotional sustenance. Most fantasies are kept secret, for if no one knows them, no one can destroy them.

Power and control are all integral aspects of the dynamics underlying the behavior of the Private Harasser. He exudes these publicly in his professional attire and presentation. He uses these to intimidate students and to secure sexual contact. Compensating for intense self-doubts about his potency (sexual and otherwise), demonstration of his power is foremost and he selects as his objects those he has direct power over. Not only does this tactic avoid challenging his fantasy and fragile self-image; it is often a required component of his secret identity. As a rule, the whole scenario is part of his fantasy.

Seducer/Demander versus Receptive Non-Initiator

A popular retort to condemnations of sexual liaisons between faculty and students makes reference to the perception that not infrequently it is the female student who is "on the make" and seduces the professor. How often this occurs is difficult to assess. For one thing, it is not always clear what constitutes an "initiation." If a student responds to a professor's attentive, solicitous, personal, and mildly flirtatious behavior with a sexual overture, where did the initiation begin? What is even more problematic is the evidence that men frequently misinterpret women's behaviors and clothing as seductive and signaling a sexual invitation. This finding includes interpretations of interactions between female students and male faculty members (Abbey 1982; Henig and Ryan 1986). Of the 235 male faculty members who responded to the Fitzgerald, et al., 1988 survey, 17.5 percent reported an experience in which a student initiated an unsolicited attempt to stroke, caress, or touch them (they were not asked whether these were sexual invitations), and only 6 percent believed they had been sexually harassed by a student.

Nonetheless, focusing on the ambiguities sidesteps the issue. The professor who is absolutely innocent of leading the student on, ceases to be innocent once he has sexual contact with her. The unequal distribution in the faculty-student relationship makes his "concession" to her overtures exploitation. The fact that the female student "asked" is not an explanation for why he complied. Yet this is the very justification offered by the Receptive Non-Initiator.

In our society a woman's offer of free sex is considered a logical explanation for a man's indulgence. A woman would never get away with offering such an excuse. We may condemn a man for "asking" but not for saying "yes."

The stereotype about men's pervasive sexual needs and dominating drive to satisfy them prevails to the degree that we consider such behavior normal, or at least understandable.

The Receptive Non-Initiator is the professor who, as a rule, does not initiate the first sexual overture but is most accommodating when the student does. The Receptive Non-Initiator draws the line between morality and immorality at who does the asking. Superego constraints are operating here and are one of the distinctions between the Receptive Non-Initiator and the professor who actively sets out to seduce a student (the "Seducer") or who uses his position to demand sex (the "Demander"). However, it is not that simple, and it would be an error to assume that this dimension can be characterized by degrees of conscience. Superego constraints and sources of guilt can be quite idiosyncratic. Rigid standards in one domain may find a formidable match in the guilt-free escapades in another. There is an idiosyncrasy in the moral price tag people place on different behaviors that only legislation can standardize and regulate.

The Receptive Non-Initiator acknowledges the power of his position. He recognizes how the imbalance of power renders blantant overtures questionable and places undue pressure on the student. He recognizes her disadvantage in the interaction and contends with this awareness by resisting making the first move. It is a transparent rationalization, but it serves to reduce his discomfort about his unethical behavior. It is true that this standard spares the student from the trauma of confronting a sexual invitation; the disinterested student is left out of the arena and direct coercion is not involved. As such, it is probably less unethical (as opposed to more ethical) than the behavior of the Seducer/Demander. Nonetheless, the roles remain intact, as does the imbalance of power and its exploitation. The Receptive Non-Initiator either blinds himself to this obvious reality or, more commonly, acknowledges it but says, "So what? She was the seducer. I put no pressure on her." He claims freedom from responsibility. To him the ethics only apply to proactive behavior, not reactive behavior.

However, the Receptive Non-Initiator's inhibitions against initiating sexual contact with students are considerably more complex than a personal morality. He would experience asking for sex, or even overtly seducing the student, as diminishing, and the resulting relationship would be less gratifying.

The Receptive Non-Initiator wants to be sought out. He needs to feel "lovable" in his own right, for *who* he is, not for *what* he is. Henry Kissinger, secretary of state under President Nixon, was much more honest about the seductiveness of status. When asked by a reporter why women found him attractive, he responded, "Power." Kissinger knew the "score." The Receptive Non-Initiator is aware of the lure of his position and likes it. He tends to try to appear desirable, either by tending to his physical appearance or by adopting a role that encourages trust and familiarity. Yet he deludes himself into believing that he is truly special if he doesn't have to ask, if the student offers the first sexual invitation. Were he to be the sexual aggressor, he would never truly trust that it is he, and not the professor, who is desirable. The fact that he and the professor are one in the same to the student is inconvenient and pushed aside.

If the Receptive Non-Initiator wants to feel loved for himself, why doesn't he just find a woman who is his equal, over whom he does not wield power? Would not this be more affirming? But the Receptive Non-Initiator does not feel particularly lovable and doubts that such women will give him the degree of acceptance he longs for. For the most part, he is right about this assessment. A peer probably would not give him what he wants and they most likely have not in his past, because his needs are excessive and his insecurities loom when he becomes involved with a woman. A partner who is an equal does not provide the unconditional affirmation of the idealized mother. And a strong and powerful woman who "mothers" her man would trigger pervasive feelings of impotence and inadequacy. A student is a promising and available alternative. Actually, some variation on this theme applies to all sexual harassers although it gets expressed differently in the interplay of power and sex. For the Receptive Non-Initiator, these feelings are compounded by an intolerance for rejection. Confronting rejection, and all it means, is avoided if one makes no requests.

Thus, the Receptive Non-Initiator is most ambivalent about power. While his professorial role is critical for his self-esteem and he capitalizes on it to establish familiarity with a student, he cannot not tolerate the suggestion that it underlies his appeal.

Power and control are at the center of the dynamics of the Receptive Non-Initiator's sexual liaisons with students. While it may appear that he is giving over control and some degree of power by his initial passivity, he is in reality staunchly holding on to all of it. While the Seducer/Demander makes himself vulnerable to rejection and scorn by inviting sexual contact, the Receptive Non-Initiator is in the position to give or not give what is requested of him. This carries considerable power and contributes to his "keeping the upper hand" throughout the duration of the relationship. As would be expected, given these dynamics, such men are likely to test the woman's devotion regularly, as they need continuous confirmation of their power as well as "proof" that they are loved. Under such circumstances, the student is likely to find herself in an abusive relationship.

The Seducer and the Demander (i.e., the "Power Broker") have been grouped together on this dimension because both actively seek and plot sexual encounters with students (in contrast to the initial passivity of the Receptive Non-Initiator). In order to obtain what they want, both men take advantage of their position and the student's vulnerability. Although the Seducer, using impressive mental acrobatics, sometimes denies the role of power in his conquests, power does not hold for him anywhere near the degree of conflict as it does for the Receptive Non-Initiator. Both the Seducer and the Demander accept sexual privilege with students as an entitlement of power and control.

There are, however, notable differences between the Seducer and the Demander, although these too may fall on a continuum. While the professor's virtual monopoly on power and control pervade all relationships with students (sexual or otherwise), the Demander literally uses his "real" power, the rights that are part of his professional duties, to "purchase" sex from students. He is the most ruthless and unethical and perverts the educational process. He views, and treats, his female students as whores.

His disdain for women is most blatant, as is his rejection of their place in the academy. The Demander reduces women students to the role of sex object, and his behavior is a clear communication that they do not belong in the academy. They are bodies, not brains, and they will have to serve him as women to obtain what he controls. He needs to demonstrate to them his "real" power and render them literally under his command and at his mercy. The Demander operates from a psychological investment in "keeping women in their place." He is threatened by the advancement of women because it challenges his male privilege—and his self-definition of masculinity is tied to control over women. He seeks gritification by exercising the limits of his power.

As is apparent from the above, the Demander's behavior is not motivated by the need to be loved or judged desirable. Although these needs may well be present, they are rigidly guarded against. Indeed, should these needs surface and enter his motivational scheme, his whole defense structure is threatened. For if he wants a woman's affection, he is vulnerable to her and she has some power. She can give or withhold something he wants and that something cannot be purchased or controlled by his position.

There is a common stereotype, frequently cited in discussions on sexual harassment, that female students sleep with their male professors for the purpose of improving their grades and obtaining favors. That is, the claim is made that these students intentionally use their bodies in order to use their professors for their own means. Such assertions are interesting in their presentation of the faculty member as the victim and the student as the victimizer, the one in control. The available research suggests that this is an infrequent occurrence (14 percent of the male respondents in the Fitzgerald, Weitzman, et al. 1988 study indicated that a student had implied or offered sexual favors or cooperation in return for some reward). Even introducing this twist into a dialogue on sexual harassment reverberates with the same belief and attitude about women students as does the behavior of the Demander: that women do not have the competence to succeed in college so they use their femininity (bodies) to compensate.

The absurdity of viewing sexual harassment through the above lens is apparent. Those occasions when it is descriptively accurate represent a sad case study of the impact of gender stratification on women and gender relationships. The male professor has all the power and control, and the female student has bought into the attitude that, as a woman, her most advantageous asset is her body and she is intellectually inadequate. The professor and student then play out this script. But she has little power or control in this interaction. "Selling one's body" is not power, it is the result of powerlessness. Additionally, the motivation, whatever it may be, that accounts for her behavior is not an explanation for the activities of the professor.

This discussion is pertinent to understanding the dynamics of the Demander. The exchange of favors for sex is the core of his script but he does not view women as an equal negotiator in the contract. In contrast to the stereotype of the student who plots to use her body as a term paper, the Demander shuns perceiving the student as having even that much autonomy and, as such, control. While acknowledging the trade-off they make, he reserves all the power and control and would be unable to tolerate the contention that it was *he* who was being used. He would be devastated to learn that a student interpreted his proposition along the lines of "I really have him where I want him. He is so 'hot' for my body, he's eating out of my hands. This will be an easy grade." Of course, rarely is this the student's perception. She knows the reality of the power dynamics.

The Seducer, like the Demander, targets specific students with whom he would like to be sexually intimate and actively sets out to achieve his goal. Like the Demander, he is willing to introduce this new twist to their relationship. Indeed, he intends and expects to. He has taken charge from the beginning, written the script and manipulated circumstances, for the purpose of seducing and is prepared to initiate sexual intimacy when he judges the time right. The Seducer is not, however, usually thrown off balance should the student "beat him to the punch," as this is merely evidence of the success of his efforts. Unlike the Demander, the Seducer needs to feel desired, "loved," and attractive. He is aware of his power but unwilling to negotiate an exchange of favors for sex. To do so would negate the motivating force behind his seduction—evidence that he, the man that he is, is desirable, even irresistable.

Unlike the Receptive Non-Initiator, the Seducer does not struggle with the lure of his position. To the contrary, he cultivates it for his purpose. It is not a narcissistic blow to the Seducer that his power is part of his appeal, and he does not interpret it as an abuse of power. The Seducer views his power as an achievement, as evidence of his value and worth and as proof of his specialness. It is the very thing that he believes earns him love. Doubting that he is lovable without the dressing, and feeling that people are loved for the outward expression of their successes, he is not conflicted by the role his power plays in his attractiveness.

The Untouchable versus the Risk Taker

There is a distinction between the professor who does not worry about, or even consider, the consequences of his behavior and the one who feels he is walking on the edge and at any moment could get pushed over. The narcissism and grandiosity that orchestrate the behavior of the former contributes to the feeling of being "untouchable." It reminds us somewhat of the egocentric reasoning of the adolescent,[6] particularly as witnesses in the notion that they are special and unique. This personal fable (Elkind 1980), which contributes to such beliefs as "It can't happen to me" and "The rules are for others, not me," often guides actions. And, like the adolescent who, according to all indications short of the behavior itself, does not want to die in a car accident but nonetheless drives drunk, the Untouchable believes there are no real risks. He is in control—beyond the ranks of censorship.[7]

Whether or not the Untouchable flaunts his liaison or is intentionally indiscrete will depend on some of the other dynamics addressed elsewhere in this paper. Although his behavior is a bold challenge to the system, this is not necessarily one of the motivating factors underlying it. The distinguishing dimension of the Untouchable is his extreme egocentricity—his poor social perspective taking in this domain.[8]

Some Untouchables, bolstered by a distorted sense of self-importance and omnipotence, simply operate as though they exist outside the system, as though the rules do not apply to them and they cannot be hurt. These men appear so oblivious to the surrounding community that it seems unlikely their behavior is designed as a statement to others. Others are almost daring the system with the statement "No one will mess with me. I make my own Rules!" (Both types tend to be more vulnerable to rejection from students, whose rebuffs can turn into denials and projections.) Either way, the Untouchable's behavior reflects poor reality testing and judgment. For example, such men might assert, and appear most sincere when doing so, an unambivalent commitment to their wives and families and a clear and determined unwillingness to sacrifice the family for the sake of the affair. They behave like model husbands and fathers with their families and conscientiously meet all family obligations. Yet these very same men will unabashedly escort their student lover to university events and seemingly not entertain the reality that this presents tremendous risks to their status quo.

Whether the Untouchable is led by the conviction "No one will mess with me; I'm better than the rest" or merely is unable to step outside of his own inner world sufficiently to assess the situation through the eyes of others, he is egocentric and grandiose.

At the opposite extreme is the Risk Taker—the professor who believes he has really stepped "out of line." He has done the forbidden, said "Fuck you" to the system, and may have to pay the consequences. He is being "naughty" and his naughtiness is a statement. He knows he is challenging the system by taking for himself what he is not entitled to. He believes he is playing with fire, but the compulsion to do so is more powerful than the fear of the consequences. At the very least, he cannot moderate his behavior by a consideration of the possible long-term consequences.

The Risk Taker does not sleep as well as the Untouchable. He does not sleep well at all during the affair and is frequently irritable with people. He fluctuates between the "high" of his naughtiness and the guilt and fear of punishment. In this latter state he is likely to project these feelings onto the woman, whom he now blames for his transgression. Since she represents his disobedience, his perception of himself as "bad" and the reason for his eventual punishment, she is viewed, and treated, as Eve, the wicked temptress. He views himself as the victim, and punishes her for the infraction. During this cycle, he can be quite cruel, and the lover might find herself the object of sadistic behavior. At such times, the Risk Taker is identifying with the system and people from whom he fears retribution as a defense against this feelings of vulnerability. While he keeps his anxiety sufficiently in check to allow him to play out some of the affair, it is not an adequate defense, and the Risk Taker's level of anxiety remains quite high throughout the duration of the affair.

The Infatuated versus the Sexual Conqueror

Little needs to be said about the Sexual Conqueror. He is a familiar depiction. Sometimes referred to as a "womanizer," other times as a "Don Juan," the Sexual Conqueror is only interested in numbers. He repeatedly, often compulsively, seduces one or many women. While the Sexual Conqueror may have preferences in the type of student targered for seduction (e.g., the aloof and disinterested; the shy and reticent; "party girls"; "virginal" types; married women; ethnic women), the individual woman, as a particular human being with her own unique qualities and life situation, is not only irrelevant, the fact that she is an individual is rarely processed. Women are interchangeable. While the Sexual Conqueror is often determined, amorous, and focused when in the process of seduction ("conquering"), his interest wanes once he has achieved his goal. "One-nighters" are common and satisfying, although he might, at any one time, maintain several lovers to fill in the inevitable gaps.

The Sexual Conqueror generally knows and remembers little about the woman. We have heard stories from women who have approached these men several months after their sexual encounter and insist that the man seemed confused about who they were. In line with this, we have had the experience of confronting men with evidence that supported a particular woman's accusations and witnessed reactions that suggested difficulty in recalling the incident or the person. Several counselors/therapists, consulted for this paper, reported anecdotes in which male clients/patients (examples included nonacademic as well as academic settings) who fit this profile could recall specific incidents but were not able to match the woman with the event, or who were unable, with any degree of confidence, to provide information about a specific woman. (Confusing women, e.g., "She was in constant conflict with her mother, . . . I think, . . . maybe that was the girl from remedial" or combining select aspects of several women in a description of one woman, were noted.)

The above examples represent an extreme, and the Sexual Conqueror is often more moderate in his behavior, needs, and ambitions. But the repetitive pattern of his behavior and the anonymity he imposes on these women suggest the extent of his pathology—the anxiety about, and need to document, his sexual potency and masculinity and the terror of intimacy with a woman.

The Sexual Conqueror is not, however, the typical male professor who engages in sexual liaisons with female students. Many professors enter into such relationships with an intensity and need that are the antithesis of those reflected in the behavior of the Sexual Conqueror.

It would be incomplete, and, as such, stilted and misleading, to imply that all faculty who engage in sexual relationships with female students are deceptive and manipulitive men who consciously use their position of power for the explicit purpose of sexually exploiting female students. There is an identifiable dimension that characterizes men who are emotionally drawn and attached to a specific female student. In short, they become infatuated. Their behavior is not designed primarily for sexual contact, but rather to establish a "meaningful" relationship. She is not an exchangeable object or part of a stable. If he is rebuffed, he does not rapidly find another—but another there will eventually be.

Sometimes these feelings evolve inadvertently out of encounters designed to be more exploitative. Often they evolve more naturally as the faculty member slowly acknowledges to himself his desire to see the student more often and recognizes that he has a "crush." Although the more impulsive and less reticent are likely to jump into a courtship once the feeling takes shape, others approach it with more forethought.

In discussions of student-faculty "dating," someone always tells anecdotes about marriages that resulted from such relationships. Such marriages do, indeed, exist, but they are the exception and make for a weak defense or explanation of the dynamics underlying student-faculty sexual liaisons. What is more, a relationship that ends in marriage is not evidence that the power element that operates in student-faculty relationships did not apply in the particular case. A faculty member's desire or willingness to marry a student does not necessarily imply equality in the relationship or erase the real and/or psychological power he wields over her. And, as the previous discussion of the academy suggests, the student may not be in a position to objectively evaluate what is in her own best interest or to resist pressure he might place on her. Actually, a faculty member's determination to marry his student may also have exploitative aspects, as it raises questions about his use of power and control in obtaining what he wants.

Couples involved in such relationships adamantly deny that their academic roles are reflected in their relationship, although that they are is often apparent to perceptive people who are familiar with the subtleties of the academy. This "passes" in public, however, because faculty-student roles parallel male-female roles in the larger society. Such couples, however, sensitive to community opinion, generally wait until the female student graduates before they tie the knot. Sound as this may be, a September marriage following a June graduation is insufficient time to erase the psychological dynamics of the academic roles upon which their relationship evolved.

Undoubtably, many of these marriages are as appropriate and successful as most marriages and it is unwise and unjust to make assumptions and blanketly categorize individual cases or situations. The focus here is patterns— there are always exceptions—and while rules and flow charts simplify life, caution is urged in readily applying them to all professor/husband–student/ wife couples (after the fact). Nonetheless, with that disclaimer in place, these couples are atypical, and raising their case in response to dialogue or policy on sexual intimacy between faculty and student is a transparent and indefensible argument for maintaining a system that encourages the sexual exploitation of women. The rule, not the occasional exception, must guide policy, educational programs, and counseling services.

Nonetheless, those exceptional cases when student-faculty affairs end in marriage suggest the genuineness and sincerity with which some faculty might pursue and participate in a relationship with a student. The Infatuated is sincere and genuinely cares about the woman, although marriage as an outcome is unlikely to even enter the range of possibilities for most of these men. Indeed, the Infatuated, like other faculty who sexually harass women students, is often married. While his marital status makes his sincerity suspect and, as with all extramarital affairs, imposes practical limitations and additional emotional complications, stresses, and pressures, the married Infatuate is quite, often intensely, attached to the woman. For the time being, he is "in love." It is not simply a sexual extracurricula activity ("quickies" on the side) he is after. He seeks a form of emotional affirmation and gratification of needs that requires greater intimacy than that supplied solely by sexual encounters. Nonetheless, for most of these men, whether married or not, the assumption that it is temporary is not only part of the appeal but also part of its justification.

In contrast to harassers who keep their emotions more in check, the Infatuated risks emotional vulnerability. He is also more likely to become dependent on the woman, for he has specifically turned to her for the gratification of his needs.

The description presented so far does not seem distinctly different from the course of events that precedes most love relationships—a person is "drawn" to another, and the two spend time together, get to know one another better, and "fall in love." It is natural, usually even desirable, to fall in love with someone who gratifies emotional needs and meets various other requirements for an intimate relationship. If the faculty member pursues and enters into a relationship with a student with the sincere intention of giving it a chance to develop, is not this simply the normal process of adult bonding in a love relationship?[9] Although student-faculty relationships may be judged unethical as a rule, why is not this the exception? Why would we classify the Infatuated as a sexual exploiter?.

The imbalance of power and control in the faculty-student relationship is also very central to these liaisons, although the faculty member will deny it most adamantly and rarely is consciously aware of it once the relationship is established. Nonetheless, during the courtship he will use the advantage of his position, as do others, to attain her affection. All people motivated to "sell" themselves (for the purpose of forming a relationship or otherwise) put their best foot forward. But the context in which this courtship occurs suggests its exploitative potential: "Winning the heart" of the object of one's affection inevitably and unavoidably (whether by conscious design or not) involves the abuse of power by capitalizing on the fact that that power renders the other vulnerable.

The Infatuated is not simply someone with the unfortunate luck of falling in love with a woman who, circumstantially, happens to be a student at the institution in which he teaches—a circumstance that complicates things but is irrelevant to the interpersonal dynamics. The Infatuated is particularly attracted to students *because they are students*. Their very status in the academy, vis-à-vis his, is part of the attraction. Thus, the power difference is integral to the relationship.

The Infatuated is in love with a relationship that veils a multitude of self-doubts. It allows him to be the man he feels unable to be in a relationship with a peer, or even someone who does not see him robed in his academic attire. Indeed, his relationship with the student is usually a marked contrast to his marriage or past love relationships.

The Infatuated thrives on being "looked up to"; on being able to teach and guide the lover; on being at the center of the relationship; on having greater "wisdom"; on doing "more important" things; and on pondering "more cosmic" thoughts. He takes pleasure in being identified with the powerful system she is up against and in being able to advise her from the inside and teach her the ropes. He thrives on telling her the nitty-gritty of his workday, the details of department politics, and trivial gossip about his colleagues. Not infrequently, these men are discontent with their own status or treatment in their department or in conflict with someone in the college who wields greater power. Indeed, the affair may well have been triggered by a series of such incidents and tensions that have undermined his self-esteem.

The professor finds in his lover an empathic, uncritical partner. He complains to her about his mistreatment and explains how it is a result of others' inadequacies, insecurities, and jealousies. He seeks from his student-lover (and finds, if she plays her part) an ally in his defensive structure— someone who assures him he is "right," confirms his assertions, and joins him in constructing an interpretation of the situation that supports his self-esteem. She may even actively reinforce it—feed it back to him in select parts—should she sense his self-doubts surfacing. Often this is subtle; other times it has a ritualistic flavor (e.g.,—He: "Maybe they are right and the problem is me. Maybe I really can't . . ." She: "Stop talking that way. You know. . . . And don't forget . . ."). She senses how critical this support is for maintaining the relationship. She might also, however, gradually develop some doubts of her own (particularly if unsuspecting people make pertinent comments about her lover, or if she obsesses about his plight and struggles to make sense out of information that appears unlikely and "questionable"). If these doubts are not somehow dismissed, they smolder, and the relationship begins to turn. Conflicts arise (usually about things that appear unrelated to the source of her doubts but can be reduced to her withdrawal of support or increased demands for more consideration from him) and the relationship becomes fragile. In the end, she is as likely to be the one who wants to terminate the relationship as is he.

The manner in which these men treat their student-lover varies considerably as a function of the professor's other psychological constellations. The "Malevolent" infatuated treats his student-lover poorly, even abusively. He is likely to deny the legitimacy of her needs, as only his are important to him, and remind her of how fortunate she is that he chose her. He may denigrate her, either overtly by referring to her inferiority or covertly by focusing on his own superiority. He might cruelly criticize her schoolwork, mock her opinions, trivialize her interests, and dismiss and discourage her ambitions. Such malevolent treatment does not camouflage his disdain for women.

The Infatuated, however, is equally likely to be "benevolent." The "Benevolent" Infatuated takes the role of nurturer and demonstrates his affection with a most reassuring consistency. He may flatter, support, and praise her. The "Benevolent" Infatuated often mentors his student-lover—guiding her through the system, providing constructive feedback, and emotionally and pragmatically supporting her ambitions, often encouraging her to set higher goals. This behavior may be based on a realistic assessment (e.g., the quality of her work warrants praise; pushing her to aim higher is supportive of her dreams but not her doubts about her ability). Or it might more accurately reflect his own dynamics (e.g., encouraging a career direction may run counter to her own ambitions and reflect his desire to see her as, or attempt to make her into, the woman whose love is most affirming).

The "Benevolent" Infatuated's adoration of his lover may be as distorted as her image of him. He might lift her from the realm of "ordinary" woman and place her on a pedestal. He might depict her as a saint, in contrast to his wife, the "ball-busting" shrew, and view her as the "good mother" he longs for, as opposed to the depriving one he recalls. Of course, no woman can measure up to this, although the student-lover may try. Her efforts will eventually leave her depleted, her humanness and needs will surface, and the relationship will deteriorate.

Nonetheless, while in full swing, the "Benevolent" Infatuated has what he wants. To be loved and adored by the near-perfect woman makes him feel very special. He resists evidence of limitations. Indeed, he takes pride in her achievements and will enter into, or create for her, rationalizations about disappointments (e.g., a poor grade) that shift (i.e., project) the blame (e.g., the teacher's incompetence). Thus, she too, might be viewed as the victim, and the two might play out this scenario and take turns as the victim and counselor.

There is a qualitative difference in the support and care the professor gives to his student-lover from that which she gives to him, and both differ from that observed in the mutual bonding of peers. This difference is inherent in the imbalance of power in their academic roles. These roles cannot be dismissed—the relationship centers around them. For example, there is a qualitative difference between compliments and the like, bestowed by the more powerful one onto an underling, and those offered by someone lower on the hierarchy to one higher up. (Think of the differences in the way in which a teacher praises a student and the way a student compliments a teacher; the way in which the praise is received and experienced by the teacher and the student.) The obvious parallel is the parent-child interaction. Both receive tremendous gratification from the caring affection of the other—but there is a qualitative distinction in the meaning carried by feedback (e.g., a parent does not attach the same meaning to their child's declaration "You're so smart" as the child does to the identical statement from the parent). Thus, there is a parental, often patronizing, element in the professor's support of the student.

And, as is sometimes seen in parent-child dynamics, the faculty member's concern is frequently rooted in the narcissistic gratification obtained from his lover's achievements. She "belongs" to him and her achievements are his and reflect on him. She, or rather the relationship, has become part of his identity.

The above dynamics appear to work smoothly as long as he stays "on top." While he remains in control, he takes credit for her successes. He is not, however, living vicariously through her (the way a parent might when something about the child mirrors his/her unrealized desires or fantasies). To the contrary, he cultivates the reverse. If she becomes too strong or more self-confident than he, their relationship "contract" is at risk and he is threatened. This sometimes happens with a graduate student-lover who begins to accrue professional credits and is judged to have more promise than the professor-lover or when an undergraduate is accepted into a graduate school that far outshines the one the professor attended. It may also happen when the student "outgrows" the relationship—no longer needs or feels gratified by what he provides, or when she begins to see beyond the roles and becomes disillusioned with him and the relationship (which is likely to happen as she develops an independent sense of her own self-worth). When he sees the changes occurring, he may loose interest or covertly attempt to sabotage her progress. This can take the form of withdrawing support, discouraging her advancement, or challenging her competence. Indeed, the "Benevolent" Infatuated may begin to demonstrate behaviors more typical of the "Malevolent" Infatuated, blurring somewhat the distinction between the two and revealing an underlying anger so well camouflaged in the previous stage. Alternatively, the Infatuated may invert the anger and embrace the feelings of inadequacy that motivated and defined the affair in the first place. With his defenses weakened, he will succumb to depression.

One last note about the Infatuated. His ripeness to "fall in love" and readiness to enter into a relationship with a student usually occur at critical periods in his life. It generally follows some event or series of events that intensify his self-doubts, undermine his masculinity, and trigger feelings of inadequacy (e.g., rejections in love relationships, professional disappointments). These feelings preceded the particular crisis and were a painful, pervasive and integral aspect of his private identity, but they were a source of turmoil that he had previously succeeded in keeping under the surface. The relationship is a band-aid designed to help heal the wound. It acts like a euphoria-inducing drug. In its initial stages and at its height the professor-lover looks like a "new man." Everyone notices. He is flying, happy, and self-confident. The effects of the "drug" wear away, but there is a high risk of addiction.

The Benevolent-Malevolent Dimension

The "benevolent-malevolent" pattern pervades all four attitudinal stances described above and is a useful dimension for gaining insight into the dynamics of sexual harassment—possible underlying motivations and the character of the relationship. All of the men profiled in this paper demonstrate some balance of malevolent behavior (i.e., the use of the relationship to repeat old themes of sadism, control, punishment, and humiliation) and benevolent behavior (i.e., assuming the kindly, caring, protective, father-teacher role). This theme was developed within the discussion of the Infatuated to provide a context for the way in which it operates. But it is always present. As is true for all four attitudinal stances, it is never all one or the other. These men fall somewhere on the continuum between the two extremes. For conceptual purposes, however, it was necessary to depict the extremes.

As noted earlier, most men who engage in sexual relations with students can be placed somewhere on the continuum of the two poles of all of the attitudinal stances, and it would have been reasonable to create a fifth "attitude" describing the "Malevolent-Benevolent" stance. However, its pervasiveness in the relationship between the faculty-lover and the student-lover, and the evidence it suggests for an underlying theme that motivates these men's behavior, encouraged setting it aside for special attention.

The theme that appears to characterize almost all men who have sex with female students is anger toward women. This hostility is clearly seen in the behavior of the malevolent, sadistic pattern, but the benevolent pattern often provides a convenient example for contradicting the generalization. However, the benevolent man is also keeping the woman "in her place" and treating her as a subordinate. The need for power and control in the relationship is clear. Whether the man takes the student as a beloved protégé or whether he dominates and debases her with anger and rage, he continues to need, and feel that he has, complete control. This undercuts her autonomy and encourages dependency. It is aggressive, hostile, and self-serving behavior. It mirrors and reinforces the stratified gender roles and oppressive nature of traditional gender relationships in our society. The surface behavior of the benevolent faculty-lover not only masks the likely rage and threat women trigger but presents an image easily warmed to. The frequency with which the benevolence turns nasty reforms the picture and suggests that the extremes of "benevolence" are in fact a reaction formation against underlying rage. It is a socially acceptable way of expressing anger, threat, and disdain.

SEXUAL HARASSMENT, MALE PSYCHOLOGY, AND CULTURAL NORMS

The attitudinal dimensions are a preliminary attempt to sketch profiles of male professors who elect to have sexual relationships with students. Additionally, while this paper describes behavioral patterns and suggests underlying psychological meaning and dynamics, the analysis is somewhat surface. The data for a more in-depth analysis that traces developmental roots of the different profiles or even distinguishes etiologies of those who harass and those who do not, are simply not available. These ideas have been put forward for scrutiny, discussion, study, and revision.

Nonetheless, the attitudinal dimensions are valuable in suggesting repetitive themes that appear as common constellations of all harassers as well as highlighting subtle differences. The profiles are useful in helping us know what the problem looks like and in developing educational programs and institutional policies to discourage harassment.

While sexual harassers represent a diverse group of men, whose psychological histories are undoubtably equally diverse, all of the profiles reflect one global theme: "manhood"—what it means to be a man and how men demonstrate to themselves and to others that they are, indeed, "real" man. But what does it mean to be a real man? Why the drive to demonstrate one's "maleness"? And how does this translate into attitudes toward women?

It is easy to see how sexual conquests are considered evidence of "manhood," but this hardly explains sexual harassment. Why students? Why must there be a victim? Why the need to control another and exploit power? The sexual aspect of the behavior of the sexual harasser is really a secondary gain of a more profound statement. The emotion expressed in their behavior is one of fear and hatred of women. Doubts about one's masculinity and ability to measure up to definitions of "male" find expression in misogyny—disdain, devaluation, and oppression of women.[10]

Are these professors distinctly different from other men! Dziech and Wiener (1984) raise this question and explore the possibility that certain types of men are attracted to academia and that the academy can exacerbate self-doubts about masculinity. In a review of the research, they suggest that during their adolescence, professors tended to be nonathletic, unpopular with the "pretty" girls, and low in status and power and self-esteem—all adolescent measures of masculinity and success. Additionally, they point out, in our society financial resources are a measure of success and the vehicle to power. While the intellectual, scholar, teacher role is socially esteemed, it is not congruent with our definition of masculinity. It also fails to provide the material evidence of success. It does, however, provide one with a position of power and control over more people than most men ever dream of "ruling." What is more, academics, immersed in a culture of youth, may be particularly ripe for experiencing an intense midlife crisis (see Levinson 1978) in which they struggle to revise their self-image, find dignity, reflect on the past, and plan their futures. Regardless of the developmental stage individual conflicts about masculinity can be traced to, the professor is in a setting that provides the opportunity to exaggerate his own self-importance, confirm feelings of power and desirability, and exploit female students in the process of expressing his own self-doubts and disdain for women.

However, sexual harassment is not limited to the academy. It exists in all settings (e.g., executive suites, construction sites, the military). Athletes, men with great wealth, blue-collar workers, and the like, sexually harass women if the setting provides the opportunity to do so. It cannot be dismissed as an occupational phenomenon.

Pleck (1984) maintains that the primary powers women have over men are "expressive power" (the power to express emotions) and "masculinity-validating power" (the power to make men feel masculine by adhering to their prescribed role) and that men's dependency on women for these needs is a major motivation to control and have power over women. Men need women to fill their emotional gaps. The fear that women will withhold this spurs desperate attempts to dominate women, their vehicle for feeling somewhat whole. Pleck analyzes men's power over women in interaction with men's power relationships with one another (e.g., competition) and power(lessness) within society and how these dynamics serve, and are promoted by, a competitive economic structure. Others trace the roots of this misogyny—disdain, devaluation, and oppression of women—to envy of women and the masculine requirement to disown aspects of the self rooted in early experiences with nurturing, caretaking women (see for example Chodorow 1978; Horney 1932; Zalk 1987).

Whichever angle one chooses to apply to the phenomenon of sexual harassment, we can speculate that these men are particularly drawn to vulnerable women (e.g., students, employees) not simply because they exaggerate the evidence of the male's own power, but because these men feel so very vulnerable themselves. In "conquering" these women, they symbolically, albeit lamely, conquer their own vulnerability. He hates in them what he hates in himself. He masters (sic!) his fear, by "mastering" them—possessing what he seeks without acknowledging it as a part of the self.

It is reasonable to hypothesize that the male dynamics that prompt harassment are much more universal and operate in diverse settings. The psychological costs of being a "man" are great. The rewards for the price paid are power. The greater the damage, the more that power is asserted, embraced, and abused in an attempt to compensate for the losses. Some men are most vigilant in protecting themselves from exposure, and that vigilance, along with poor coping skills, can easily lead to acting out.[11] Sexual harassment is acting out, and acting out serves to avoid confronting and constructively addressing the conflict.

All men are forced to confront the perverting influence of pressures to conform to the demands of a gender-stratified society. Why some men rise above, or somehow seem to sidestep, its influence and others are shaped by it in ways that stunt their development, remains in the domain of speculation and theory. But men certainly fall on a continuum in their perspective on, and comfort with, being a "man."

Male sexual harassers in the academy and the academy itself may well be a model institutional structure to study for an understanding of the multiple factors that promote the exploitation of women. Male faculty, in general, may be an ideal sample for gaining insights on male development and the psychology of men. It may be that the academy has a tendency to attract men whose emotional development resulted in pervasive self-doubts about their masculinity, intense disdain and fear of women, and the need to exert and witness the evidence of their power. And the unique nature of the academy, with rewards that do not measure up to stereotyped evidence of male achievement and success, its power hierarchy that distorts and aggrandizes the image of the professor, disempowers students, and "minds its own business" in the arena of faculty-student interactions, encourages the abuse of power. Certain men may be attracted to the academy because it shields them from the highly competitive world of men outside its walls while providing a profession in which they are surrounded by people over whom they have power and control.

MALE FACULTY WHO DEFY THE PROFILES

The above indictment of male faculty is unfair and one-sided. Not all male professors sexually harass women students. Our experiences with sexual harassment programs and the male faculty who have been our partners in these efforts (as well as other men we have worked with) leave no question in our minds that there is another, very different profile of the male professor. Many men pursue careers as academicians for psychologically "healthy" reasons, and the choice is evidence of maturity and ego strengths. These professors have not been scarred (or the scars have long since healed) by the dissonence and conflict created by gender roles and demands. They have rejected stereotypical definitions of masculinity and its expression. They are comfortable with themselves as people and men, and with the multiple dimensions of their identity. They have chosen to pursue knowledge and to contribute to society through intellectual pursuits and by nurturing the intellectual development of others. The challenge of stimulating ideas, the excitement of witnessing change, the satisfaction of producing something others judge worth reading, and institutional involvement designed to enhance the educational environment are their sources of gratification and evidence of success and achievement. Such men are more comfortable empowering students than dominating them. They are a marked contrast to the sexual harasser.

There is much we can learn about male psychological development and the function of institutions in perpetuating an oppressive society from these men, working alongside of the sexual harasser, as well as from the harasser, and much to be learned from studying their behaviors within the organizational structure of the academy.

CONCLUSION

How can the information provided in this chapter serve the campaign to stop sexual harassment in the academy? If the pervasive practice of sexual harassment is an outcome of the impact of gender-stratified roles, demands, and limitations on male psychological development, how can it be stopped? Of what use is this perspective? While the transformation of societal structures is the ideal, it is hardly a realistic tactic for eliminating sexual harassment.

However, the institution of the academy can be changed, and can be changed in ways that will discourage the exploitation of women. The very fact that sexual harassment is one of many culturally ingrained and promoted expressions of women's oppression, and serves to perpetuate that oppression, means that academic institutions *must* take responsibility for programs, policies, and structural revisions that will discourage and create a hostile environment for the exploitation of women.

Other chapters in this book address the needed institutional reforms and methods and policies for confronting sexual harassment. The material presented in this paper underscores the need for institutional responsibility and suggests directions for reform. It is essential that *all* students be empowered, that they know their rights and the parameters of appropriate behaviors for all institutional roles. The empowerment of female students, in particular, is essential. Women, more than men, experience the academy as hostile and disempowering. While some pedagogical techniques and teacher attitudes may empower women more than others, an institutional atmosphere, promoted and supported from the top, that publicly and consistently endorses gender equality and reflects it in curriculum, projects, programs, policies, and the like, is a most effective and implementable vehicle for the empowerment of women students. Empowered women are much less likely to tolerate abuse, and faculty will find such an environment much less conducive to exploitation. Women students who have been exposed to women's studies and are knowledgeable about and supportive of women's rights are more likely to report incidences of sexual harassment than those who are not (see the Preface to this book).

Sexual harassment *must* be an open issue on campus. It must be publicly dissected for both students and faculty. While peer support groups are valuable for the victims of harassment, students will feel safe reporting incidences only if they are supported and protected at all levels of the system. Faculty and administrators need to educate student about sexual harassment and must guarantee, through policies and procedures, that they will not let the student down. We cannot encourage students to "blow the whistle" and then leave them open and vulnerable by our inaction.

While we cannot hire or retain faculty based on "types," the forms and shapes in which harassment gets enacted should be part of the educational campaign. Faculty evaluations can include questions about gender discrimination in the classroom, and students' reports should be considered in hiring aand tenuring decisions. Indeed, interviews for faculty positions should include issues pertinent to attitudes toward women students and women's advancement.

Most importantly, the veil of secrecy must be lifted. Colleagues frequently know who among them is harassing students. It is not only through the grapevine; students often confide in trusted professors. But it usually stops there. It is risky to turn one's colleague in, and the student accurately learns "What's the use? Nothing will be done. I'm on my own." Everyone must take this seriously.

Notes

1.   The focus is on male faculty–female student sexual liaisons, as these represent the preponderance of harassment incidences in the academy as well as the workplace (e.g., Fitzgerald, Chullman, et al., 1988; Fitzgerald, Weitzman, et al. 1988; Gutek and Morasch 1982; Sandler 1981).

The gender stratification of most societies is such that it hardly strikes us as surprising or even unacceptable when the older, more accomplished male professor is attracted to his younger, eager, often admiring female student. Although this is, in and of itself, worthy of critical analysis, it is not an explanation for sexual harassment. There is a large, qualitative jump between feeling something and acting on those feelings. Yet for some, the former is sufficient justification for the latter and requires little consideration of the context and the consequences.

That it is not simply a function of the two roles (i.e., student and professor), but an interaction of roles and gender, is evident by the fact that women professors rarely sexually harass male students. Indeed, we would find it curious, at best, if a female professor invested time and energy, took risks, and used the power of her position to secure sexual encounters with younger male students. She would undoubtedly be the object of conjiderable speculation about "her problem." The male faculty–female student affair is sufficiently frequent and compatible with social roles that its existence elicits little surprise.

2.   There are many fine publications that provide a historical perspective on the status of women faculty and students in higher education (e.g., Cham-

berlain 1988; Simeone 1987). Additionally, the Project on the Status and Education of Women of the Association of American Colleges (Washington, D.C.) has a publication that regularly addresses these issues, and the interested reader is encouraged to obtain this material and take advantage of the valuible service they provide.

3. I am disregarding maintenance workers, support staff, and the like. While their work is essential, their role is not part of the definitional purpose of the academy.

4. While these psychological profiles, based on attitudes and behavior, draw upon the research and writings of others, the substance of this material comes from personal experiences with sexual harassment and harassers. This material was based on information provided from the following sources: colleagues' observations of, and interactions with, sexual harassers; sexual harassers' perceptions of encounters and affairs; stories told by students who were the object of harassment; anecdotes and perceptions shared by people who were confidants of harassers, many of whom were privy to (often witnessing) the details of one or more sexual encounters with students (usually as they unfolded) and several of whom had established a relationship with the student and socialized with the couple; and clinical material provided by counselors and therapists who treated men with a history of sexual liaisons with students or employees. Thus, the "data" were subjective reports. Patterns appeared to emerge and were subjected to a psychodynamic theoretical framework. Undoubtedly, when viewed through a different theoretical lens a different picture is likely to emerge.

5. In speculating on the psychological roots motivating male professors to sexually harass female students, Dziech and Weiner (1984) explore the possibility that this behavior reflects unresolved adolescent crisis. In their review of other research on adolescent males' definitions of masculinity, power, and status and histories of male professors, they note that, as adolescents, professors were "outies," not part of the in-group (an experience that negatively affects self-esteem), lacked the adolescent markers of status (e.g., athletics) and, like their more popular peers, wanted to date the best-looking girls rather than the smartest.

6. Egocentrism is also descriptive of the functioning of the infant and the preschooler. The egocentrism of the infant stems from the lack of awareness of self as distinct from others. As such, they experience themselves as the center of the universe—their needs, perceptions, feelings, and so forth are absolute. The egocentric reasoning of preschoolers entails an inability to take the perspective of others, to be simultaneously aware of themselves and the

outside world. Elements of both these stages may also be operating, in a somewhat developed form. for the Untouchable.

7. It is recognized that reckless, life-threatening behavior by adolescents may, present a "death wish," but the point pertinent here is the element of egocentric reasoning.

8. Pryor (1987) found that male college students who scored high on his paper-and-pencil measure of "likelihood of sexually harassing" a woman, given a risk-free opportunity to do so, also scored low on the measure of perspective taking (i.e., they had difficulty taking another's perspective).

9. Disregard, for the moment, the possibility that the faculty member could be married. While this fact certainly throws suspicion on his sincerity and intentions, it is not germane to the argument being presented.

10. Pryor (1987) found that male college students who scored higher on his "likelihood to sexually harass" measure also scored a higher rape proclivity and authoritarian measure, and had negative feelings about sexuality. Additionally, these men were more likely to describe themselves in socially undesirable masculine terms or masculine terms that strongly differentiated them from the stereotypical female.

11. *Acting out* is a psychological term for expressing emotional conflicts through a series of behaviors that are symbolic of the conflict. That is, rather than recognize the conflict or tolerate the anxiety it elicits, the individual plays out some version of it. An example would be the adolescent who runs away from home in response to struggles around separation issues.

References

Abbey, A. (1982). Sex differences in attributions for friendly behavior: Do males misperceive females' friendliness? *Journal of Personality and Social Psychology, 42*, 830–38.

Chamberlain, M. (1988). *Women in academe: Progress and Prospects.* New York: Russell Sage Foundation.

Chodorow, N. (1978). *The reproduction of mothering.* Berkeley: University of California Press.

Dziech, B.W., and Weiner, L. (1984). *The lecherous professor. Sexual harassment on campus.* Boston: Beacon Press.

Elkind, D. (1980). Strategic interactions in early adolescence. In J. Adelson (Ed.), *Handbook of adolescent psychology* (432–44). New York: Wiley.

Fitzgerald, L., Shullman, S., Bailey, N., Richards, M., Swecker, J., Gold, Y., Ormerod, M., and Weitzman, L. (1988). The incidence and dimensions of sexual harassment in academia and the workplace. *Journal of Vocational Behavior*, *32*, 152–75.

Fitzgerald, L., Weitzman, L., Gold, Y., and Ormerod, M. (1988). Academic harassment: Sex and denial in scholarly garb. *Psychology of Women Quarterly*, *12*, 329–40.

Gutek, B., and Morasch, B. (1982). Sex-ratios, sex-role spillover, and sexual harassment of women at work. *Journal of Social Issues*, *38*, 55–74.

Henig, S., and Ryan, J. (1986). Sex differences in levels of tolerance and attribution of blame for sexual harassment on a university campus. *Sex Roles*, *15*, 535–49.

Horney, K. (1932). The dread of women. *International Journal of Psychoanalysis*, *13*, 348–66.

Levinson, D. (1978). *The seasons of a man's life*. New York: Ballantine.

Pleck, J. (1984). Men's power with women, other men and society: A men's movement analysis. In P.P. Rieker and E.H. Carmen (Eds.), *The gender gap in psychotherapy*. New York: Plenum Press.

Pryor, J. (1987). Sexual harassment proclivities in men. *Sex Roles*, *17*, 269–90.

Sandler, B. (1981). Sexual harassment: A hidden problem. *Educational Record*, *62*, 52–57.

Simeone, A. (1987). *Academic women: Working towards equality*. Boston: Bergin & Garvey.

Tangri, S., Burt, M., and Johnson, L. (1982). Sexual harassment at work: Three explanatory models. *Journal of Social Issues*, *38*, 33–54.

Zalk, S.R. (1987, July). *Women's dilemma: Both envied and subjugated*. Paper presented at the Third International Interdisciplinary Congress on Women, Dublin, Ireland.

6

What's Wrong with Faculty-Student Consensual Sexual Relationships?

M. Cynara Stites

Although college catalogs never mention professors' intimate relationships with students, in almost every college and university in the United States, at some time, a professor has fallen in love with one of his students, married her, and lived happily ever after. So, what's wrong with this picture of the "happy couple"?

This "happy couple" picture does fit the profile of the genders of the most frequent participants in faculty-student sexual relationships—male faculty members and female students, particularly female graduate students (Dziech and Weiner 1990; Fitzgerald, Shullman, et al. 1988; Hoffman 1986; Hughes and Sandler 1986; Pope, Levenson, and Schover 1979; Reilly, Lott, and gallogly 1986; Sandler and Associates 1981; Truax 1989). However, this "happy couple" picture does not depict the only—nor the most common—circumstances of faculty-student consensual sexual relationships. More often, a faculty-student sexual relationship is a one-night stand, a sexual fling, an affair a time-limited romantic relationship (which might end with bad feelings between the couple), or a professor's sexual harassment of the student. Although the precise prevalence of faculty-student sexual relationships is unknown and the extent of mutual consent in such relationships is unknown, studies of former women graduate psychology students indicate that 12 to 17 percent were sexually involved with a male professor or clinical supervisor during graduate school (Bond 1988; Glaser and Thorpe 1986; Pope, Levenson, and Schover 1979; Robinson and Reid 1985). In one study, 26 percent of male faculty members reported they had had sexual encounters or sexual relationships with women students (Fitzgerald, Weitzman, et al. 1988).

Another scenario that is more common than the "happy couple" picture is a professor's attempts to indicate his sexual interest in female students through flirting, sexual advances, sexual propositions, sexual invitations, seductive behavior, attempts to establish romantic/sexual relationships, or unwanted sexual attention, which are experienced by 2 percent to 48 percent of women students (Benson and Thomson 1982; Bond 1988; Fitzgerald, Shullman, et al. 1988; Oshinsky 1981; Reilly, Lott, and Gallogly 1986; Robinson and Reid 1985; Rowland, Crisler, and Cox 1982; Wilson and Kraus 1983). One student describes a professor's efforts to seduce women students as follows:

> Through the journal [required for the class], I began to share my personal experiences with the professor, at his initiation and with his encouragement. Because he was so self-disclosing in class, and because we were supposed to relate what we were reading to our own experience, I shared my feelings with him. His responses to my journal entries became more and more personal. In this way, I thought a rare friendship was developing with someone whose politics and commitment to ethics in education I shared. I was extremely flattered by his interest in me. . . . By displacing our student-teacher relationship onto nonacademic ground, symbolically and literally, he masked the inherent power imbalance between my role as a student and his as a professor. The relationship thus seemed to be one between two consenting adults. And, indeed, this professor was not a lecherous powers-monger, pinning students against his desk and promising a good grade for sexual favors. He never said he desired me sexually, he never threatened me with academic retribution if I didn't submit to his demands, he was not overtly coercive. . . . His pattern was to use the journal to establish a close relationship, and the political groups to increase access to women and to encourage them to think of him not as a professor but as a friend, *a man*. Then he would encourage any physical advances the context would allow. For me it stopped with kissing, but with one of the women [students], he engaged in [sexual] intercourse in the department lounge. (Peter 1990, 17–18)

The major problem with the "happy couple" picture is that the couple's happiness should not be the basis for judging faculty-student consensual sexual relationships. Instead, a university community should be concerned about faculty ethical responsibilities, favoritism and equal educational opportunity, the detrimental consequences of faculty-student consensual relationships (particularly for the women students who participate in these relationships and for other women students), and the potential for sexual harassment.

FACULTY MEMBERS' ETHICAL RESPONSIBILITIES

When faculty-student consensual sexual relationships are scrutinized in the context of ethics, questions arise about the professional ethical obligations of university professors, conflicts of interest in dual-role relationships, and the potential for a professor's abuse of power over his student-lover. "Unlike employers, educators have a professional and ethical responsibility to provide a learning environment that fosters students' academic performance and intellectual development" (Robertson, Dyer, and Campbell 1988, 807). Inherent in the concept of professional ethical respnsibility is the expectation that professionals apply their specialized knowledge to serve the interests of their clientele above the professionals' personal interests (Kitchener 1988).

> Insofar as . . . teaching is taken seriously as a professional activity, there arises a tension between the concepts of professional relationship and the relationship of sexual intimacy. Historically, sexual, or for that matter, familial intimacy has been seen as distorting clear professional judgment. The Hippocratic Oath, for example, prohibits sex between physicians and their patients. Beyond the issue of professional judgment, the professional may be viewed not so much as one who has achieved some high level of useful, specialized skill (an apt description of an accomplished athlete or good plumber), but rather as someone who is accorded special status, income, or security in exchange for which he or she agrees to an ethic of placing the client's interest above all else. A teacher who gains satisfaction for sexual wants and needs through students may have considerable difficulty maintaining the student's interests as primary (Pope, Schover, and Levenson 1980, 158)

The university teaching profession, like any other profession, should have professional ethical standards that emphasize protection of the student over the personal interests of the professor (Ingulli 1987). Ethical codes prohibiting other professionals such as attorneys, social workers, physicians, and psychologists from engaging in sexual relationships with their patients or clients are models for academic professionals' conduct in their relationships with their students (Glaser and Thorpe 1986; Kitchener 1988; Pope, Schover, and Levenson 1980; Schover, Williams 1982). "Codes of ethics for most professional associations forbid professional-client sexual relationships. . . . The professor-student relationship is one of professional and client" (University of Minnesota 1990, 206).

The American Association of University Professors (AAUP) Statement on Professional Ethics is the most widely used ethical code for the university teaching profession. Unlike many other professions' ethical codes, the AAUP code does not specifically address sexual relationships between a professor/ professional and a student/client. Instead, the AAUP ethical statement generally addresses the need for professors to avoid misusing the power of their position with students. It states that faculty members should avoid "any exploitation of students . . . for private advantage" (American Association of University Professors 1990, 42).

Although the AAUP Statement on Professional Ethics does not directly address faculty-student consensual sexual relationships, it was cited as the basis for a court decision allowing a university to dismiss a faculty member who had engaged in a consensual sexual relationship with a student. In *Korf v. Ball State University* (1984), the court ruled that the professor was fired for "unethical conduct by exploiting students for his private advantage" (1230). The court explained the professional ethical obligations of faculty members who engage in consensual sexual relationships with students as follows:

> While there is no evidence that the young student Dr. Korf admitted having a sexual relationship with did not consent to engage in sexual activity with him, Dr. Korf's conduct is not to be viewed in the same context as would conduct of an ordinary person on the street. Rather, it must be judged in the context of the relationship existing between a professor and his students within an academic environment. University professors occupy an important place in our society and have con- commitant ethical obligations. The AAUP Statement of Professional Ethics makes this clear:
>
> > "1) The professor, guided by a deep conviction of the worth and dignity of the advancement of knowledge, recognizes the special responsibilities placed upon him. . . .
> >
> > 2) . . . He demonstrates respect for the student as an individual and adheres to his proper role as intellectual guide and counselor."
>
> (*Korf v. Ball State University* 1984, 1227)

Even when a university has no faculty ethical code or consensual rela- tionship policy, a professor may be disciplined for unethical behavior when he engages in a faculty-student consensual sexual relationship ("College Sus- pends Professor" 1991). A Louisiana State University instructor who was involved in a sexual relationship with a student for whom the instructor had no teaching or supervisory responsibilities was disciplined for a breach of ethics despite Louisiana State University's lack of any written faculty conduct standards, ethical code, or consensual relationship policy (*Naragon v. Wharton* 1983, 1984). In upholding the university's action against the instructor, the court explained the instructor's professional ethical responsibilities as follows:

> The fact that the student was not enrolled in a specific class being taught by [the instructor], or that [the instructor] was not in a position to assign grades to the student's work, does not make the relationship between

the teacher and the young student acceptable behavior. Contained in University regulations pertaining to teachers is the specific requirement that teachers should be "positive role models" for students, and should govern themselves accordingly. The regulations do not contain specifics concerning the conduct expected of teachers, but it does not seem unreasonable to suggest that by implication, at least, it should be understood by teachers and professors that "deep, personal romantic relationships" with students in the University could reasonable be viewed by University officials as conduct which is unprofessional and unbecoming a teacher or professor, and detrimental to the best interests of the University. . . . Such romantic relationships between teacher and student may give the impression of an abuse of authority; it may appear to create a conflict of interest even if in fact no such conflict directly results; it tends to create in the minds of other students a perception of unfairness; it tends to and probably does affect other students' opinions of the teacher; it may affect other professors' opinions of the student and the teacher; and it might well affect prospective students' opinions of the University. . . . [The University] has a right to expect and demand the highest standards of personal behavior and teaching performance from its teachers and professors. (*Naragon v. Wharton* 1983, 1121)

A professor who engages in a dual-role relationship with a student as both her teacher and her lover has an unethical conflict of interest. Professors and students in any mentoring relationship often have difficulty balancing the professional and personal aspects of their relationship (Brooks and Haring-Hidore 1987). However, the conflicting role expectations of a professional relationship and a sexual relationship may affect the professor's objectivity and damage the professor-student relationship at the student's expense (Walker, Erickson, and Woolsey 1985). The professor faces conflicts when the expectations of his role as professor are incompatible with the expectations of his role as lover; and these conflicting roles compete for his time and energy (Kitchener 1988):

As the obligations of different roles diverge, the potential for divided loyalties and loss of objectivity increases. . . . The primary obligation of a professional is to promote the welfare of the consumer whether the consumer is a client, supervisee, or student. By contrast, in a personal relationship, for example, there is an expectation that the needs of both parties will be met in a more or less reciprocal manner. It is difficult to consistently put the consumer's needs first if one is also invested in meeting one's own needs. (219)

Another ethical concern regarding faculty-student consensual sexual relationships is the potential for the professor's *unintended* abuse of power or coercion in a relationship that is inherently unequal (Kennedy 1980; Tuana 1985). The larger the power difference is between the professor and the student, the greater the potential may be for the professor to exploit the student—even without intention or awareness that he is exploiting her (Kitchener 1988). A professor may be unaware that his expectations or suggestions "may come across as demands or threats to students because of the inherently unequal nature of the relationship or as the 'gospel' to be introjected in order to bolster an unsure professional identity" (Pope, Schover, and Levenson 1980, 158). Since professors, like attorneys and psychologists, are professionals with certain ethical responsibilities, they have ethical responsibilities to avoid the conflicts of interests in a dual-role relationships and the subtle potential for coercion inherent in their superior power position with students.

Research findings reveal that faculty members as well as students believe that professors are behaving unethically when they have sexual relationships with their students. At least 80 percent of male faculty members and female graduate students surveyed at a large Eastern state university agreed that the following ethical problems are inherent in faculty-student consensual sexual relationships (Stites 1993): (1) A professor cannot avoid professional conflicts of interest when he has a sexual relationship with a student whom he teaches, advises, or supervises (Stites 1993). (2) The professor's objectivity in evaluating a student's academic work is compromised when he has a sexual relationship with the student (Stites 1993) and (3) The professor in such a relationship has the potential to abuse the power of his professional position over the student and has a subtle yet powerful potential to coerce the student (Stites 1993). One woman graduate student wrote, "I feel very strongly that it is totally unethical for a faculty member to engage in a sexual relationship with a student" (Stites 1993, 101). Another student commented:

> Although I understand that a consensual relationship might be seen as a relationship between two consenting adults, there is still an inherent power imbalance with the potential for abuse. No matter what the situation and/or attraction, I believe it is the professor's responsibility to abstain from such a relationship with a graduate student. The professor has a responsibility to graduate students' academic/professional growth. (Stites 1993, 101)

Another graduate student commented: "College teachers are professionals and are expected to act as such" (Stites 1993, 101). Noting the power a professor has over a student, another student commented: "I view sexual relationships between faculty and students as unprofessional in the same way I view such intimate relationships between employees and employers" (Stites 1993, 102).

Over two-thirds of female graduate students and 87 percent of male faculty members in the Stites (1993) study agreed that a faculty member is behaving *un*ethically if he continues to teach, advise, or supervise a graduate student with whom he is having a sexual relationship. Numerous male faculty members and female graduate students in the Stites (1993) study volunteered written opinions that a professor who starts a sexual relationship with a student should remove himself from teaching, advising, or supervising that student or should refrain from the sexual relationship until after the student graduates.

A 1986 study of former women graduate students in psychology who had sexual relationships with professors or clinical supervisors during graduate school revealed that their attitudes changed somewhat after they left graduate school (Glaser and Thorpe 1986). At the time of the sexual relationship, 72 percent of the women students felt that they were not at all coerced by the professor into the sexual relationship; only 49 percent still feel that way after leaving graduate school (Glaser and Thorpe 1986). While still in graduate school, 49 percent of the women who had sexual relationships before or during their working relationship with the professors believed that the sexual relationships were ethically problematic, but 68 percent of them later believe when they look back after graduate school, that the relationships were ethically problematic (Glaser and Thorpe 1986). Eighty percent of female psychology graduate students who had received sexual advances from a professor in graduate school viewed such sexual advances by faculty members as "somewhat or highly ethically inappropriate" when the sexual advances occurred; and 95 percent of them hold this view in retrospect after leaving graduate school (Glaser and Thorpe 1986).

Schneider (1987) reports that a few of the 46 women graduate students she surveyed who had dated a faculty member at least once while they were in graduate school were

> focused on the general ethical issue of the propriety of an academic relationship in which romance has intruded. A twenty-six year old woman who had recently married a faculty member in her own department comments: "I don't think it is the most ethical situation for either party for a female student to be personally or intimately involved with a faculty member that is in a position to evaluate them [sic] either by grade as in the case of a course or by serving on their committee. (54)

One study of male faculty members' attitudes about faculty-student consensual sexual relationships revealed that a tiny minority (5 to 15 percent) of male faculty members surveyed believe that the ethics of a faculty-student sexual relationship hinge on certain situational circumstances of that relationship (Fitzgerald, Weitzman, et al. 1988). Those situational circumstances include the mutual consent of the participants, the professor's responsibility for evaluating the student, the student's initiation of the relationship, and the outcome of the relationship, such as marriage (Fitzgerald, Weitzman, et al. 1988). These male professors' concept of mutual consent as a legitimizing factor in faculty-student consensual sexual relationships focuses only on the mutual consent of two adults, regardless of any authority the professor may have over the student. As one male professor wrote, "Just because I personally haven't engaged in close personal or sexual relationships [with students] doesn't mean that I disapprove. Whatever two adults feel that they must do, as responsibly as they can, is just fine" (Fitzgerald, Weitzman, et al. 1988, 337).

Another legitimizing factor for a small minority of male faculty members is the student's initiation of the sexual relationship with the faculty member (Fitzgerald, Weitzman, et al. 1988):

> A few [male] faculty reported being the object of female students' sexual interest, such interest constituting the legitimizing factor in the relationship. Faculty who reported this tended to describe themselves as passive and non-initiating, and occasionally appeared to feel taken advantage of by the student with whom they had become involved. One respondent wrote: "It has been my observation that students, and some faculty, have little understanding of the extreme pressure a male professor can feel as the object of sexual interest of attractive women students. (337)

At a large Eastern state university, only 22 percent of the female graduate students and 17 percent of the male faculty members who were surveyed agreed that if a graduate student seeks to initiate a sexual relationship with a professor who teaches, advises, or supervises her, then it would be ethical for the professor to have a consensual sexual relationship with her (Stites 1993).

Another legitimizing factor for professor-student consensual sexual relationships cited by a few male faculty members is the eventual marriage of the professor to his student-lover (Fitzgerald, Weitzman, et al. 1988). Only 26 percent of the male faculty members and 33 percent of the female graduate students surveyed at a large Eastern state university agreed that a professor can be viewed as behaving ethically if his consensual sexual relationship with a graduate student whom he teaches, advises, or supervises leads to marriage (Stites 1993). Whereas only 22 percent of male faculty members and female graduate students in the Stites (1993) study would recommend no university action against a professor who has a consensual sexual relationship with a graduate student whom he teaches, advises, or supervises, 37 percent of the male faculty members and 33 percent of the female graduate students would recommend no university action if the couple recently got engaged. A few male faculty members objected to marriage's being viewed as equivalent to other types of faculty-student consensual sexual relationships, such as affairs and romantic relationships (Stites 1993). One male faculty member pointed out that "many ethical and well respected faculty members married students" and asked, "Can the wife of a professor obtain a graduate degree in his department?" (Stites 1993, 103).

The professor's lack of professional responsibilities for the students—grading or other evaluations, teaching, advising, supervising—is a very strong legitimizing factor in professor-student consensual sexual relationships. Fitzgerald, Weitzman, et al. (1988) report that the male professors they surveyed

> suggested that personal relationships are acceptable if the student is not taking the professor's class, and/or is not in the same department, or is not being evaluated by the professor in any way. For instance: [one male professor commented] "the only time I have ever gone out with female students occurred *after* they had completed my class, and this only on two occasions. I would not subject one of my currently-enrolled students to the pressures or conflicts og being both a student or mine and a personal friend or lover. (337)

Regarding a professor who has a consensual sexual relationship with a graduate student from a different academic department, 75 percent of male faculty members and female graduate students in one study would recommend no university action against the professor (Stites 1993). If the professor removes himself from teaching, advising, and supervising a student when he begins a consensual sexual relationship with her, 58 percent of male faculty members and 74 percent of female graduate students in that study would recommend no university action against the professor (Stites 1993). However, recognition of the potential for a future conflict of interest may account for the lower percentages of male faculty members (45 percent) and female graduate students (51 percent) who would recommend no university action against a professor who has a consensual sexual relationship with a new graduate student in his academic department whom he has never taught, advised, or supervised (Stites 1993).

FAVORITISM AND EQUAL EDUCATIONAL OPPORTUNITY

When a professor's sexual relationship with a student creates a conflict of interest for the professor, other students assume that the professor is unfairly favoring his student-lover over other students in his professional responsibilities (DeChiara 1988; Little 1989; Pope, Schover, and Levenson 1980). Consequently, the professor appears to be denying other students their rights to equal access to educational opportunities.

The perception that the student involved in a faculty-student sexual relationship has an unfair advantage over other students is heightened when the student appears to pursue the professor for a sexual relationship in order to gain specific favors in her academic work. Although there is little evidence in the workplace that women can use their sexuality to advance professionally (Gutek 1985; Schneider 1984),

> when it is the student who initiates sexual overtures, the issue of faculty ethics and conflict of interest is even more sharply focused. The possibility that the student may have academic gain rather than sexual gratification as a purpose cannot be overlooked. The rights of other students to educational experiences in which all students in the class are treated fairly and equally must be considered. (Walker, Erickson, and Woolsey 1985)

The Howard University consensual relationship policy ackowledges the problems of favoritism and unequal educational opportunity that are inherent in faculty-student sexual relationships as follows:

> Even genuinely consensual relationships between faculty members and students and supervisors and supervisees may be problematic. For example, they may result in favoritism or perceptions of favoritism that adversely affect the learning or work environment. Consensual relationships involving a power differential, therefore, may violate University policy and equal opportunity law. (*Howard University Sexual Harassment Policy and Procedures* 1990, 220)

Faced with a professor-student sexual relationship, other students could sue the university for violation of their Fourteenth Amendment rights to equal protection (Connolly and Marshall 1989; Little and Thompson 1989). Male students could also claim that they are denied equal protection on the basis of sex. Employees have brought lawsuits against employers for sex discrimination under Title VII when the employees felt that a supervisor had unfairly favored an employee with whom the supervisor had a sexual relationship; and an employee sued her employer after a sexual relationship with her supervisor ended with her being discharged from her job (Hustoles 1990). Court rulings have gone both ways on the issue of whether a consensual relationship that affects other workers constitutes sex discrimination.

> One line of cases has held that consensual relationships which impact others can give rise to a cause of action based upon traditional notions

of sex discrimination, when the plaintiff asserts some discriminatory treatment because of the consensual relationship. Another line of cases holds that a consensual relationship (and/or its break-up) does not give rise to discrimination based upon "sex", but rather is due to one's status of being a party to or non-party to a relationship, so that a sex discrimination theory is not viable. (Hustoles 1990, 254)

Observers of the professional relationship between a professor and his student-lover almost universally perceive the professor as guilty of favoritism. In the Stites (1993) study, 97 percent of the female graduate students and 98 percent of the male faculty members who were surveyed agreed that other graduate students may believe that a professor who has a consensual sexual relationship with a graduate student whom he teaches, advises, or supervises is unfairly favoring this graduate student over others in his professional responsibilities. One female graduate student wrote, "If I was a student and knew my professor was having an affair with another student in my class, I would be very upset. The situation is even worse in the advisee/advisor graduate school relationship" (Stites 1993, 105). Another commented, "It is not fair to the less superior person in the relationship and to the struggling peers of that person for him or her to gain any sort of reward from inappropriate personal relations with the 'boss' " (Stites 1993, 106). Yet another person offered these observations about the effects of favoritism:

As a female graduate student and teaching assistant in a department where a very visible consensual relationship between a professor and a student he teaches, advises, and supervises occurred, and as a teacher who has experienced attraction and a potential relationship with a student of my own, I *know* a few things: 1) Relationships between professors and students can ruin a department. The graduate students in my department feel betrayed and compromised, and several faculty members have been put in awkward and impossible positions. 2) When a student-teacher relationship becomes intimate, objectivity is *impossible.* (Stites 1993, 106)

A male faculty member offered similar observations about the assumptions students and faculty members make regarding a professor's favoritism of his student-lover as follows:

I have had the unpleasant experience of other faculty in my department having consensual sexual relationships with students they supervised. The experience strongly suggested to me and my colleagues that such relationships a) create a climate in which unbiased judgements are almost impossible to achieve, b) unnecessarily denigrate the stature of the faculty member involved, c) cause considerable demoralization among the graduate students, and d) to a very considerable extent disrupt the normal functioning of the department. Yet I married a graduate student on whose committee I served as a minor advisor. Even the nonsexual, artificially distanced relationship we had prior to her receiving her doctorate was a stressful experience for both of us and I am sure was a source of some concern for her committee chair and her department faculty. (Stites 1993)

As this faculty member suggests, besides perceptions of favoritism of the professor's student-lover and the consequent unequal educational opportunity for other students, faculty-student consensual sexual relationships can cause other detrimental consequences.

DETRIMENTAL CONSEQUENCES OF FACULTY-STUDENT SEXUAL RELATIONSHIPS

Faculty-student consensual sexual relationships may damage the university's reputation (DeChiara 1988; *Naragon v. Wharton* 1983, 1984) and sometimes tarnish the credibility of the professors who seek or have such relationships (Haring-Hidore and Inguilli 1987; Kantor 1990). At least 80 percent of the male faculty members and female graduate students surveyed at a large Eastern state university agreed that when faculty members have consensual sexual relationships with graduate students whom they teach, advise, or supervise, the university's credibility as an educational institution is compromised in the public's eyes and an academic department's integrity is compromised in the eyes of graduate students when faculty members tolerate such faculty-student sexual relationships (Stites 1993). One male faculty member commented that, when he was a graduate student at another university, he had "lived through disillusionment" with his academic department's faculty who tolerated a professor's sexual relationship with a student (Stites 1993). When women students are aware that faculty members seek and/or have sexual relationships with other women students, they may view the university and their academic department as unsupportive of women's professional and academic development (Bond 1988; Schneider 1987).

Most of the detrimental consequences of faculty-student consensual sexual relationships fall on women students (Schneider 1987)—both the women students participating in sexual relationships with faculty members and other women students. The student who has a sexual relationship with a faculty member often incurs the resentment and hostility of other students (DeChiara 1988). Other students and faculty members may accurately or inaccurately perceive the professor's student-lover as receiving academic rewards for her participation in the sexual relationship, doubt her academic abilities, and characterize her as "sleeping her way to the top" (Haring-Hidore and Paludi 1989; Horn and Horn 1982; Hughes and Sandler 1986; Jamison 1983).

A woman student who is having a sexual relationship with a male professor often experiences the strain of attempting to keep the relationship secret (Hughes and Sandler 1986; Williams 1982). To maintain the appearance that no sexual relationship exists, the professor may limit the student's professional opportunities by such actions as refusing to take the student with him to out-of-town professional conferences (Haring-Hidore and Paludi 1989) or refusing to choose her to give a department seminar. Studies of workplace romances indicate that efforts to hide the sexual relationship usually fail, although co-workers and supervisors might not reveal their awareness of the sexual relationship to the couple (Quinn 1977). Such failed attempts at secrecy isolate the woman from her co-workers (Quinn and Lees 1984) or other students.

A professor's student-lover may feel that her academic progress becomes precariously linked to her sexual relationship with the professor. When a professor has advising, teaching, or supervisory responsibilities for a student with whom he is sexually involved, the student's confidence in her academic abilities may be undermined by doubts about the basis of her professor's-lover's evaluations (Hughes and Sandler 1986; McCormack 1985). "She may fear that his praise is a form of seduction and that his letters of recommendations for her have been won in bed" (Walker, Erickson, and Woolsey 1985, 427). In a study of 46 women graduate students who had dated a professor at least once, Schneider (1987) notes that

> five women expressed feelings quite consistent with the remarks of one woman in the social sciences: "My one sexual relationship with a male faculty member was in no way coerced and would have progressed similarly had we known each other in any other context, but I *did* react a lot to the fact that he was my teacher. I realized then and now that a female graduate student is putting herself in a potentially vulnerable situation, even in the best of circumstances, and can rarely come out of such a relationship without having lost some degree of control over her academic life. (54)

The student-lover of a faculty member may experience other adverse consequences of the sexual relationship. A professor-student consensual sexual relationship may permanently disrupt the student's other intimate relationships or her marriage (Williams 1982). If the student becomes aware that the professor has had similar sexual relationships with other students, she may feel betrayed and humiliated (Peters 1990). Other detrimental consequences for women students include the inherent power difference in a professor-student sexual relationship, which negates the possibility of a relationship between equals (Hughes and Sandler 1986). Hite (1990) describes the particularly adverse consequences experienced by a graduate student who, after informing her program head that she was a patient in intensive psychotherapy because she had been raped by her father, was then seduced by the program head. She was admitted to a psychiatric hospital (while the program head took the university's offer to resign and moved to a very good faculty position at another university) (Hite 1990). Some of the male faculty perceived this program head's successive affairs with female graduate students as "normal" and "usual" for a bachelor; and one male faculty member blamed the graduate student by commenting that "any woman who can't handle that sort of pressure has no business in this program" (Hite 1990, 13).

Should the professor-student sexual relationship end, especially if it ends with negative feelings between the couple, the student may experience severe loss of confidence about her academic ability and doubt about her student status (Schneider 1987; Williams 1982). Hughes and Sandler (1986) warn students of the potential pitfalls of breaking off an intimate relationship with a professor, as follows:

> If the [professor-student dating relationship] ends badly with a lot of hard feelings on both sides, depending on his position, 1) he could sabotage your grade, or at least leave you wondering if his personal feelings influenced the grade; 2) he could talk about you to other teachers and negatively influence how they perceive you; 3) if he is the only one teaching any courses that you must take, it will be very awkward being in those classes. It will be difficult to ensure that his personal feelings wouldn't affect his behavior toward you in class or at grading time; 4) if he teaches in your major department, you might feel very uncomfortable not only with him but with others in the department as well. Indeed, some women go out of their way to avoid both a professor who is an ex-boyfriend and his department in general, and end up feeling alienated by the whole experience; 5) it would be extremely difficult to use him as a reference. (9)

Some of the most severe detrimental consequences of professor-student consensual sexual relationships occur when the relationship is or becomes unwanted by the student, even if the professor does not threaten any reprisals or promise any rewards. Sometimes the student feels compelled to maintain an unwanted sexual relationship with a professor because of the implied coercion of his position over her and her fears of reprisals should she break off the relationship (Haring-Hidore and Paludi 1989). A graduate student may feel particularly trapped into maintaining a sexual relationship with a professor to avoid major setbacks to her professional career should she leave graduate school or to avoid risks of reprisals from a professor who has a lot of power over her professional future (Schneider 1987). One doctoral student described the dilemma she faced in starting and continuing a sexual relationship with her faculty adviser, as follows:

> [My faculty adviser] cried and so forth [about his marital problems] and I responded as if he were my friend. It was the wrong thing to do; he was soon making real [sexual] advances. I was utterly repulsed but I was terrified to say no. He just had too much authority over me. It was absolute. It was even more than the authority that a boss has over you in a job, it has parental aspects to it because this whole graduate experience is an apprenticeship system. . . . It always seemed at the time that I would rather be sexually exploited than risk my whole career. You see, nobody else [other than your major adviser] really knows that much about what you're doing academically. The whole way they judge you is by what your adviser says to them at coffee and over lunch and so forth. Everything depends on his opinion and I thought if I get him pissed off at a personal level he's going to communicate negativity about me to the others. I knew I couldn't overcome that because I'd seen it happen before, and once you get a reputation for not being a good student they don't ever give you a chance to perform otherwise. ("Diane" in Farley 1978, 75–76)

In order for a professor to initiate a consensual sexual relationship with a student, he must indicate that he is interested in sex with the student. Even a professor's indication of sexual interest in a student can have detrimental consequences for the student. Students do not respond to sexual invitations from professors by simply saying no and continuing their professional relationship as if the sexual invitation never happened (Dziech and Weiner 1990). "Once a student is propositioned [by a professor], all her future interactions with, and evaluations by, the professor are tainted and suspect, whether a promise or threat was ever made or carried out" (Crocker 1983, 705). When the unwanted sexual advance from a professor occurs in a well-established faculty-student relationship, the woman student might lose her confidence in her academic ability and become disillusioned with all male professors (Benson and Thomson 1982). Women students who are the object of professors' unwanted sexual advances and/or are aware that other students are being approached by professors often implement avoidance strategies that can limit their educational experiences. They may consciously avoid appearing interested in intimacy with professors by dressing modestly, mentioning their boyfriends or husbands to the professors, and avoiding contact with certain professors— not taking his classes, avoiding meeting with him, not having him serve as an adviser, avoiding his research, and avoiding informal contacts (Adams, Kottke, and Padgitt 1983; Cammaert 1985; Olson and McKinney 1989; McKinney, Olson, and Satterfield 1988; Rabinowitz 1990; Sandler and Associates 1981; Schneider 1987; Scott 1984). Some of these avoidance strategies may be disadvantageous to the women student's academic prospects. "Without comfortable access to the informal channels of professional socialization, women ultimate experience less control over their academic lives" (Benson and Thomson 1982).

Students' other possible reactions to unwanted sexual advances from professors include numerous somatic complaints, decreased concentration, depression, feeling helpless and hopeless that anything can be done, and even changing study or career plans (Sandler and Associates 1981). A female student who experiences unwanted sexual advances from a male professor might also blame herself for somehow exciting his sexual interest, deny to herself that the professor is really making sexual advances or that such advances are offensive to her, or deny that there is any coercive element to his sexual advances (Farley 1978; Olson and McKinney 1989; Rabinowitz 1990).

One graduate student describes how she experienced a professor's attempt to seduce her, as follows:

> I had a class with [this professor] when I started my doctoral program. He left notes on my papers asking me to come in and see him. I was really impressed—he seemed to take such a genuine interest in my program. I asked him to be my [major adviser]. He changed. He began to touch me, my arms and legs, giving me neck rubs, kissing me. I would try and pull away, he'd pull closer. He kept asking to come to my house. He came and brought wine. He began touching me again, only going farther. I told him I didn't think a sexual relationship for us was a good idea because he was my [major advisor], married, etc. He assured me it was a good idea. I got him to leave without having sex but his pursuits became heavier. He frequently said he wanted to be sure that I know that I didn't have to make love to him to get through the program. Finally, when I couldn't take it any longer, I tried to politely but firmly tell him "no". Once again I was chastised for my "coldness". About three weeks later, out of the blue, he threatened go give me an incomplete in a class. He began to be bitter and sarcastic with me. I confronted him with what I thought was unfair—he said he knew now I didn't want him, so why hadn't I told him. It was obvious the man was out of touch. I tired to placate him but kept my distance. I have not finished my

program so I still have to deal with him. I have married . . . which I have really played up to keep him at a distance. He remains periodically unfair to me, was a complete jerk during my comprehensives, and generally makes life difficult. I stay away from him as much as possible. (Till 1980, 26–27)

Once students are aware that sexual relationships have intruded into faculty-student relationships, each woman student may experience conflicts between her gender role as a sexual woman and her student role as a competent student. This conflict presents a dilemma. She may struggle with her desire to be treated as a competent student and her perception that a male professor is expecting her to behave according to the stereotypical female gender role (Olson and McKinney 1989; Popovich and Licata 1987). Male students are not faced with such role conflicts because social conditioning allows men to be viewed as sexual people and competent professionals at the same time (Gutek 1985). Should a woman respond to a male professor's sexual overtures positively and, consequently, reinforce his perception of her as a sex object? Or should a woman act like an asexual, competent student and risk being demeaned by men as being "old-fashioned," "frigid," a "prude," or an "old maid" (Gutek 1985; Gutek and Dunwoody 1987; Guteck and Morasch 1982; Levy 1982)? Whichever alternative she chooses may not adequately resolve the dilemma of her perception that her sexuality as a woman is perceived by a male professor as more salient than her competence as a student.

When universities tolerate male professors' pursuit of sexual relationships with female students, male students—and, in turn, female student—also can be negatively impacted.

Some [male students] are sophisticated enough to see the embarassment and panic felt by women students targeted by instructors. Some feel frustrated as men because their status as students prevents them from intervening on behalf of women. Others are less sensitive. They conclude that women possess unfair advantages. Subordinated to the sexual power of the female and the academic power of the professor, men students feel bewildered and angry. Frecguently, their social conditioning and self-interest lead them to turn their hostility toward the victims [female students] rather than the offenders [male professors]. (Dziech and Weiner 1990, 60)

A very high rercentage (83 to 90 percent) of the male faculty members and female graduate students surveyed at a large Eastern state university agreed that potential detrimental consequences exist for the women students who have sexual relationships with their professors (Stites 1993). They agreed that a student's participation in such a relationship diminishes that student's credibility as a competent scholar in the eyes of other faculty members, undermines her confidence in her academic ability because of her perception that the professors' evaluation of her work is not based solely on its scholarly merit, and does not enhance her learning experiences or academic progress. They also agreed that if a student breaks off a consensual sexual relationship with a professor who teaches, advises, or supervises her, she can risk incurring the professor's unfair reprisals in his professional responsibilities for her. One women graduate student commented, "I know for a fact that reprisals against female graduate students exist." Another noted that,

> as a female student, it is hard to not believe that you may be risking your academic career because of the relationship. I've had an involvement myself as an undergraduate and, although it worked out o.k., I could have been really screwed professionally if it hadn't. I can't help but think there is an inherent vulnerability for a female student in this type of relationship. (Stites 1993, 104–5)

Another study reveals that only 2 percent of a sample of former psychology graduate students (both male and female) believe that sexual relationships between students and their professors or clinical supervisors are beneficial to both the student and the professor (Pope, Levenson, and Schover 1979). Such detrimental consequences for women students of faculty-student consensual relationships are similar to the adverse consequences for women students when faculty members harass women students.

CONSENSUAL SEXUAL RELATIONSHIPS AND SEXUAL HARASSMENT

Although, at first glance, consensual sexual relationships appear to be antithetical to sexual harassment, distinctions between consensual sexual relationships and sexual harassment in professor-student relationships often can be difficult to make (Keller 1988). Distinctions between a consensual sexual relationship and sexual harassment can blur with a professor-student "romance which sours before the end of the term, leaving hurt feelings on both sides and possibly an atmosphere ripe for sexual harassment" (Ross and Green 1983, 4). Sexual harassment is most clear-cut when a professor deliberately uses his power over a student by threatening her with reprisals or promising her a reward to endure her participation in a sexual relationship. In this way, a professor-student consensual sexual relationship may "degenerate" into *quid pro quo* sexual harassment (DeChiara 1988).

More commonly, but perhaps more subtly, a consensual sexual relationship can constitute a second type of sexual harassment, known as "hostile environment" sexual harassment. In federal courts, a hostile environment sexual harassment claim hinges on severe and persistent harm to the student and on the student's perception that she did not want or welcome the sexual contact. In 1991, a Ninth Circuit Court ruled in *Ellison v. Nicholas* that the standard to determine what is unwanted or unwelcomed should be a "reasonable woman's" view because women, as targets of men's sexual advances, may have different perceptions of objectionable behavior than men have (Marcus 1991; National Association for Women in Education 1991). A student who is involved sexually with a professor could have a valid claim that the professor is sexually harassing her, should the professor's request for sex be or become *unwanted* or *unwelcomed* by the student even if she voluntarily participates in the sexual relationship with the professor and even if she cannot demonstrate that she resisted this sexual involvement (American Council on Education 1988; Cole 1988; Connolly and Marshall 1989; Keller 1988; Little and Thompson 1989; *Meritor Savings Bank v. Vinson* 1986; Robinson, Delaney, and Stephens 1987; Welzenbach et al. 1986).

CONCLUSION

All members of a university community need to face what is wrong with consensual sexual relationships between faculty members and students for whom faculty members have professional responsibilities. We no longer can just feel good about those rare "happy couples." We can no longer ignore the adverse consequences for the students and for the academic departments where such improper faculty-student sexual relationships occur. University communities need to address the real problems of professors' breaches of their ethical responsibilities, favoritism, equal educational opportunities for students, the detrimental consequences of such relationships, and the opportunities for sexual harassment when a faculty member has a sexual relationship with a student for whom he has professional responsibilities such as teaching, grading, advising, or supervising.

References

Adams, J., Kottke, J., and Padgitt, J. (1983). Sexual harassment of university students. *Journal of College Student Personnel, 24*, 484–90.

American Association of University Professors. (1990). Sexual harassment: Suggested policy and procedures for handling complaints. *Academe, 76* (5), 42–43.

American Council on Education. (1988). Sexual harassment on campus: Suggestions for reviewing campus policy and educational programs. In Joan Van Tol (Ed.), *Sexual harassment on campus: A legal compendium* (123–28). Washington, DC: National Association of College and University Attorneys.

Benson, D. and Thomson, G. (1982). Sexual harassment on a university campus: The confluence of authority relations, sexual interest, and gender stratification. *Social Problems, 29,* 236–51.

Betz, N. and Fitzgerald, L. (1987). *The career psychology of women.* New York: Academic Press.

Bond, M. (1988). Division 27 sexual harassment survey: Definition, impact, environmental context. *Community Psychologist, 21,* 7–10.

Brooks, L. and Haring-Hidore, M. (1987). Mentoring in academe: A comparison of mentors' and proteges' perceived problems. *International Journal of Mentoring, 1* (2), 3–9.

Cammaert, L. (1985). How wide spread is sexual harassment on campus? *International Journal of Women's Studies, 8* (4), 388–97.

Cole, E.K. (1988). Recent legal developments in sexual harassment. In Joan Van Tol (Ed.), *Sexual harassment on campus: A legal compendium* (pp. 153–171). Washington, DC: National Association of College and University Attorneys.

College suspends professor for publicizing affair with student. (1991). *Chronicle of Higher Education,* 15 May, p. A14.

Connolly, W. Jr., and Marshall, A. (1989). Sexual harassment of university or college students by faculty members. *Journal of College and University Law, 15* (4), 381–403.

Crocker, P. (1983). An analysis of university definitions of sexual harassment. *Signs: Journal of Women in Culture and Society, 8* (4), 696–707.

DeChiara, P. (1988). The need for universities to have rules on consensual relationships between faculty members and students. *Columbia Journal of Law and Social Problems, 21* (2), 137–62.

Dziech, B. and Weiner, L. (1990). *The lecherous professor: Sexual harassment on campus* (2nd ed.). Boston: Beacon Press.

Farley, L. (1978). *Sexual shakedown: The sexual harassment of women on the job.* New York: McGraw-Hill.

Fitzgerald, L., Shullman, S., Bailey, N., Richard, M., Swecker, J., Gold, Y., Ormerod, M., and Weitzman, L. (1988). The incidence and dimensions of sexual harassment in academic and the workplace. *Journal of Vocational Behavior, 32* (2), 152–75.

Fitzgerald, L., Weitzman, L., Gold, Y., and Ormerod, M. (1988). Academic harassment: Sex and denial in scholarly garb. *Psychology of Women Quarterly, 12* (3), 329–40.

Glaser, R., and Thorpe, J. (1986). Unethical intimacy: A survey of contact and advances between psychology educators and female graduate students. *American Psychologist, 41*, 43–51.

Gutek, B. (1985). *Sex and the workplace: The impact of sexual behavior and harassment on women, men, and organizations.* San Francisco: Jossey-Bass.

Gutek, B., and Dunwoody, V. (1987). Understanding sex in the workplace. In Ann Stromberg, Laurie Larwood, and Barbara Gutek (Eds.), *Women and work: An annual review* (Vol. 2, 249–69). Beverly Hills, CA.: Sage.

Gutek, B., and Morasch, B. (1982). Sex ratios, sex role spillover and sexual harassment of women at work. *Journal of Social Issues, 38* (4), 55–74.

Haring-Hidore, M., and Paludi, M. (1989). Sexuality and sex in mentoring and tutoring: Implications for opportunities and achievement. *Peabody Journal of Education, 64* (4), 164–72.

Hite, M. (1990). Sexual harassment and the university community. *Initiatives, 52* (4), 11–16.

Hoffman, F. (1986). Sexual harassment in academia: Feminist theory and institutional practice. *Harvard Educational Review, 56* (2), 105–21.

Horn, P., and Horn, J. (1982). *Sex in the office.* Reading, MA: Addison-Wesley.

Howard University Sexual Harassment Policy and Procedures. (1990). In Elsa Kircher Cole (Ed.), *Sexual harassment on campus: A legal compendium* (2nd ed., 219–20). Washington, DC: National Association of College and University Attorneys.

Hughes, J. and Sandler, B. (1986). *In case of sexual harassment: A guide for women students. We hope it doesn't happen to you, but if it does.* Washington, DC: Project on the Status and Education of Women, Association of American Colleges. (ERIC Document Reproduction Service No. 268 920.)

Hustoles, T. (1990), Consensual relations issues in higher education. In Elsa Kircher Cole (Ed.), *Sexual harassment on campus: A legal compendium*

(251–55). Washington, DC: National Association of College and University Attorneys.

Ingulli, E. (1987). Sexual harassment in education. *Rutgers Law Journal, 18* (2), 281–341.

Jamison, K. (1983). Managing sexual attraction in the workplace. *Personnel Administrator, 28* (8), 45–51.

Kantor, M. (1990, Nov./Dec.). Confessions of a lonely T.A. *Issues and Insights for the College Women in View,* 3.

Keller, E. (1988). Consensual amorous relationships between faculty and students: The Constitutional right to privacy. *Journal of College and University Law, 15* (1), 21–42.

Kennedy, M.S. (1980). "A" for affairs with the professors: What happens when a student falls in love with her teacher? *Glamour,* August, 237, 241.

Kitchener, K. (1988). Dual role relationships: What makes them so problematic? *Journal of Counseling and Development, 67,* 217–21.

Korf v. Ball State University. 726 F.2d 122 (7th Cir. 1984).

Levy, P. (1982). Surviving in a predominantly white male institution. In Sue Vartuli (Ed.), *The Ph.D. experience: A woman's point of view* (45–59). New York: Praeger.

Little, D. (1989). *Addressing the issue of appropriate professional ethics on community college campuses.* Paper presented at the annual convention of the American Association of Community and Junior Colleges. (ERIC Document Reproduction Service No. ED 306 999.)

Little, D., and Thompson, J. (1989). Campus policies, the law, and sexual relationships. *Thought and Action, 5* (1), 17–24.

Marcus, R. (1991). When is flirting at work sexual harassment? *Washington Post National Weekly Edition,* 25 February–3 March, p. 32.

McCormack, A. (1985). The sexual harassment of students by teachers: The case of students in sciences. *Sex Roles, 13* (1/2), 21–32.

McKinney, K., Olson, C., and Satterfield, A. (1988). Graduate students' experiences with and responses to sexual harassment: A research note. *Journal of Interpersonal Violence, 3* (3), 319–25.

Meritor Savings Bank v. Vinson, 477 U.S. 57 (1986).

Naragon v. Wharton, 572 F. Supp. 1117 (M.D. La. 1983).

Naragon v. Wharton, 737 F. 2d 1403 (5th Cir. 1984).

National Association for Women in Education Women's Issues Project. (1991). Reasonable woman. *About Women on Campus, 1* (1), 10.

Olson, C., and McKinney, K. (1989). Processes inhibiting the reduction of sexual harassment in academe: An alternative explanation. *Initiatives, 52* (3), 7–13.

Oshinsky, J. (1981). Sexual harassment of women students in higher education. *Dissertation Abstracts International, 42* (2–A), 555.

Peters, L. (1990). A student's experience. *Initiatives, 52* (4), 17–21.

Pope, K., Levenson, H., and Schover, L. (1979). Sexual intimacy in psychology training: Results and implications of a national survey. *American Psychologist, 34* (3), 682–89.

Pope, K., Schover, L., and Levenson, H. (1980). Sexual behavior between clinical supervisors and trainees: Implications for professional standards. *Professional Psychology, 11* (1), 15–62.

Popovich, P., and Licata, B.J. (1987). A role model approach to sexual harassment. *Journal of Management, 13* (1), 149–61.

Quinn, R. (1977). Coping with Cupid: The formation, impact, and management of romatnic relationships in organizations. *Administrative Science Quarterly, 22* (1), 30–45.

Quinn, R., and Lees, P. (1984). Attraction and harassment: Dynamics of sexual politics in the workplace. *Organizational Dynamics, 13* (2), 35–46.

Rabinowitz, V. (1990). Coping with sexual harassment. In Michele Paludi (Ed.), *Ivory power: Sexual harassment on campus* (103–18). Albany: State University of New York Press.

Reilly, M.E., Lott, B., and Gallogly, S. (1986). Sexual harassment of university students. *Sex Roles, 15* (7/8), 333–58.

Robertson, C., Dyer, C., and Campbell, D'A. (1988). Campus harassment: Sexual harassment policies and procedures at institutions of higher learning. *Signs, 13* (4), 792–812.

Robinson, R., Delaney, J.K., and Stephens, E. (1987). Hostile environment: A review of the implications of *Meritor Savings Bank v. Vinson. Labor Law Journal, 38,* 179–83.

Robinson, W., and Reid, P. (1985). Sexual intimacies in psychology revisited. *Professional Psychology: Research and Practice, 16* (4), 512–20.

Ross, C., and Green, V. (1983). Sexual harassment; A liability higher education must face. *Journal of the College and University Personnel Association, 34* (1), 1–9.

Rowland, D., Crisler, L., and Cox, D. (1982). Flirting between college students and faculty. *Journal of Sex Research, 18* (4), 346–59.

Sandler, B., and Associates. (1981). Sexual harassment: A hidden problem. *Educational Record, 62* (1), 52–57.

Schneider, B. (1984). The office affair: Myth and reality for heterosexual and lesbian women workers. *Sociological Perspectives, 27* (4), 443–64.

————. (1987). Graduate women, sexual harassment, and university policy. *Journal of Higher Education, 58* (1), 46–65.

Scott, D. (1984). Sexual harassment behaviors, management strategies, and power-dependence relationships among a female graduate student population. *Dissertation Abstracts International, 44* (10–A), 2983.

Stites, M.C. (1993). *Faculty-student consensual sexual relationships and university policy.* Unpublished doctoral dissertation, University of Connecticut, Storrs.

Till, F. (1980). *Sexual harassment: A report on the sexual harassment of students. Washington, DC: U.S. Department of Education, National Advisory Council on Women's Educational Programs.*

Truax, A. (1989). *Sexual harassment in higher education: What we've learned. Thought and Action, 5* (1), 25–38.

Tuana, N. (1985). Sexual harassment in academe: Issues of power and coercion. *College Teaching, 33* (2), 53–64.

University of Minnesota. (1990). Presidential statement and policy on sexual harassment. In Billie Dziech and Linda Weiner (Eds.), *The lecherous professor: Sexual harassment on campus,* (2nd ed., 203–4, 206). Boston: Beacon Press.

Walker, G., Erickson, L., and Woolsey, L. (1985). Sexual harassment: Ethical research and clinical implications in the academic setting. *International Journal of Women's Studies, 8* (4), 424–33.

Welzenbach, L. et al. (Eds.). (1986). *Sexual harassment: Issues and answers. A guide for education, business, industry.* Washington, DC: College and University Personnel Association. (ERIC Document Reproduction Service No. 275 270.)

Williams, R. (1982). In and out of relationships: A serious game for the women doctoral student. In Sue Vartuli (Ed.), *The Ph.D. experience: A woman's point of view* (78–82). New York: Praeger.

Wilson, K., and Kraus, L. (1983). Sexual harassment in the university. *Journal of College Student Personnel, 24,* 219–24.

7

Individual Training of Sexual Harassers

Jan Salisbury and Fredda Jaffe

Although sexual harassment literature has grown exponentially since the Hill-Thomas hearings, very little research or writing has focused on the harasser. When harassers are described in terms of job classifications, socio-economic background, age, or race, their descriptions are vague and unhelpful: "the average man with no easily identifiable characteristics" (Fitzgerald and Weitzman 1990). Other authors (Zalk 1990) have written persuasively about the academy and its patriarchy as well as the seductive role-classification system used to identify profiles of sexual harassers. John Pryor (1992; Pryor, LaVite, and Stoller 1993) has conducted the most credible research in this area, but only focusing on those harassers who may have a propensity to commit *quid pro quo* harassment. His research about harassment that involves the exchange of sexual favors and job favoritism suggests that both situational and individual factors contribute to harassment. The research does not, however, address what to do with harassers who commit the more common and sometimes subtle harassment offense of creating a hostile work environment.

Thus, the rehabilitation of perpetrators of sexual harassment who remain in the workplace is a new area, with a dearth of written materials and few practitioners. While there may be few precedents, organizations have a critical need to help harassers they do retain to "get it" so they will not reoffend. During the last eight years, this organizational need stimulated a handful of Seattle-area mental health professionals and organizational consultants to experiment with a training approach to rehabilitating sexual harassers.

This chapter is based on the experiences of three trainers working with over twenty-five individuals accepted for individual training. Their occupations included vice president of human resources, clergy, professor, plumber, engineer, banker, lineman, and manager. One was female. As we outline our methods and philosophies, we will also share our successes, our failures, and our questions about the rehabilitation of harassers in workplaces.

TRAINING VERSUS COUNSELING

Managing harassers is a legal, moral, and practical challenge for organizations. For legal reasons and because good leadership should be consistent and fair, discipline has been the major tool for the rehabilitation of harassers. Some organizations have also sought help from employee assistance programs (EAPs) or licensed mental health professionals. These methods for addressing rehabilitation have *not* proven reliable. Most EAP and private practitioners do *not* have the organizational, legal, and psychological experience with sexual harassment to provide valid, short-term help for employees who harass. The other practical obstacle involved with traditional mental health resources is the confidentiality inherent in those relationships. Because of the potential harm to others and the legal liabilities involved when employees reoffend, organizations need to be fully informed about the rehabilitation process. The failure of a "therapeutic" model to meet the complex needs of organizations led the authors to adopt a training approach.

The first standard of a successful individual training model is a legal one. Training must potentially meet the legal standards of "prompt corrective action" and "doing something that reasonably deters the behavior from occurring again" (*Ellison v Brady* 1991). Organizations that administer fair discipline, vigilant follow-up, and supervision accomplish much to meet these standards. Discipline for sexual harassment must be decided separately from training and fit the degree of severity as well as the accused's history. Management expects legal and moral propriety from employees, and disciplining offenders communicates this expectation. Managerial follow-up further establishes the organization's commitment to eradicating harassing behaviors from the workplace and serves notice that repetition of such behaviors threatens job status.

However, organizations also recognize that many of their best employees who harass appear confused, incredulous, and unable to translate the organization's actions into the requisite behavioral changes. Following an investigation, harassers often leave debriefing session conducted by human resources personnel and/or management with little understanding of why their behavior was so egregious. Consequently, few understand what behaviors they need to change or why they should try.

Individual training is intended to fill this psychological gap. Effective individual training can help the harasser achieve understanding and translate this into behavioral change. Although no educator or trainer can guarantee the outcome of their services, they can truthfully state: "We have done all that is reasonably possible to facilitate an employee's success." Once the harasser is personally involved in learning about the legal, psychological, and social antecedents and consequences of their specific behaviors, it is up to him or her to make certain these behaviors are not repeated.

WHO SHOULD DO THE TRAINING AND WHO SHOULD BE TRAINED

Ideally, the training/education should be conducted by an independent consultant who has been involved *neither* in the investigation *nor* in resolving aftermath issues of the workplace *nor* in advising the organization about discipline. The significance of sending the harasser outside the "workplace walls" should not be underestimated: Being able to physically leave the workplace setting and enter a new, less accusatory environment is the first step toward effective training for the harasser.

Assessing the suitability of the employee (harasser) for training is also essential. It is our experience that harassers involved in *quid pro quo*, those with histories of sexual assault/obsession, and harassers with characterological problems and other serious patterns of long-lasting abuses of power are not likely to be positively affected by our individual training model. In one recent case, a sexually obsessive male employee admitted during the initial interview that he had recently "ended" a long-term involvement with drug dealing and addiction. Further questioning revealed that the employee was not committed to a recovery program. The combination of drug and sexual addiction indicated that this employee was a candidate for intensive mental health treatment, rather than short-term, content-focused, sexual harassment training.

It is also important that the organization *not* use individual training as a replacement for discipline. Training should be reserved for the education and rehabilitation of employees who are *appropriately* retained by organizations.

While our experiences have been mostly with male harassers, we believe this training is also applicable to the rehabilitation of female harassers. In fact, the complexity of nontraditional harassment (female-female, female-male, and male-male) may more clearly call for individual training.

Up to this point, individual training has been conducted by mental health professionals with substantial experience in sexual harassment and other workplace issues. They have been well trained in the legal and organizational response to sexual harassment and discrimination, the psychology of power, gender dynamics and differences, sexual abuse, and the effects of sexual harassment on victims and work groups. They also understand the distinctions between training and counseling. A sexual harassment trainer should also possess objectivity and critical judgment. Harassers often have highly developed social skills and strong denial regarding the implications of their behavior. For this reason and to provide a consistent standard of treatment, the trainer needs a conscious degree of healthy skepticism.

THE TRAINING PHILOSOPHY

In recent years there has been a shift in the psychological community toward more systemic, brief treatment approaches to therapy. These approaches view the individual within a context (the family, the workplace, the social service system). The perspective of an individual employee caught within the confines of a shifting society and workplace helped us develop a focus for both the content and the process of our training.

For our training, we borrowed a self-ratingg caring/critical grid developed for use in work with sex offenders (see fig. 7.1). According to this model, a highly caring trainer would place in the upper left quadrant, while a more critical trainer would place in the lower right quadrant. Trainers who work with sex offenders agree that the most effective treatment approach is to remain dubious and critical. We recommend a blend of mild caring with moderate criticality. The more caring, Rogerian model is typically not effective in treating sexual harassers. A slightly biased critical approach more effectively diffuses denial and minimization. Caring, uncritical professionals are more easily manipulated and more apt to lose their objectivity and, as a result, more likely to reduce their effectiveness. Too critical a position aligns the trainer with punishment and will undoubtedly elicit defensiveness.

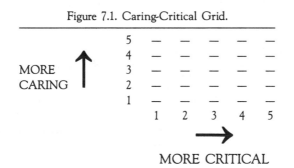

Figure 7.1. Caring-Critical Grid.

SETTING UP TRAINING WITH THE ORGANIZATION

How the harassment trainer defines the contract and the expectations with the organization is critical to the success of the training. Organizations are likely to have misconceptions about this relatively new training approach. They will be uncertain about the organization's role, the trainer's role, how to communicate expectations to the harasser, and what outcomes to expect. The trainer must take time to explain each part of the process before agreeing to do the work and before the employer communicates to the harasser about the training.

First Contact

Typically, a representative from human resources, personnel, or affirmative action/EEO or an operations manager will contact the trainer. They should do so *only* after they have investigated the incident and administered discipline and other consequences. During the initial contact, trainers should elicit enough information about the discriminatory behaviors to decide whether the employee is suitable. As we have previously discussed, the trainer should screen out those whose behaviors and personalities preclude probable training success.

Following the screening, the trainer should review the purpose, content, time/cost, and outcome of the training. Cost and method of payment should always be clarified in the initial contact. Our position is that the organization is responsible for all costs of the training and will pay within thirty days of billing; missed appointments are billed in full.

Organizations wishing to further penalize the accused by making them pay the trainer personally may sabotage the training by creating further resentment. Making the accused pay usually sets up a dynamic between the trainer and the employee that undermines the trust needed for successful training. We tell organizations that individual training is a worthy investment in the rehabilitation and mitigation of liability. Individual training reflects a commitment from organizations that states, in effect: "We are committed to eliminating hostile and intimidating behavior and we will do whatever we can to help employees to understand our work ethos. As a valuable employee you are worth the effort to help you become successful in our workplace."

Second Contact/Meeting

If possible, arrange a face-to-face meeting with the person in charge of the process as well as the supervisor of the harasser. At this meeting trainers should reiterate in greater detail the process and their role. Trainers and employers should then agree on what will be said to the harasser about the process, how long it will take, and what the harasser is expected to produce at the end of the training. Management should never use the word *counseling*. Management should make it clear that the trainer will be meeting with management to give them feedback about the employee's progress. Because this is training and not counseling, confidentiality is neither implied nor guaranteed.

To conduct training that is individually focused, trainers must receive *very* specific information about the outcome of the complaint. Harassers often have a very different experience of the events. It is easy for the trainer to get bogged down in confusing details colored by the harasser's perceptions when they do not have the investigative report in hand. The best information usually comes from reading the investigative report and/or talking with the investigating agent. This information should be sent before the first meeting so that the trainer is prepared to ask pertinent questions at the meeting.

Content of Training Sessions

Our training sessions last from four to eight hours, often in one- to two-hour blocks. The training sessions can be divided into four basic stages.

Stage 1: Establishing Rapport and Expectations. In the first stage, an overview of the training is presented and discussed. The nonjudgmental nature of the training is established, and the harasser begins to describe his/her feelings. This often includes anger, shame, betrayal, frustration, and other kinds of defensiveness. To begin the process of personal accountability, the harasser is asked to define his goals for the training.

Stage 2: Creating an Education Dynamic. After the incidents are thoroughly discussed, the trainer begins to provide verbal, written, and recorded educational materials. A precursor to selecting materials is ascertaining and determining the employee's preferred learning style (observing, watching, analyzing, etc.). Appropriate articles, graphs, statistics, books, and videos are shared, and homework assignments are made. Typically, the employee is asked to compile questions, concerns, and reactions to the material for discussion at the next session.

Stage 3: Personal Insights and Applications. During this stage, the trainer helps the harasser make sense of the shared information as it is applied to his and other's behaviors. Questions and feelings are clarified. In one situation a manager known for his noncommunicative demeanor suddenly became aware that he didn't need to resolve all of this employees' complaints, but simply acknowledge that they had been heard. Other managerial employees realized that their belief that they could be a friend to employees (or one of the gang) was not accurate. They learned that their behavior as a boss is *always* interpreted in the context of their power, whether the supervisor perceives it that way or not. Jokes and innuendoes by a co-worker may be annoying to employees but can easily be perceived as threatening when expressed by a boss. The workplace power differences, the exploration of male and female differences in perceptions of sexual harassment (Gutek 1985), the effects of sexual harssment on victims and the extent of sexual behaviors and abuse in society were also themes that generated insight.

Stage 4: Written/Oral Reports. Harassers are asked by the organization (at the trainer's request) to write or deliver an oral report on their learning and its applications. During the last session, the trainer and the employee discuss how the report represents what has been learned in the sessions.

The Trainer Reports Back to the Organization

Final reports by the trainer to the organization have been verbal. However, organizations may want written reports to help them keep a record of their "corrective/preventive action." Reports should be addressed to the employer representative(s) with whom the trainer has been meeting. Communication can be either through a conference call or in a meeting.

Our verbal reports have typically focused on the following:

1. The employee's response to homework and their timeliness with appointments and other agreements
2. The employee's willingness to ask questions or otherwise honestly engage in the content
3. Particular insights into the situation or behavior that the employee acknowledged
4. Reported changes in the employee's behavior at work
5. "Blind spots" and other issues that continue to be difficult for the employee to acknowledge or understand
6. Observed changes in the employee between the initial session and the last training session
7. Analysis of the report written by the employee for the employers
8. Suggestions for further training or supervision of the employee

Follow-Up by the Organization

Organizations need a plan to follow up on the lessons learned in the training. The *best* person to do this is the employee's manager or supervisor in consultation with a human resources representative. This manager should observe not only whether the employee is reverting to old behavior but also note positive changes in their communication, style of management, or other work behavior. Failure to commit to follow-up often undermines the successful resolution of sexual harassment complaints.

CASE EXAMPLE

"Harold Stevens" was a fifty-year-old archaeology professor. His college had just received a second complaint in two years from a female student (senior) accusing him of discriminatory harassment. She described him as making sexist comments, inquiring into her private life, making abusive comments about her class performance, and giving her an unsolicited hug on a field trip.

During the investigation, Dr. Stevens admitted to most of the alleged behaviors. The context and intent he described were very different. Rather than admit to a pattern of discrimination, Dr. Stevens talked about isolated incidents "taken wrong," such as referring to female students as "girls" and male students as "men," stating the opinion that archaeology fieldwork may be very hard on women who want relationships and children. He acknowledged he was gruff and highly critical with *all* students on occasion and that during field trips he did ask about students' families and dating as a way of getting to know them. The hug was done in a group of people as a spontaneous reaction to his joy in finding an important relic. Finally, he stated to the investigator that he felt aggrieved the time he had spent mentoring the complainant. Because it was the second complaint against this professor for similar behaviors, the college felt he needed individual training.

Preliminary Work

The trainer talked to the affirmative action officer as well as the department chair about the professor. Discipline was a formal letter of reprimand stating that termination could result if the behavior continued. It was agreed that the professor would meet for two sessions of two hours each.

First Session

Professor S. was highly agitated and defensive when he came to the trainer's office. He protested: How could he change something he had not admitted to (i.e., harassment)? He also stated that he felt this was counseling and that he ought, therefore, to be able to vent his feelings.

The trainer carefully acknowledged Professor S.'s feelings and discomfort. She then slowly summarized her role, her agreement with the college, and the purpose of the "training." She then informed him of what she had read and whom she had talked to at the college. She also shared her credentials and résumé and talked about the articles and video he was required to read and see. She assured him that while it was important to understand his feelings, it was also important to acknowledge the feelings of the complainant and come to an understanding of how what had transpired could result in such a serious complaint. The trainer pointed out the cost of the training and how that symbolized the college's belief in him as a valued colleague in the academic community. The trainer and Professor S. agreed that he had nothing to lose and everything to gain by committing to the process. Finally, the trainer assured the professor that she was not there to judge him, but to help him understand what had happened and how he might do things differently in the future.

Most accused harassers have an understandable need to tell "their side of the story." Professor S. was no exception. He spent the remainder of the session talking in great detail about the incidents and *his* experience of them.

He admitted feeling puzzled about why two students, especially one that excelled academically, would perceive him as a discriminatory teacher.

The trainer paraphrased his viewpoint carefully. As his story wound down, she began to compare his viewpoint with that of the complainant. She shared some of the research on male/female culture, men and women's perceptions of sexual harassment, and the "nontraditional" aspects of archaeology. The trainer ended by giving the professor several of articles and books, including *Ivory Power* (Paludi 1990); the articles "Counseling Victims of Sexual Harassment" (Salisbury et al. 1986), "The Power and Reasons behind Harassment" (Stringer et al. 1990), as we as handouts from a training class on sexual harassment and the video *The Issue Is Respect* (Roselle 1992).

The professor left visibly less upset and defensive and committed to reading the materials.

Second Session

Professor S. returned, having read all the materials. At first he was eager to point out all the behavior listed that he had not committed. He asked several questions about the law. The trainer spent time clarifying the law, the university's liability, and the effects of harassment. She asked Professor S. to review the different behaviors sustained by the complaint and look at them from another perspective. The trainer then discussed how, by virtue of Professor S.'s powerful position as a full professor, even isolated incidents could have long-lasting effects on his teaching relationship with female students majoring in his field.

Professor S.'s reaction to this deeper look at his behavior was mixed. On the one hand, he was shocked at the young woman's perspective. He was told that students may feel excluded, discounted, not good enough, intruded upon—even intimidated and threatened—by the behaviors described. On the other hand, his surprise led him to say that he wondered if he could work with women again and risk offending in these ways. The trainer pointed out that if he and others like him acted on the belief that they could never overcome feelings of gender differences, women students would never get an education.

The last half hour was spent talking about how the professor might try new behaviors and learn about women's perspective on learning and interacting at the college. The trainer asked Professor S. to identify groups and activities on campus in which he could invest time to learn and even lead in this arena. He identified two and agreed to involve himself. He wanted to write a letter to the student apologizing for the his effects of behavior and assuring her of his esteem for her abilities. He wanted the trainer to review the letter before he sent it. The trainer then suggested he also ask his chair and EEO office to review the letter. Finally, they discussed what he had learned and what he would write about his learning.

Professor S. thanked the trainer for her knowledge and time. Although he continued to feel victimized and excessively punished by the process, he was engaged in applying his new insights about professorial power, male/female differences, and the law.

College Follow-Up

The sessions were summarized in a phone conference with the department chair. The trainer suggested that the chair involve Professor S. with other female professors on committees and projects as well as meet with him about his final training paper and expectations for the future. She encouraged Professor S.'s management to support him and to work out a way to evaluate his classes and his new behaviors with students in a way mutually agreeable and responsive to the issues of the investigation.

OUTCOMES

Of the two dozen male and one female harasser we have seen, at least three of them have reoffended in some way. Usually this has taken the form of a sexual joke or comment. As far as we know, no escalation in the harasser's behavior has occurred. Some harassers have gone through a dramatic period of withdrawal before psychologically reintegrating themselves into the workplace. Since we have conducted no outcome studies of our work, it is difficult to evaluate long-term effectiveness. We do know, however, that employees who reoffend are apt to receive greater punishment without hesitation and to tell their organizations they now know why the punishment has been leveled against them.

The strength of individual training is also its greatest weakness. Some employees, those with hidden personality disorders or emotional blocks, may need long-term therapy to fully dislodge their behavior pattern. Quick screening may not ferret out these factors. However, when an educational/training approach is combined with the clout of organizational power, some employees will consider the information, determine its applicability, and finally shift their attitudes and behaviors. Some harassers have even become more vigilant in their workplaces toward bias, prejudice, and harassment.

SPECIAL ISSUES WITH ACADEMIA

The work culture of academicians is a particularly difficult arena in which to resolve harassment. Professors are often not regarded as regular employees requiring supervision and training. Rather, they are treasured sources of knowledge and power expected to self-manage and self-train. Many decisions about personnel matters in universities are decided by politically polarized, ineffective committees. And finally, chairs of departments are widely regarded as peer leaders who do administrative work and do not actively manage members of the department. In contrast, the individual training model requires accountability. Chairs and deans must take on the role of supervising and following up with harassers throughout and following the training process. Without their active participation, the training is not likely to work.

The ombudsman approach currently being used in a number of universities (Rowe 1990) to resolve low levels of sexual harassment can also use this training model. The ombudsman may be neutral enough in the eyes of the harasser to undertake a similar training role with low-level harassment that has not been formally investigated.

CONCLUSIONS

Individual training is a practical method for addressing the educational and emotional needs of some harassers who remain in workplaces and are motivated to change. There have been as many clear successes as there have been failures. Further experimentation and research is needed, particularly to track the variables affecting the effectivness of harrasser training programs. Though we lack scientific validation, trainers using this process have been impressed with its power to help employees stop their harassment and even take leadership positions on diversity and gender issues. The individual attention to their specific situations persuades most harassers that the organization cares enough to help them change. Most importantly, however, this individual training gives employees the support to change.

References

Ellison v. Brady, (9th Cir 23 January 1991). No. 89-15248 in BNA's Dally Reporter System 18.

Fitzgerald, L.F., and Weitzman, L.M. (1990). Men who harass: Speculation and data. In M.A. Paludi (Ed.), Ivory power: Sexual harassment on campus. Albany: State University of New York Press.

Gutek, B. (1985). Sex and the workplace. San Francisco: Jossey-Bass.

Paludi, M. (Ed.). (1990). Ivory power: Sexual harassment on campus. Albany: State University of New York Press.

Pryor, J.B. (1992). The social psychology of sexual harassment: Person and situation factors which give rise to sexual harassment. In *Proceedings of Sex and Power Issues in the Workplace: A National Conference to Promote Men and Women Working Productively Together.*

Pryor, J.B., LaVite, C.M., and Stoller, L.M. (1993). A social psychological analysis of sexual harassment: The person/situation interaction. *Journal of Vocational Behavior, 42*, 68–83.

Roselle, R. (1992). *The issue is respect: Subtle sexual harassment for employees and managers* [Video]. Seattle: Media Resources.

Rowe, M.P. (1990, October). *The ombudsman as part of a dispute resolution system.* Paper presented at the annual SPIDR conference, Dearborn, MI.

Salisbury, J., Ginorio, A., Remick, H., and Stringer D. (1986). Counseling victims of sexual harassment. *Psychotherapy: Research and Practice, 23* (2), 316–24.

Stringer, D., Remick, H., Salisbury, J., and Ginorio, A. (1990). The power and reasons behind sexual harassment: An employers guide to solutions. *Public Personnel Management, 19* (1).

Zalk, S.R. (1990). Men in the academy: A psychological profile of harassment. In M.A. Paludi (Ed.), *Ivory power: Sexual harassment on campus.* Albany: State University of New York Press.

8

University Consensual Relationship Policies

M. Cynara Stites

University consensual relationship policies were introduced in American colleges and universities in the early 1980s after it became apparent that sexual harassment policies were inadequate to address the problems inherent in faculty-student consensual sexual relationships—such as faculty ethical obligations, favoritism, and the detrimental consequences of such relationships on the students involved in the relationships and on other students. Sexual harassment policies tend to focus on coercive sexual advances and repeated, unwanted sexual invitations and tend to ignore conflict-of-interest issues or the implied coercion involved in a professor's power over a student in faculty-student consensual sexual relationships (Robertson, Dyer, and Campbell 1988). Therefore, consensual relationship policies can address professors' unethical behaviors that are not adequately covered by sexual harassment policies (Ingulli 1987; Keller 1990).

Consensual relationship policies, however, are still relatively rare. One survey revealed that only about 17 percent of colleges and universities have consensual relationship policies or faculty eithics codes that specifically address faculty-student sexual relationships (Little and Thompson 1989). The scarcity of consensual sexual relationship policies may reflect a lack of consensus on campuses about the extent to which a university is capable of regulating faculty-student consensual sexual relationships, concern that such policies might constitute unwarranted intrusion into the private lives of faculty members and students, and the preference of many administrators to avoid a potentially complicated issue (DeChiara 1988; Fitzgerald 1991; Hustoles 1990). However, only 24 percent of male faculty members and 22 percent of female graduate students in a study at a large Eastern state university would accept a university's having no policies regulating faculty-student consensual sexual relationships (Stites 1993).

Appropriate policy making about faculty-student consensual sexual relationships is complicated by the diverse range of sexual relationships and motivations for sexual relationships that university policies attempt to address. Horn and Horn (1982) note that there are six types of sexual behaviors in the workplace: (1) flirting, (2) one-night stand (a brief sexual encounter based on a seized opportunity), (3) casual dating (which may include sexual intercourse), (4) affair (a long-term relationship irrespective of the marital status of the participants), (5) sexual harassment, and (6) committed relationship (engagement, cohabitation, or marriage). Quinn (1977) identifies three types of motivations for sexual relationships between people in the workplace: (1) flings (temporary sexual relationships motivated by intense excitement), (2) true love (motivated by love), and (3) utilitarian relationships (typically where the man seeks ego satisfaction, excitement, or sexual gratification and the women seeks some organizational/academic rewards). Policy making is further complicated by the possibility that the participants in a faculty-student sexual relationship might have different motivations for engaging in the relationship, different concepts of what type of relationship they have, and different perceptions of how freely the student consented to the relationship with the professor. Policy making is even further complicated by the possibility that the participants' perceptions and motivations might change over the course of a relationship.

PURPOSES OF UNIVERSITY CONSENSUAL RELATIONSHIP POLICIES

Despite these potentially complicating factors, university consensual relationshp policies have been developed for several sound policy making purposes. Because there is no universal consensus that professors' sexual relationships with students are wrong, faculty members should be informed of what behaviors a university prohibits (Connolly and Marshall 1989; DeChiara 1988; Keller 1990). When a clear policy is in place, professors and students are not subjected to the whims, prejudices, and blind spots of university administrators (Keller 1990). Consistent enforcement of a clear policy can help to alleviate male professors' fears about engaging in appropriate professional and mentoring relationships with women students (DeChiara 1988; Sandler and Associates 1981; Wagner, 1990). Such policies help to establish higher ethical standards for faculty behavior in faculty-student professional relationships (Inguilli 1987; Little and Thompson 1989; Schneider 1987). Consensual relationship policies can also help to reinforce prohibitions against more egregious sexual harassing behaviors by drawing the line of prohibited behavior more narrowly (DeChiara 1988).

Students may be spared the stress of coping with professors' sexual advances when a university has a consensual sexual relationship policy (DeChiara 1988). In the absence of any policy forbidding a professor from dating a student, a university may be unable to take army disciplinary action against a professor who makes only one sexual advance toward a student (*Brown v. California State Personnel Board* 1985). A Temple University profesor was charged by six women students with sexual harassment for asking them for dates or making sexual advances to them. " 'All he did was ask someone out. Is this harassment?' asked the professor's lawyer in his defense" (Dreifus 1986, 308). When a university has a sexual harassment policy that does not address consensual sexual relationships, professors can

> disguise sexually harassing behavior as academic or personal atten-
> tion . . . and students have no way of knowing whether or not they can
> fairly categorize a faculty member's behavior as harassment. A single
> request for a date, for example, unaccompanied by a threat of retaliation
> or the promise of gain, may not constitute sexual harassment under
> certain policies that focus on more intimidating and coercive behavior.
> (Keller 1990, 30–31)

Because of this ambiguity in differentiating personal attention from sexual harassment, some universities have developed consensual relationship policies in order to set clear standards of conduct for faculty members, to assure that faculty members fulfill their professional ethical responsibilities, and to address areas of misconduct that are not adequately covered by sexual harassment policies. With these policy-making goals in mind, different types of consensual relationship policies have been developed in some American universities.

PROHIBITION POLICIES

Some universities have consensual relationship policies that prohibit sexual relationships between a professor and a student over whom the professor has some authority, such as an advising role, supervisory responsibility, or teaching and grading responsibilities. The University of Iowa consensual relationship policy, which was adopted in 1986, was one of the first prohibition-type consensual relationship policies. The University of Iowa policy explicitly states that "no faculty member shall have an amorous relationship (consensual or otherwise) with a student who is enrolled in a course being taught by the faculty member or whose academic work (including work as a teaching assistant) is being supervised by the faculty member" (University of Iowa 1988, 110). The University of Iowa policy includes a rationale for the policy as follows:

The University's educational mission is promoted by professionalism in faculty-student relationships. Professionalism is fostered by an atmosphere of mutual trust and respect. Actions of faculty members and students that harm this atmosphere undermine professionalism and hinder fulfillment of the University's educational mission. Trust and respect are diminished when those in positions of authority abuse, or appear to abuse, their power. Those who abuse, or appear to abuse, their power in such a context violate their duty to the University community.

Faculty members exercise power over students, whether in giving them praise or criticism, evaluating them, making recommendations for their further studies or their future employment, or conferring any other benefits on them. Amorous relationships between faculty members and students are wrong when the faculty member has professional responsibility for the student. Such situations greatly increase the chances that the faculty member will abuse his or her power and sexually exploit the student. Voluntary consent by the student in such a relationship is suspect, given the fundamentally asymmetric nature of the relationship. Moreover, other students and faculty may be affected by such unprofessional behavior because it places the faculty member in a position to favor or advance one student's interest at the expense of others and implicitly makes obtaining benefits contingent on amorous or sexual favors. Therefore, the University will view it as unethical if faculty members engage in amorous relationships with students enrolled in their classes or subject to their supervision, even when both parties appear to have consented to the relationship. (University of Iowa 1988, 109–10).

Temple University's sexual harassment policty also spcifically prohibits professor-student sexual relationships when the professor has professional responsibilities for the student. The policy even explicitly prohibits professors' sexual advances or requests for dates from students as well as professors' continuing to evaluate a student with whom a sexual or romantic relationship has developed (Temple University 1985).

Harvard University holds a faculty member responsible for a consensual relationship with a student for whom the faculty member has professional responsibilities. Harvard's policy reads as follows:

Amorous relationships that might be appropriate in other circumstances always have inherent dangers when they occur between any teacher or officer of the University and any person for whom he or she has a professional responsibility (i.e., as teacher, advisor, evaluator, supervisor). Implicit in the idea of professionalism is the recognition by those in positions of authority that in their relationships with students or staff there is always an element of power. It is incumbent upon those with authority not to abuse, nor to seem to abuse, the power with which they are entrusted. Officers and other members of the teaching staff should be aware that any romantic involvement with their students make them liable for formal action against them. Even when both parties have consented at the onset to the development of such a relationship, it is the officer or instructor who, by virtue of his or her special responsibility and educational mission, will be held accountable for unprofessional behavior. (Harvard University 1990, 196).

Policies that prohibit professor-student consensual sexual relationships when the professor has professional responsibilities for the student constitute the best type of policy, because the professor's authority over the student is easily discerned and because the professor's authority over the student gives the university a legitimate reason for prohibiting such relationshigs. Such policies can "maintain the integrity of the academic missions while safeguarding the privacy interests of faculty members and students" (Keller 1990).

A majority of female graduate students (57 percent) and male faculty members (60 percent) surveyed at a large Eastern state university would accept a university policy that prohibits faculty-student consensual sexual relationships when a faculty member teaches, advises, or supervises a student (Stites 1993). However, they had reservations about a prohibition-type policy. Over half of the female graduate students and 42 percent of the male faculty members in that study believed that such a prohibition policy would violate individuals' rights to privacy. Some female graduate students expressed cynicism about a university's willingness to prohibit faculty members from having sexual relationships with students. One student commented that "the only way to keep [such relationships] to a minimum is to make a rule with teeth in it which clearly forbids them. I don't think the university will do it because it would lose some of the most able, young professors and because scholarship will be seen as more important than ethics" (114). Another female student commented, "I am pessimistic about the creation of a university policy and its subsequent implementation. In the end, it seems like the 'old boys' in the university simply protect one another" (115). Some male faculty members indicated that a prohibition policy would not work, due to the ineffectiveness of university administrators. One faculty member commented, "I found the use of the word 'prohibit' amusing. A university administration cannot effectively prohibit anything, even parking" (115). Another faculty member suggested that "the university should have a policy as a guide and should then stay the hell out of it. When it meddles, the university generally screws up, I do not have confidence that it treats individuals fairly" (115). A discouragement-type policy received stronger endorsements.

DISCOURAGEMENT POLICIES

A discouragement-type university consensual relationship policy was chosen most frequently as acceptable by the male faculty members (88 percent) and female graduate students (87 percent) in the Stites (1993) study. This finding is consistent with the findings that most of those respondents believed that some policy is necessary because faculty-student sexual relationship are fraught with ethical problems and detrimental consequences; and they believed that a discouragement-type policy is more workable than a prohibition policy (Stites 1993).

A discouragement-type policy is a statement of a university's preference regarding faculty members' sexual relationships with students. Such discouragement-type policies express concern, discourage, or warn professors about engaging in consensual sexual relationships with students over whom they have some authority. For example, the University of Minnesota (1990, 206) has a discouragement-type policy that states that "consenting romantic and sexual relationships between faculty and student or between supervisor and employee, while not expressly forbidden, are generally deemed very unwise." Similarly, the University of Connecticut policy (1990, 1) states that "the University strongly discourages romantic and sexual relationships between faculty and student or between supervisor and employee even when such relationships appear, or are believed to be, consensual." Even more tentatively stated is the New York University School of Law (1988) policy, which states that "it is the sense of the faculty that a person should not enter into a sexual relationship with a person during the time that the person has a direct authority over the student." The Massachusetts Institute of Technology (1985) policy is another example of a discouragement-type policy; it warns faculty as follows:

> It is presumably not the intention of the Institute to interfere with the course of true love, but it is appropriate to consider that a faculty member or teaching assistant who has a supervisory or educational responsibility for an employee, other faculty member, or student should divest himself or herself of that responsibility if a personal involvement develops between the two people. (61)

Such discouragement-type consensual relationship policies address only those relationships where the faculty member has authority over the student. However, because such policies are only warnings, they give faculty members "only a vague notion that such relationships are suspect and subject to unspecified consequences" (Keller 1990, 31). Discouragement-type policies are also difficult, if not impossible, to enforce because they are nothing more than statements of the university's preference. Should universities try to discipline professors based on a discouragement-type consensual relationship policy, "the institution opens itself to claims of selective punishment and unfair process" (Keller 1990, 31).

Despite the drawbacks of a discouragment-type consensual relationship policy, some of the male faculty members and female graduate students in the Stites (1993) study suggested that a discouragement-type policy is more acceptable than a prohibition policy. One female graduate student commented that "although it would seem like a good idea to discourage such relationships, I do not think you can forbid them. If people are going to get involved, a rule will not stop them. If it is discouraged, maybe it will not happen so often" (114). Another female graduate student commented that "sexual relationships, especially when they are not emotional, should be discouraged by a university when they occur between faculty and students. However, since graduate students are adults, I do not believe [such] relationships should be prohibited" (117).

Another argument for choosing a discouragement-type policy over a prohibition-type policy is that regulation of faculty conduct should be the province of faculty colleagues and not the province of administrators. A discouragement-type policy better fits the collegial faculty governance model with its reliance on informal persuasion by colleagues instead of a prohibiton-type policy with its reliance on administrative enforcement procedures. As one male faculty member in the Stites (1993) study commented, "Certainly these relationships are improper, but any attempt by the university to 'prohibit' them is doomed. Peer pressure can be more effective" (116.) One male faculty member describes his experience with collegial resolutions of a problematic faculty-student consensual sexual relationship as follows:

> It would be best if such matters could be dealt with within the framework of the academic department. In one instance in my experience, the situation was discussed among colleagues, then with the department chair, who then discussed the matter with the offending faculty member. When this produced no desired effect, those members of the faculty who wished to do so (almost all) confronted the faculty member and sucessfully demanded a change in the advisor/teaching relationship with the student. In another situation, however, it was the chair [of the academic department] who was offending. This became a very serious situation and required strong intervention by the dean. Here not only the stature of the faculty, but of the students, had been affected. (Stites 1993, 116).

Despite such endorsements of collegial solutions to discouraging faculty members from engaging in sexual relationships with their students, it has been this author's observations as a therapist in a university mental health service for twenty years that collegial solutions and discouragement-type policies often serve as means for academic departments to avoid addressing the conflicts of interest in faculty-student sexual relationships. In one academic department where several graduate students complained about a male faculty member's sexual relationship with a female graduate student whom he taught, advised, supervised, and recommended for admission to the doctoral program, the department head characterized the graduate students' objections to this professor's unethical relationship as "immature" and unsuccessfully tried to "counsel" the professor into abandoning his extra

TOTAL-BAN POLICIES

Apparently no public university has a policy that bans all sexual relationships between professors and students regardless of the professors' professional role (or lack thereof) with the student. Such an outright ban was proposed at the University of Virginia (Gross 1993), but the faculty senate approved a prohibition only when the faculty members teaches the student ("Faculty Approves Sex Ban" 1993). The faculty council at the University of Iowa successfully objected to the first draft of a proposed consensual relationship policy that appeared to ban all sexual relationships between professors and students (Small and Mears 1988). Only 23 percent of female graduate students and male faculty members surveyed at a large Eastern state university found acceptable a total ban of faculty-student consensual sexual relationships that would extend to a faculty member who does not teach, advise, or supervise a student (Stites 1993). Moreover, 85 percent of the female graduate students and 78 percent of the male faculty members in that study believed that a university ban on all faculty-student sexual relationships would violate individuals' rights to privacy when the professor has *no* professional responsibilities for the student. Seventy-five percent of the male faculty members and female graduate students would recommend no university disciplinary action against a professor who has a consensual sexual relationship with a student from a different academic department (Stites 1993).

A university cannot justify its interest in prohibiting a sexual relationship between a professor and a student from unrelated academic departments who meet through social activities and never leave a professional relationship. If *all* faculty-student sexual relationship were prohibited, faculty members and students might fear that any close associations, mentorships, or friendships between professors and students would be misconstrued (Keller 1990). However, a sexual relationship between a faculty member and a student who currently have no professional relationship but could eventually have a professional relationship is problematic for university policymakers.

POTENTIAL CONFLICT-OF-INTEREST POLICIES

Some university consensual relationship policies address the *potential* for a professor to have a future conflict of interest regarding a student with whom he has a consensual sexual relationship but with whom he does not currently have a professional relationship. Harvard University's guideliness for faculty on sexual harassment and unprofessional conduct address this issue as follows:

> Amorous relationships between members of the Faculty and students that occur outside the instructional context can lead to difficulties. In a personal relationship between an officer [i.e., a faculty member] and a student for whom the officer has no current professional responsibility, the officer should be sensitive to the constant possibility that he or she may unexpectedly be placed in a position of responsibility for the student's instruction or evaluation. This could involve being called upon to write a letter of recommendation or to serve on an admissions or selection committee involving the student. In addition, one should be aware that others may speculate that a specific power relationship exists even when there is none, giving rise to assumptions of inequitable academic or professional advantage for the student involved. Relationships between officers and students are always fundamentally asymmetric in nature. (Harvard University 1990, 196)

The University of Iowa policy addresses the potential for a conflict of interest or perception of conflict of interest even when the professor is not currently teaching his student-lover by stating that

> amorous relationships between faculty members and students occurring outside the instructional context may lead to difficulties. Particularly when the faculty member and student are in the same academic unit or in units that are academically allied, relationships that the parties view as consensual may appear to others to be exploitative. Further, in such situations (and others that cannot be anticipated), the faculty member may face serious conflicts of interest and should be careful to distance himself or herself from any decisions that may reward or penalize the student involved. A faculty members who fail to withdraw from participation in activities or decisions that may reward or penalize a student with whom the faculty members has or has had an amorous relationship will be deemed to have violated his or her ethical obligation to the student, to other students, to colleagues, and to the University. (University of Iowa 1988, 110)

Such potential conflict-of-interest sections of university consensual relationship polices attempt to address those circumstances where a faculty member may eventually have some power and authority over the student's academic progress. However, such warnings about potential conflicts of interest could inhibit sexual relationships between professors and students where no conflict of interest ever arises and appear to some faculty members to be an unfair intrusion by the university on their personal lives.

DISCIPLINARY ACTIONS AGAINST OFFENDING PROFESSORS

What type of personnel disciplinary actions are appropriate for professors who violate a university consensual relationship policy? In the Stites (1993) study at a large Eastern state university, male faculty members and female graduate students most often chose informal reprimand or formal reprimand as the appropriate penalty for an offending professor's first offense. However, the three most egregious situations elicited recommendations from 32 to 42 percent of the male faculty members and female graduate students to temporarily suspend the professor, to demand the professor's resignation, or to fire the professor. The more egregious situations were that (1) the student's consent to the relationship with the professor was partly based on her fear that her academic progress would suffer if she had not consented, (2) the student believed that the professor treated her unfairly in his professional responsibilities after she ended their sexual relationship, and (3) several faculty members and graduate students believed that the professor unfairly favored his student-lover in grading and recommendations for an assistantship.

One male professor suggested that "the [university] administration should be firm in disallowing conflicts of interest due to sexual relationships and yet be lenient in the manner of sanctions. Emphasis should be put on solving situations rather than punishing" (Stites 1993, 118). A female graduate student believed that "actions such as termination of employment and even suspension should only be used in extreme cases where favoritism or harassment is supported by statements from several faculty and/or student and the issue has been thoroughly investigated and it is proven that less severe actions have been ineffective" (118).

The key to a university's successful implementation of a consensual relationship policy lies in establishing fair investigatory and disciplinary procedures that begin with collegial solutions within the offending professor's academic department. Also, an effective policy should emphasize flexible university actions regarding the offending faculty member. For a professor's first violation of a consensual relationship policy, the university's actions should emphasize removing the professor's conflict of interest by removing the professor from his professional responsibilities for his student-lover before further disciplinary actions are taken. Disciplinary actions should primarily be informal reprimands or formal reprimands of the professor the first time the professor has a consensual sexual relationship with a student whom he teaches, advises, or supervises. More severe disciplinary actions such as temporary suspension, demanding the professor's resignation, or firing should be reserved for repeated violations or particularly egregious behavior by the professor in his conduct of a sexual relationship with a student.

FALSE COMPLAINTS

Although only a small minority of universities have adopted any type of consensual relationship policy, proposals of such policies have engendered controversy at some universities about the possibility of false complaints. Some University of Iowa faculty members expressed concerns that students would bring false complaints against professors if the University adopted a consensual relationship policy (Small and Mears 1988). False charges might include a student's claim that she was harmed merely because her relationship with a professor ended unhappily. Professors' fears of false complaints under consensual relationship policies may be similar to their fears of false sexual harassment complaints in that their fear is actually fear of the student's power to define the professor's behavior as unwanted or unwelcomed.

If the university prohibits a faculty-student relationship when a professor teaches, advises, or supervises a student, then a false complaint would be a claim that a sexual relationship existed when it never existed. Women tend to underreport professors' sexual harassment behaviors, which are more egregious and harder to prove than the existence of a consensual sexual relationship. In surveys of hundreds of universities, intentionally fabricated complaints constitued less than 1 percent of the sexual harassment complaints brought by women (Robertson, Dyer, and Campbell 1988; Sandler 1990). A woman student who has consented to a sexual relationship with a professor (for whatever reason) might view her consent as mitigating the professor's responsibility and, therefore, be even more reluctant to report a professor for violating a consensual relationship policy than would a woman who has been sexually harassed. However, even if false complaints are likely to be quite rare, university consensual relationship policies and enforcement procedures, like any other complaint procedures, should provide for due process and confidentiality for any accused professors so that false complaints cannot unfairly affect a professor's professional life and reputation.

STUDENT'S CONSENT AND SEXUAL HARASSMENT CHARGES

Some university consensual relationship policies offer some protection for the student-participant in a faculty-student sexual relationship should the student complain that the relationship was or became unwanted or unwel-comed. If the student feels that she was coerced or induced in any way or that she was sexually harassed, she might be denied any recourse by some university sexual harassment policies because she consented to the relationship at one time. Some universities have instituted consensual relationship policies that clarify that the student's previous consent will not provide the professor any immunity from subsequent sexual harassment findings (Welzenbach et al. 1986). Such a policy has a strong legal basis in the 1986 *Meritor* decision, in which the Court ruled that the victim's consent or voluntary participation in a sexual relationship with a supervisor is no defense against a sexual harass-ment charge against that supervisor (Ingulli 1987; Keller 1988; *Meritor Savings Bank v. Vinson* 1986).

The University of Minnesota policy (1990) addresses the role of the student's prior consent in subsequent disciplinary proceedings against the faculty member as follows:

> Faculty are warned against the possible costs of even an apparently consenting relationship, in regard to the academic efforts of both faculty member and student. A faculty member who enters into a sexual rela-tionship with a student (or supervisor with an employee) where a pro-fessional power differential exists must realize that if a charge of sexual harassment is subsequently lodged, it will be exceedingly difficult to prove immunity on grounds of mutual consent. (206)

A similar policy at the University of Pennsylvania (1987) states:

> In order to discourage such [faculty-student sexual relationships], in acting on complaints that come to the University's attention, it will be presumed that any complaint of sexual harassment by a student against an individual is valid if sexual relations have occurred between them while the individual was teaching or otherwise had supervisory responsibility for the student. The presumption might be overcome, but the difficulties in doing so would be substantial. In short, any teacher or person in a supervisory capacity enters at peril into sexual relations with a student. (iii)

Similarly, the section on consensual relationships in Howard University's *Sexual Harassment Policy and Procedures* states that "in internal proceedings, the University generally will be unsympathetic to a defense based on consent when the facts establish that the accused had the power to affect the complainant's academic or employment status or future prospects" (*Howard University Sexual Harassment Policies and Procedures* 1990, 220).

Over 60 percent of the male faculty members and the female graduate students surveyed at a large Eastern state university doubted the legitimacy of a sexual harassment claim by a female student who had agreed to have a sexual relationship with a professor who did not coerce or threaten her (Stites 1993). Despite their doubts on the legitimacy of such a sexual harassment claim, less than 25 percent of both groups would accept a university policy that disallows official findings of sexual harassment or ethical misconduct by a professor if the student at any time consented to the sexual relationship with the professor. The female graduate students and male faculty members differed significantly (.00002 significance level) on whether a professor should be permitted to use the student's consent as a defense against a sexual harassment charge. A slight majority (57 percent) of the female graduate students but only a minority (31 percent) of the male faculty members agreed that university policy should *not* permit a faculty member facing sexual harassment or ethical misconduct charges to use as his defense the fact that the student at one time consented to the sexual relationship with the professor. As one person noted, "the professor should be able to use any *defense* he desires. The graduate student's charge of sexual harassment should not be ignored because she at one time consented to sex" (112).

Disallowing a professor's defense that his relationship with a student was once mutually consensual protects the educational interests of students who engaged (however freely or not) in sexual relationships with professors. Such policies place the responsibility on the professor for an unethical practice. However, taking away the professor's main defense argument that the student consented to the relationship may seem to be a violation of due process to an accused professor.

INDIVIDUALS' CIVIL RIGHTS

At some universities that have proposed to institute consensual relationship policies, concerns have been raised about how such policies might infringe upon individuals' rights to privacy, individuals' rights to freedom of speech and association, and faculty members' rights to academic freedom. Most Americans believe that their civil rights include the right to be free of governmental intrusion into their intimate relationships (Keller, 1988). Many University of Washington at Seattle faculty members opposed a proposed ban on faculty-student consensual sexual relationships because such a ban seemed to be an inappropriate intrusion into people's private lives by trying to legislate morality (Gross 1993). In 1986, faculty at both the University of Texas at Arlington and the University of California rejected proposed consensual relationship policies. In doing so, they objected to the university's intrusion into individuals' private, interpersonal relationships, which are, as one faculty member noted, "none of the university's business" (Keller 1988; McMillen 1986; "Romance Is Not Dead" 1986).

The constitutional right to privacy for employees of public universities has been established in several court rulings that rely primarily on the Fourteenth Amendment (DeChiara 1988; Keller 1988).

> Given the emphasis by the Court on the inter-relationship among the right to privacy, marriage, and child-rearing, the formation of consensual amorous relationships viewed as natural precursors to the more formal bord of marriage, should similarly be protected by the right to privacy. . . . The right to privacy, however, is not absolute. As with any constitutionally guaranteed individual right, a compelling state interest permits certain infringements on that right. Laws [or public university policies] which limit the fundamental freedoms of an individual must serve a compelling state interest and also must be narrowly drawn to serve only that interest. (Keller 1988, 32–33)

A compelling state interest clearly exists when a professor has some professional authority over a student such as teaching, advising, or supervising. Court cases have affirmed that a public university may discipline a faculty member who has a sexual relationship with a student, because of the university's legitimate interest in maintaining the integrity of its educational mission, avoiding professors' conflicts of interest and abuse of authority, avoiding a perception of unfairness in professors' treatment of students, or maintaining the university's good reputation (DeChiara 1988; Kelelr 1988; *Korf v. Ball State University* 1984; *Naragon v. Wharton* 1983, 1984). One court found that Louisiana State University had a legitimate interest in disciplining an instructor even when the instructor had no grading or other professional responsibilities for the student-lover (*Naragon v. Wharton* 1984). Courts, too, could very well uphold private universities' consensual relationship policies just as they have upheld private companies' policies forbidding fraternization between managers and nonmanagers. Courts have held that such policies do not invade employees' privacy because private companies have "a legitimate interest in avoiding the appearance of favoritism, employee dissension, or possible claims of sexual harassment" (Keller 1988, 29).

Further objections to university consensual relationship policies have been based on the belief that consensual relationship policies abrogate individuals' rights to freedom of speech and association. However, the *Naragon* court specifically rejected the instructor's claim that the university violated her freedom of association when it disciplined the instructor for engaging in a consensual sexual relationship with a student (*Naragon v. Wharton* 1983). Universities must consider which group—students or faculty—is more harmed if its rights are limited (Crocker 1983). The harm done to students when the university tolerates consensual sexual relationships must be weighed against the harm done to faculty in having to refrain from making sexual advances to students and engaging in sexual relationships with students.

In order to successfully implement a consensual relationship policy, a university would need to educate the university community that a university policy that prohibits a consensual sexual relationship between a professor and a student for whom the professor has professional responsibilities would not violate individuals' rights to privacy. This educational effort seems necessary in light of some faculty members' and graduate students' concerns that consensual relationship policies might violate their right to privacy (Stites 1993).

Professors, rights to academic freedom may be cited as a basis for objecting to university consensual relationship policies. Sometimes "educational institutions have an unfortunate tendency to wrap policy decisions in the sacred mantle of First Amendment freedom, as though the persons and practices of academic life were exempt from the examination to which most professions are routinely subjected" (Winks 1982, 465). Faculty's autonomy "tempts arrogance. It is easy—and convenient—to confuse the principle of academic freedom with license to behave and speak irresponsibly" (Dziech and Weiner 1990, 44). However, the Stites (1993) study found that only a small minority of female graduate students (29.8 percent) and an even smaller minority of male faculty members (13.1 percent) believed that university policies that restrict faculty-student consensual sexual relationships impinge on faculty rights to academic freedom.

CAN STUDENTS FREELY CONSENT?

One of the most controversial objections raised to consensual relationship policies is the assertion that students—especially graduate students and non-traditional-age undergraduate students—should be treated as consenting adults. Universities have come to regard students as adults and have moved away from in loco parentis rules and paternalistic roles with students. In this regard, consensual relationship policies may constitute a step backward (Hoffman 1986). When the University of California academic senate voted down a proposed consensual relationship policy in 1986, one professor pointed out that the relationships the university wanted to regulate were "romantic relationships between consenting adults" ("Romance Is Not Dead" 1986).

The controversy about treating students as consenting adults centers on these questions: Is a student free to consent to a relationship with a professor who has power over her? Is it possible for the student to ignore the power the professor has over her academic life and career in order to give consent free of any implied coercion or indirect pressure (Wagner 1990)? Should the university attempt to protect the student who may not be able to objectively assess the risks of a sexual relationship with a faculty member?

Hoffman (1986) argues that universities should not have consensual relationship policies because students should be treated as consenting adults. She argues that

> amorous relationship statements go beyond the observation that sexual harassment arises from the interaction between power and status differences in sexual expression to argue that all sexual relationships between faculty and student, whether exploitative or not, are inherently suspect because of the danger of exploitation. The logic of the argument is as follows: since sexual harassment occurs most frequently between individuals with asymmetric degrees of status and power, and since faculty and students have such asymmetric relationships with one another, *all* sexual relationships between faculty and all students are appropriately proscibed to prevent abuse (or perception of abuse) of *some* students. . . . Amorous relationship statements assume that the relatively powerless group—students—is incapable of empowerment and, in seeking to prevent its victimization, reinforce and perpetuate its powerlessness and vulnerability. Amorous relationship policies reflect the difficulty of devising strategies that correct some forms of victimization of women without introducing new ones. . . . [Such policies] reinforce status hierarchies and ignore or deny the right of individuals to establish relationships when, with whom, and where they choose. (112–14)

Sheila Tobias, former Wesleyan University associate provost, also objects to university consensual relationship policies on the basis that women students should not be protected from learning about the realities of the adult worlds— how to handle sexual politics, their emotions, and their professors' emotions (Munich 1978, 108).

An opposing point of view is held by Dziech and Weiner (1990), who assert that it is a myth that a student participant in a faculty-student sexual relationship is a consenting adult.

> If a professor becomes involved with a student, his standard defense is that she is a consenting adult. Few students are ever, in the strictest sense, consenting adults. A student can never be a genuine equal of a professor insofar as his professional position gives him power over her. Access to a student occurs not because she allows it but because the professor ignores professional ethics and chooses to extend the student-faculty relationship. Whether the student consents to the involvement or whether the professor ever intends to use his power aganst her is

not the point. The issue is that the power and the role disparity always exist, making it virtually impossible for the student to act as freely as she would with a male peer. In a normal romantic situation, both the man and the women make efforts to assess each other's reasons for pursuing the relationship, to understand their true feelings and desires, and to predict their own and the other's future behaviors and attitudes. In a faculty-student relationship, the enormous role (and frequently age) disparity inhibits the woman so that she herself may have trouble understanding and predicting her feelings. (74)

The view that a male professor's sexual interest in a female student is normal or that the student should be flattered by this sexual interest as in any peer relationship between a man and a woman ignores the power differences inherent in the faculty-student relationship (Benson and Thomson 1982). The student role may engender powerlessness and encourage the student to accommodate to the "almost absolute power" the professor seems to have over her academic work and professional future (Zalk, Paludi, and Dederich 1990, 119). A student who tries to avoid a professor's sexual invitations usually fears that the professor will use his power over her to inflict negative consequences (Rochelle 1980).

> Regardless of faculty intention, potential coercion can influence students to consent to sexual involvement with faculty. Students may consent to unwanted sexual liaisons because of uncertainty regarding the academic consequences of noncompliance. Therefore, what may appear to be an adult, consensual, private relationship may be the product of implicit or explicit duress. (Keller 1988, 27)

Of the male faculty members surveyed at a large Eastern state university 94 percent agreed that a subtle yet powerful potential for coercion (by the professor) exists in any consensual sexual relationsip between a professor and a graduate student when the professor teaches, advises, or supervises her; and 95 percent agreed that even when a professor and a graduate student mutually consent to a sexual relationship, potential exists for the professor to abuse the power of his professional position over a graduate student whom he teaches, advises, or supervises (Stites 1993). Howard University (*Howard University Sexual Harassment Policies and Procedures* 1990) recognize that consent might not necessarily be freely given by a student who is involved in a faculty-student sexual relationship by stating in its consensual relationship policy that "the powers faculty members exercise in evaluating students' work, awarding grades, providing recommendations, and the like will generally constrain a student's actual freedom to choose whether to enter into or to end a romantic or sexual relationship with a faculty member" (219).

The potential coercion inherent in a professor-student sexual relationship can be disguised by the professor's gradual and covert sexual pursuit of the student, should he take advantage of the wide latitude of the professor's role. He might give a woman student extra help, extend deadlines, be flexible in grading, and extend unusual friendliness in order to lay the groundwork for eventual sexual overtures to her (Benson and Thomson 1982). The student's gratitude and sense of obligation to the professor as well as confusion about the professor's motives may impair her objectivity in consenting to a sexual relationship with him.

Students' exaggeration of professors' power over them and their awe of professors' knowledge and power can impair their ability to consent freely to sexual relationships with faculty members. The larger the power differential is between the professor and the student, the more the student may lose her objectivity about her own best interests in engaging in a faculty-student sexual relationship (Kitchener 1988). A student's infatuation with a professor may stem primarily from her fascination with his role as a powerful figure and as an expert in an academic subject in which they have a common interest (Taylor 1981). One male faculty members who had stopped having sexual relationships with students noted that "most of my encounters ended unhappily after I learned that the students were mostly actualizing their fantasies, and were not sincerely interested in me" (Fitzgerald et al. 1988, 337). As one teaching assistant learned, a student enrolled in his course lost her previous interest in dating him once he was "no longer her all-knowing T.A." (Kantor 1990, 3). A student might uncritically idealize her sexual relationship with a professor and deny the risks inherent in such a relationship (Zalk, Paludi, and Dederich 1990). A professor might promote the student's dependency on him by treating her as a modern-day Galatea awaiting Pygmalion's touch to give her "intellectual and sexual vitality" (Dziech and Weiner 1990, 71). These factors impair students' ability to act as consenting adults in faculty-student consensual sexual relationships.

The question of a female student's ability to consent freely to a sexual relationship with a male professor is further complicated by the interaction of gender roles and university status, which can exaggerate the power differences between a male professor and a female student (McKinney, Olson, and Satterfield 1988). The prticipants in most of the faculty-student sexual relationships in American universities are male faculty members and female students (Stites 1993). The interaction of gender roles and university status plays out in a different way when the professor is a man and the student is a woman than when the relationship is between a female professor and a male student or between a professor and a student of the same gender. Male professors have informal power because of their male gender and formal power because of their position in the university hierarchy (Farley 1978; Fitzgerald 1990; Winks 1982). In our society, men have the sexual prerogative that gives them informal power to make sexual advances to women, especially when the woman has a lower status, as a student does (Fitzgerald 1990; Winks 1982). Schneider (1985, 99) asserts that "most sexual approaches at work are not voluntary sexual interactions or sexual relationships. More often, [they are] a means of asserting male privilege; the sexual interest and content is secondary."

> There is . . . *a nexus of power and sexual prerogative* often enjoyed by men with formal authority over women. Men in such positions can engage in (or "get away with") overt sexual behaviors that would be rebuffed or avoided were the relationship not one of superior and subordinate. They can also discharge selectively the power and rewards of their positions as a means to obligate women sexually. (Benson and Thomson 1982)

Women's gender-role expectations, combined with their lower status as students, contribute to powerlessness. "Women are not only socialized to regard all men as powerful, but also they are socialized to equate power with sex appeal" (Walker, Erickson, and Woolsey 1985, 427). Women are socialized to defer to men's expectations and to trust male authority figures. "Forced into a choice between a teacher's wishes and their own, some [women] students do what they have learned to do best—defer, submit, agree" (Dziech and Weiner 1990, 78). The norm for women students who are approached sexually by male professors, then, might be to attempt to please the professors as men and to accommodate men's expectations that women should be sexual objects (Olson and McKinney 1989). The powerlessness that women feel often prevents them from overtly rejecting male professors' sexual advances. Instead, they often resort to indirect communications and avoidance strategies.

The image of the woman as a "naive student swept into bed by her brilliant professor" may be a fantasy that tries "to soften the linking of sexual dominance with the powerful and of sexual submission with the powerless" (Franklin et al. 1981, 3). Given this interaction of gender-role conditioning and formal power differences between male professor and female student, the image of the women student freely weighing her options as a consenting adult in a relationship with a male peer becomes quite troublesome in judging faculty-student sexual relationships.

Viewed in this light, students—particularly women students—need the protection of clear, enforceable, and enforced university consensual relationship policies. Faculty members, too, need clear and enforced rules about what ethical misconduct is prohibited by the university.

References

Benson, D., and Thomson, G. (1982). Sexual harassment on a university campus: The confluence of authority relations, sexual interest, and gender stratification. *Social Problems, 29* (Feb.), 236–51.

Brown v. California State Personnel Board. 213 Cal. Rptr. 53 (Cal. App. 3 Dist., 1985).

Connolly, W., Jr., and Marshall, A. (1989). Sexual harassment of university or college students by faculty members. *Journal of College and University Law, 15* (4), 381–403.

Crocker, P. (1983). An analysis of university definitions of sexual harassment. *Signs: Journal of Women in Culture and Society, 8* (4).

DeChiara, P. (1988). The need for universities to have rules on consensual relationships between faculty members and students. *Columbia Journal of Law and Social Problems, 21* (2), 137–62.

Dzeich, B., and Weiner, L. (1990). *The lecherous professor: Sexual harassment on campus* (2nd ed.). Boston: Beacon Press.

Faculty approves sex ban. (1993). *Hartford Courant,* 23 April, p. A2.

Farley, L. (1978). *Sexual shakedown: The sexual harassment of women on the job.* New York: McGraw-Hill.

Fitzgerald, L. (1990). Sexual harassment: The definition and measurement of a construct. In Michele Paludi (Ed.), *Ivory power: Sexual harassment on campus* (21–42). Albany: State University of New York Press.

———. (1991). *Sexual harassment in higher education: Concepts and issues* (Monograph). Washington, DC: National Education Association.

Fitzgerald, L., Weitzman, L., Gold, Y., and Ormerod, M. (1988). Academic harassment: Sex and denial in scholarly garb. *Psychology of Women Quarterly, 12*)3), 329–40.

Franklin, P., Moglin, H., Zatling-Boring, P., and Angress, R. (1981). *Sexual and gender harassment in the academy: A guide for faculty, students, and administrators.* New York: Modern Language Association of America, Commission on the Status of Women in the Profession.

Gross, J. (1993). Love or harassment? Campuses bar (and debate) faculty-student sex. *New York Times,* 14 April, p. B9.

Hoffman, F. (1986). Sexual harassment in academia: Feminist theory and institutional practice. *Harvard Educational Review, 56* (2).

Horn, P., and Horn, J. (1982). *Sex in the office.* Reading, MA: Addison-Wesley.

Howard University Sexual Harassment Policy and Procedures. (1990). In Elsa Kircher Cole (Ed.), *Sexual harassment on campus: A legal compendium* (2nd ed., 219–20). Washington, DC: National Association of College and University Attorneys.

Hustoles, T. (1990). Consensual relations issues in higher education. In Elsa Kircher Cole (Ed.), *Sexual harassment on campus: A legal compendium* (2nd ed., 251–55). Washington, DC: National Association of College and University Attorneys.

Ingulli, E. (1987). Sexual harassment in education. *Rutgers Law Journal, 18* (2), 281–341.

Kantor, M. (1990, Nov./Dec.). Confessions of a lonely T.A. *Issues and Insights for the College Woman in View,* p. 3.

Keller, E. (1988). Consensual amorous relationships between faculty and students: The Constitutional right to privacy. *Journal of College and University Law, 15* (1), 21–42.

————. (1990). Consensual relationships and institutional policy. *Academe, 76* (1), 29–32.

Kitchener, K. (1988). Dual role relationships: What makes them so problematic? *Journal of Counseling and Development,* 67 (Dec.), 217–21.

Korf v. Ball State University. 726 F.2d 122 (7th Cir. 1984).

Little, D., and Thompson, J. (1989). Campus policies, the law, and sexual relationships. *Thought and Action, 5* (1), 17–24.

Massachusetts Institute of Technology. (1985). Report of the ad hoc faculty-student committee on sexual harassment. In Nancy Tuana, Sexual harassment in academe. *College Teaching, 33* (3), 61.

McKinney, K., Olson, C., and Satterfield, A. (1988). Graduate students' experiences with and responses to sexual harassment: A research note. *Journal of Interpersonal Violence, 3,* (3), 319–25.

McMillen, L. (1986). Many colleges taking a new look at policies on sexual harassment. *Chronicle of Higher Education,* 17 December, pp. 1, 16.

Meritor Savings Bank v. Vinson 477 U.S. 57 (1986).

Munich, A. (1978). Seduction in academe. *Psychology Today,* February, pp. 82–84, 108.

Naragon v. Wharton. 572 F. Supp. 1117 (M.D. La. 1983).

Naragon v. Wharton. 737 F. 2d 1402 (5th Cir. 1984).

New York University School of Law. (1988). *Policy regarding sexual harassment and gender bias.* New York: New York University School of Law.

Olson, C., and McKinney, K. (1989). Processes inhibiting the reduction of sexual harassment in academe: An alternative explanation. *Initiatives, 52* (3), 7–13.

Quinn, R. (1977). Coping with cupid: The formation, impact, and management of romantic relationships in organizations. *Administrative Science Quarterly, 22* (1), 30–45.

Robertson, C., Dyer, C., and Campbell, D'A. (1988). Campus harassment: Sexual harassment policies and procedures at institutions of higher learning. *Signs, 13* (4), 792–812.

Rochelle, L. (1980). Sex roles on campus: Does professor Charles really get his angels? *Community College Frontiers, 8* (4), 11–20.

Romance is not dead. (1986). *Chronicle of Higher Education,* 3 September, p. 44.

Sandler, B. (1990). Sexual harassment: A new issue for institutions. *Initiatives, 52* (4), 5–10.

Sandler, B., and Associates. (1981). Sexual harassment; A hidden problem. *Educational Record, 62* (1), 52–57.

Schneider, B. (1985). Approaches, assaults, attractions, affairs; Policy implications of sexualization of the workplace. *Population Research and Policy Review, 4,* 92–113.

————. (1987). Graduate women, sexual harassment, and university policy. *Journal of Higher Education, 58* (1), 46–65.

Small, M.J., and Mears, J. (1988). To draft a more perfect policy: The development of the University of Iowa's sexual harassment policy. In Joan Van Tol (Ed.), *Sexual harassment on campus: A legal compendium* (135–49). Washington, DC: National Association of College and University Attorneys.

Stites, M.C. (1993). *Faculty-student consensual sexual relationships and university policy.* Unpublished doctoral dissertation, University of Connecticut, Storrs.

Taylor, R. (1981). Within the halls of ivy the sexual revolution comes of age. *Change, 13* (4), 22–29.

Temple University. (1985). Policy prohibiting sexual harassment of students. In Elaine Ingulli. (1987). Sexual harassment in education. *Rutgers Law Journal, 18* (2), 327–28.

University of Connecticut. (1990). President's policy on harassment. In 1 May
· 1990 Memorandum from Thomasina Clemons, Director, Office of Affirmative Action Programs, to Vice Presidents, Deans, Directors, and Department Heads.

University of Iowa. (1988). University of Iowa policy on sexual harassment consensual relationship. In Joan Van Tol (Ed.), *Sexual harassment on campus: A legal compendium* (109–10). Washington, DC: National Association of College and University Attorneys.

University of Minnesota. (1990). Presidential statement and policy on sexual harassment. In B. Dzeich and L. Weiner (Eds.), *The lecherous professor: Sexual harassment on campus* (2nd ed., 203–4, 206). Boston: Beacon Press.

University of Pennsylvania. (1987). Harassment policy. *Almanac Supplement,* p. iii. Philadelphia: University of Pennsylvania.

Wagner, K.C. (1990). Prevention and intervention: Developing campus policy and procedures. *Initiatives, 52* (4), 37–45.

Walker, G., Erickson, L., and Woolsey, L. (1985). Sexual harassment: Ethical research and clinical implications in the academic setting. *International Journal of Women's Studies, 8* (4), 424–33.

Welzenbach, L., et al. (Eds.). (1986). *Sexual harassment: Issues and answers. A Guide for education, business, industry.* Washington, DC: College and University Personnel Association. (ERIC Document Reproduction Service No. 275 270.)

Winks, P. (1982). Legal implications of sexual contact between teacher and student. *Journal of Law and Education, 11* (4), 437–77.

Zalk, S.R., Paludi, M., and Dederich, J. (1990). Women student assessment of consensual relationships with their professors: Ivory power reconsidered. In Elsa Kircher Cole (Ed.), *Sexual harassment on campus: A legal compendium* (2nd ed., 103–32). Washington, DC: National Association of College and University Attorneys.

Part III
Campus Interventions for Effectively Dealing with Sexual Harassment
Individual and Institutional Approaches for Change

Editor's Notes

As was pointed out by the contributors to Part 2, women might not label their experiences as academic sexual harassment, despite the fact the experiences meet the legal definition of this form of victimization. Consequently they might not label their stress-related responses as being caused or exacerbated by the sexual harassment. Their responses are attributed by classmates and perhaps faculty and administrators to other events in their lives—biological and/or social. However, several reports have documented the high cost of sexual harassment to women. In this sextion, Kathryn Quina and Vita Rabinowitz note that the outcomes of the harassment/victimization process in academia can be examined from three main perspectives: school/ work-related, psychological or emotional, and physiological or heath-related:

School work-related outcomes. Research has documented decreased morale and absenteeism, decreased satisfaction with one's career goals, performance decrements, and damage to interpersonal relationships on campus.

Psychological outcomes. The consequences of being harassed to students and campus employees have been devastating to their emotional health; such consequences include depression, feelings of helplessness, strong fear reactions, loss of control, disruption of their lives, and decreased motivation. Research has indicated that, depending on the severity of the harassment, from 21 to 82 percent of women report that their emotional condition deteriorated as a result of the sexual harassment. Furthermore, like victims of rape who go to court, sexual harassment victims experience a second victimization when they attempt to deal with the situation through legal and/or institutional means. Stereotypes about sexual harassment and women's victimization blame women for the harassment. These sterotypes, as Kathryn Quina suggests in her chapter, center around the myths that sexual harassment is a form of seduction, that women secretly want to be sexually harassed, and that women do not tell the truth.

Physiological outcomes. The following physical symptoms have been reported in the literature concerning academic sexual harassment: headaches, sleep disturbances, disordered eating, gastrointestinal disorders, nausea, weight loss or gain, and crying spells. Recently, researchers and clinicians have argued that victims of sexual harassment can exhibit a "post-abuse" syndrome characterized by shock, emotional numbing, constriction of affect, flashbacks, and other signs of anxiety and depression

These responses are influenced by disappointment in the way others react and the stress of harassment-induced life changes, such as moves, loss of student loans, loss in teaching or research fellowships, and disrupted educational history. Other direct costs stemming from academic sexual harassment include legal expenses, medical costs, and psychotherapy costs. Campus employees might lose health benefits, life insurance, pensions, or other benefits as a result of the alleged harassment. Furthermore, a loss or change in job status can affect one's access to day-care arrangements.

Both Kathryn Quina and Vita Rabinowitz offer suggestions for advocates, counselors, and educators who work with victims of seuxal harassment for (1) empowering these individuals, (2) facilitating their appropriate labeling of the victimization, and (3) helping them to view sexual harassment as resulting from the opportunities presented by power and authority relations that derive from the hierarchical structure of the college/university system. Each of these contributors points out that cognitive reappraisals of beliefs shattered by sexual harassment will contribute to women's ability to become self-reliant, adapt, grow, and become confident in their abilities once again.

Both Dr. Quina and Dr. Rabinowitz alert us to the continuum of issues in the area of academic sexual harassment that are not addressed by policy statements and laws. They agree that faculty responsibility is the way to ensure a campus setting free of sexual harassment. And they express the sentiment of this entire volume: that we need to change the relative power of women in college/university settings that underlies sexual harassment. Women and women's experiences must be placed in the center of the academic environment.

To effectively meet this goal, the following components are typically recommended: an effective and enforced policy statement, an effective and enforced grievance procedure, and education/training programs for all members of the campus community. In this section, the contributors focus more attention on each of these three components.

Maryka Biaggio and Arlene Brownell also address interventions on a college campus that can be implemented by a panel or other designate. These interventions include (1) placing items relating to sexist comments or sexual invitations on teaching evaluations, (2) publishing articles on sexual harassment in student newspapers, (3) disseminating information about institutional policies that prohibit sexual harassment at new student orientations and dormitories, and (4) setting up community activist strategies to raise public awareness and to protest particular instances of sexual harassment.

Helen Remick, Jan Salisbury, Donna Stringer, and Angela Ginorio aptly point out that educational interventions concerning sexual harassment increase the likelihood that complaints will be brought on campus. They offer suggestions for working with unions, how to handle investigations of sexual harassment, and the effects of these investigations for individuals as well as the campus climate.

Dorothy O. Helly, discusses major issues in establishing a sexual harassment panel on a college campus, including handling informal and formal complaints by students, faculty, administrators, and staff; the establishment of an explicit policy against sexual harassment on campus; and the makeup of such a panel.

All of the contributors to this section support Meg Bond's (1988) plea for an ecological perspective—educational, psychotherapeutic, legal, and sociocultural—for handling sexual harassment on campus. As Bond suggested:

> The use of an ecological perspective can move beyond finger pointing to a more comprehensive understanding of a complex social problem that has been a critical barrier to women's professional development for many years. . . . Continued development of an ecological approach will provide a more solid basis for developing policies and preventive interventions to reduce the negative impact sexual harassment has on women's professional development. (6)

References

Bond, M. (1988). Sexual harassment in academic settings: Developing an ecological approach. *Community Psychologist, 21*, 5–6.

9

Sexual Harassment and Rape:
A Continuum of Exploitation

Kathryn Quina

In the comic strip "Beetle Bailey," common forms of sexual harassment are carried out by harmless characters whom we are supposed to love, or at least feel a kind of charitable forgiveness toward. General Halftrack is the archetypical older gentleman whose dowdy wife starves him for affection. His secretary Miss Buxley—who can't type—drives him wild with her sexy figure and short skirts. "Killer" (short for *lady-killer*, a curiously violent name) is always whistling at "chicks" (who love it), accompanied by Beetle, who is equally aggressive but not as successful. Zero just stares at women's bodies.

Played out in the real world, these scenarios are not funny. The similarity of a university department to a comic strip seems especially incongruous, yet many of us have had to cope with Generals, Killers, Beetles, and Zeros in our professional as will as personal lives. In my first five years as an academic, I experienced an older professor literally chase me around a desk, similar-aged colleagues determined to bed me, and a dean who simply could not stop staring at my chest (and I'm not Miss Buxley!). Sadly, I am not the only one to relate these experiences. In most of the instances described above, I learned about other victims of the same offenders; in my research on sexual harassment and rape, I have met many more victims of other offenders.

The striking thing about sexual harassment is that it is also not harmless. In this chapter, I will argue that all forms of sexual harassment share important commonalities with rape. While harassment is usually less physically intrusive and less violent or life-threatening, it is not substantially different structurally or socially from rape. This conceptual framework defines rape and harassment as sexual assaults lying on a continuum of sexual exploitation, varying in degree of physical intrusion and potential physical injury to the victim.[1] At the pole of the least physically violent, this continuum begins with verbal assaults, including sexually offensive jokes or degrading comments, also caled "gender harassment" (e.g., Fitzgerald and Ormerod 1991). At the pole of the most violent are rape, murder, and femicide. On such a scale, sexual harassment and rape are relatively close together. In fact, many assaults now called "harassment"—those involving sexual contact—are legally the equivalent of rape.

This continuum perspective allows us to utilize the extensive literature on rape victimization and recovery to gain insight into and understanding of the sexual harassment situation and survivor reactions. In fact, much of the recent research in sexual harassment began as an extension of research on rape offenders, attitudes toward rape victims, and the like.

COMMONALITIES

Six major commonalities underlying this continuum are discussed here, illuminated with stories from students and colleagues and from my own life to provide a glimpse of the reality of these sexual assaults. These areas of commonality are (1) power dynamics, (2) gender roles and relationships, (3) offender characteristics, (4) cultural stereotyping, (5) emotional reactions of victims, and (6) costs to the survivor. Paths to resolution, suggested from work with rape and harassment survivors, will be explored.

Power Dynamics

The rapist is likely to have greater physical size and strength than the victim, or to wield a gun or knife (Brownmiller 1975). The sexual harasser uses age or social position, or wields economic power and authority, as weapons (Alliance Against Sexual Coercion 1981; Fitzgerald et al. 1988). In all cases, however, a power advantage is essential to the act.

Gender, age, hierarchical status, and race are important points of vulnerability to a sexual harasser's power. By far, the sexual offender is most likely to be a male: An estimated 99 percent of rapists (Groth 1979) and 75 to 90 pecent of sexual harassers (Reilly, Lott, and Gallogly 1986) are men. The victim is most likely to be female and young (Finkelhor 1979; Reilly et al. 1986; Terpstra and Baker 1988a). Minority women are more frequently asked for sexual favors or dates, and subject to more sexually offensive gestures, than nonminority women are. Bingham and Scherer (1993) found that 78 percent of the harassed academic faculty and staff women were victimized by men of greater or "equal" status (although, in academia, nontenured and tenured faculty are clearly not equal), compared to 42 percent of comparable men.

Ann was a new assistant professor, the only woman in a large department. Only one colleague had welcomed her arrival and had informally begun to mentor her. Late one night, he called her to "discuss a problem." He began talking about her future tenure decision and her need to be more "friendly." He also suggested they have dinner to discuss their relationship, since he knew it would "help her get ahead," At the same time, he warned her not to associate with students (the only other women) or the women's group on campus, because such associations would "look bad" in the eyes of her colleagues. Already isolated, she now avoided him as well as the women.[2]

When harassment is "contrapower," that is, involves subordinates as harassers, other vulnerabilities for women emerge. Faculty women, who should be at the upper levels of the power hierarchy in universities, find themselves subjected to sexual harassment by male students in substantial numbers (Grauerholz 1989). Underscoring women's tenuous existence within the ivory halls, almost 9 percent of those who knew the student harassing them chose to remain silent for fear of personal or professional repercussions.

Increasing attention has been paid to the work environment as a source of power for the sexual abuser. In society at large, media and other images of women create a culture that is, if not supportive, at least not opposed to sexual violence (e.g., Check and Malamuth 1985). Academic and other organizations can be characterized by their level of support for harassment victims (Gallant and Cross 1993; Gutek 1985; Terpstra and Baker 1988b). In nonsupportive environments, it may be assumed that the harasser can tap into the organizational "power base" (fraternities are one such context [Copenhaver and Grauerholz 1991]).

Finally, rapists and harassers gain enormous power when victims do not report the incident, or when institutions designed to protect victims do not respond to reports. It is estimated that less than 10 percent of victims of all sexual assaults report them to the police or other authorities (e.g., Mynatt and Allgeier 1990; Schneider 1987). Among those who do report sexual harassment, fewer than a third find favorable decisions from authorities (Terpstra and Baker 1988a).

Gender Roles and Relationships

Beyond gender, cultural expectations of masculinity and femininity seem to be extremely important to rape and harassment. Rapists endorse, and perhaps attempt to act out, extreme versions of the cultural stereotype of masculinity as dominance over women (Groth 1979; Scott and Tetreault 1987; Zaitchik and Mosher 1993). There is evidence that sexual harassers hold the same stereotypes and desire the same macho image. Mosher and Sirkin (1984) found that men with hypermasculine patterns held more callous attitudes toward women, and suggested they were more likely to harass as well as rape. On a larger level Jaffe and Straus's (1987) state-by-state analysis of sexual assault data revealed a relationship between higher rape rates and evidence of hypermasculine cultural gender roles (e.g., sex magazine readership).

Women who accede to cultural demands on women to be "feminine"—that is, to be passive, submissive, helping, and nurturant—probably have an increased likelihood of being victims of rape or harassment (Bart and O'Brien 1985).

For several monthes, Beth remained silent about her major professors sexual comments and the way he touched her whenever they were alone. She tried to be nice, partly to avoid his wrath and partly because she didn't know what else to do. As a southern woman, she had only been taught "niceness." Meanwhile, other graduate students were beginning to tease her about him. One day, as she described it, she "freaked out." She yelled at him to get out of her of office and quit bothering her. She was deeply embarrassed by her outburst, but held back her urge to apologize. Not only did his abuse stop, but the other students, who overheard the interaction, began to treat her with greater respect. Until she spoke up, they had assumed she was "using her femininity."

Characteristics of the Abuser

Rapists and child molesters are "habitual" offenders; many commit various kinds of assault, some with hundreds of victims (Freeman-Longo and Wall 1986; Rosenfeld 1985). Pope (1990) has observed a high repetition (recidivism) rate among therapists who have sex with clients, an act he effectively argues is similar to rape and incest, and which structurally is similar to seduction of students by teachers.

Sexual offenders often carry out their repeated assaults in a highly stereotyped fashion, or *modus operandi*. Even those rapists who claim to be in love with their victims are likely to have a characteristic pattern of behaviors leading up to, during, and following the assault (Holroyd and Brodsky 1977). Although data are not widely available on harassers, it is likely that many practice "personal favorite" styles (Zalk, this volume).

Cindy, a student tutor, was assaulted by a client, who accused her of "exuding sexuality all over the place." She remained silent, embarrassed by the experience and frightened by the powerful message she felt she must be projecting. A month later, a co-worker filed a complaint of sexual assault against the same man, and Cindy spoke up. In the ensuing legal proceedings, another student victim came forward, and records revealed that several previously reliable tutors had resigned after working with this client.

This has important implications for any victim: Someone else probably has a similar story to tell. Unfortunately, we have a tendency to view each assault as an isolated incident, attributing the cause to the individual's character or behavior (Hamilton et al. 1987; Holcomb et al. 1991), and fail to look for a pattern. The legal implications are also important: It might be possible to identify others who have shared the experience and to pursue a group grievance.

Cultural Myths and Attitudes

Brownmiller (1975) provided an excellent review of the cultural mythologies surrounding rape, and the images of rape victims, extending back to biblical writings. Thanks to extensive educational efforts and the willingness of some victims to speak up, these attitudes now are less prevalent with respect to rape (Kanarian and Quina-Holland 1981). Raising awareness about sexual harassment was initially difficult because offensive behaviors had never been named or defined (Fitzgerald 1993). Increasingly, however, men and women respond similarly in making judgments about severe harassment (Dietz-Uhler and Murrell 1992). Studies have found that well over 90 percent of male and female college students labeled certain behaviors (sexual bribery, coercion, and assault) as harassment or rape (e.g., Konrad and Gutek 1986).

Stereotypes and misinformation continue to be applied to less severe forms of sexual assault. There is considerable disagreement even among women over whether verbal or other gender harassment and seductive approaches constitute harassment (Fitzgerald and Ormerod 1991; Tata 1993). Gender differences are stronger for these forms of harassment; women more likely than men to label them as harassment and less likely to attribute responsibility to the victims (reviewed in Rubin and Borgers 1990). Similar gender relationships in labeling and attributions of blame are found for stranger-versus date-rape scenarios (e.g., Holcomb et al. 1991). Both men and women who hold conservative attitudes about gender roles in society find harassment less serious or offensive (e.g., Dietz-Uhler and Murrell 1992).

Beliefs and myths about their (female) victims most likely allow sexual abuse as well. Perpetrators of rape and harassment (or both) also believe myths about women and rape (Malamuth 1988; Zaitchik and Mosher 1993). Pryor (1987) found high correlations among college men's scores on measures of likelihood to rape, likelihood to sexually harass, and related attitudes such as accepting rape myths and rejection of feminism, as well as behavioral measures of unnecessary sexual contact with women confederates in a neutral setting (a poker game). Bartling and Eisenman (1993) gave an extended set of measures to men and women, and confirmed these intercorrelations, though they were weaker for women. On the positive side, Mosher and Anderson (1986) showed increases in guilt, shame, and awareness among high-likelihood-to-rape college men after a guided rape fantasy.

The most common of the myths shared by rape and sexual harassment offenders (and other members of society) fall into the following three categories.

1. *Sexual assault is harmless and a form of seduction.* Throughout history, from ancient literature (e.g., Homer's Sirens) to our contemporary culture (e.g., Cindy's case), rape images are imbued with images of women as temptresses and men as helpless slaves to powerful sexual drives. In a study of college

students' attitudes toward date rape by Holcomb et al. (1991), one in three college men agreed that women "often" provoke rape, and 14 percent disagreed that a man could "control his behavior no matter how attracted he feels toward someone" (439). Meyer et al. (1981) advised women in the workplace to be careful about the way they dress and talk, because it could cause their co-workers to harass them. Fitzgerald et al. (1988) found that professors who dated students were more likely (than nondating professors of the same students) to perceive that women students had approached them.

2. *Women secretly need/want to be forced into sex.* Young men are taught by peers from an early age that women like to be forced into sex (Malamuth and Briere 1986) and that they "say no but mean yes."[3] Holcomb et al. (1991) found that nearly one in two college men endorsed the item "Some women ask to be raped and may enjoy it," and one in three agreed that a woman "means 'maybe' or even 'yes' when she says no" (493). It is not surprising, then, that harassment usually continues or escalates when the victim has given no positive response (Benson and Thomson 1982) or even a negative response (Alliance Against Sexual Coercion 1981). Harassers offer such excuses as "I know her better than she knows herself," while onlookers—like Beth's fellow graduate students—may suspect the victim really enjoyed the attention.

3. *Women do not tell the truth.* Until the 1970s, charges of rape had to be corroborated by a witness in some states, and judges' instructions to juries included a warning that rape is easy to accused and hard to prove (Brownmiller 1975). Such suspicion clouds victims of sexual harassment as well. Among the forms this mistrust take are questions of whether the victim has any grudge against the alleged offender or any other motive for complaining. Summers (1991) found more victim blame by college students if the harassed woman was described either as competing for the same job (a personal motive) or as a feminist (presumably, a political motive).

At a conference I attended a few years ago, a university counsel (a woman!) recommended that any time a sexual harassment case ended in acquittal, the university should consider bringing charges of false accusation against the alleged victim.

Victim Reactions

Sexual assaults across the continuum can cause severe trauma. Even when their lives are not in danger, victims of harassment report fear (Alliance Against Sexual Coercion 1981), loss of control, and disruption of their lives—experiences shared with victims of more physically dangerous traumas such as rape or natural disasters (Goodman et al. 1993; Quina and Carlson 1989). Ninety percent of the harassed graduate student women surveyed by Schneider (1987) reported negative reactions, and two thirds worried about potential and actual consequences.

"Looking back I don't know what I was afraid of," mused Deborah some years after her traumatic experience, as a student worker, of being fondled by a professor, "but I was terrified each time this man came toward me." At the end of the semester, Deborah wrote a short note about the professor's advances, gave it to her dorm advisor, and left school. She gave up her ambitions to become a scientist, and didn't return to college for many years.

Like other sexual assaults, harassment is also a violation. Physical contact is not necessary to create intense disgust, as noted in the reactions of women who receive obscene phone calls or street harassment (Sanford and Donovan 1984; Sheffield 1989). Because in sexual harassment the victim usually knows the offender, a violation of trust is almost always experienced. Most survivors also report feeling degraded by the experience, "stripped" of their dignity by the abuser. In these last two dimensions, harassment bears important similarities to incest (Hamilton et al. 1987).

When a nationally known scholar asked her to participate in his research project, Ellen was thrilled. Flattered by his attentiveness and excited by promises of a letter of recommendation to top graduate schools, she worked long hours, collecting data and writing up a paper herself. Shortly before it was to be sent for publication Dr. X delivered his ultimatum: no sex, no authorship. Ellen submitted, although disgusted by him physically, because she was so invested in the project. After they had sex, he laughed at her tears. The next day, he told her he did not consider her contributions very thoughtful or important, certainly not sufficient to deserve authorship, and that he had allowed her to work on these projects only because he knew how much she wanted to be near him. Ellen lost a year of work, her chance for a good graduate placement, and two publications. More importantly, she lost her confidence. Dr. X's comments were emotionally devastating, and ultimately felt more degrading to her than the sexual acts.

Costs to the Survivor

Emotional responses to rape and sexual harassment, of course, vary widely as a function of the severity of the assault, the number of experiences with assault, personal coping style, emotional vulnerability, and the availability of social support (reviewed in Quina and Carlson 1989). However, survivors of all the sexual assaults on our continuum have described long-term emotional aftereffects: grief, anger, fear, lowered self-esteem, helplessness, self-blame, shame, body image distortion, sexual dysfunction, and problems in other relationships (reviewed in Goodman et al. 1993 and Quina and Carlson 1989; see also Gutek and Koss 1993; Hamilton et al. 1987).

Emotional reactions are compounded by social losses. Among Schneider's (1987) graduate women, 29 percent reported a loss of academic or professional opportunities, and 14 percent reported lowered grades or financial support, because of sexual harassment. Employees who file charges of sexual harassment face a range of negative responses, including being demoted or fired (Fitzgerald 1993), lack of support or continued harassment by co-workers (Loy and Stewart 1984), and other insults. In too many cases, the survivor experiences revictimization by institutions during the complaint process, as administrators become defensive or even attack the victim. Academia has long maintained a facade of civilized, nonviolent behavior, and the disillusionment (in the value-free nature of scholarship and science, as well as the revered institution) can create emotional distress as well (Hamilton et al. 1987).

Too often, survivors find little comfort and support from others after rape or harassment. Those who remain silent, like Ann, often become increasingly isolated and begin to view themselves as deviant. To those who tell, family, friends, and co-workers might respond with rejection, blame, or disbelief. These secondary betrayals increase the severity of long-term emotional reactions, and interfere with healthy resolution.

At first, Faye didn't tell her mother about the abuse she was experiencing at work, or about the charges she had filed against the department chair. Unfortunately, a local newspaper picked up the story, and her mother learned about the case when a friend who lived near the university called her. Faye's mother, embarrassed by the publicity, accused Faye of "bringing shame upon the family," and said, "None of my friends would have gotten themselves into a mess like this—I raised you to know better!" Faye had to deal with the private anger of her family along with the public humiliation of a media-interest trial. Eventually she dropped the case, too emotionally exhausted to testify. Her family relationships continue to be strained.

Two other potential effects of sexual harassment are essential to understanding its long-term impact. First, sexual harassment can revive wounds from the survivor's past, including prior rape or incest (e.g., Crull 1982). Past sexual abuses have been shown to increase fear of sexual harassment (Holgate 1989) and to cause the survivor to reexperience the emotions of prior sexual abuse (Hamilton et al. 1987).

In addition, women who fear sexual assault tend to avoid potentially dangerous or abusive situations (Gordon and Riger 1989; Junger 1987; Schneider 1987), As women define a wider scope of situations as abusive, they restrict their scope of activities. In academia, this can translate directly into reduced willingness to seek out mentoring or related contacts, loss of opportunities for joint projects, and ultimately career damage. The costs to the organization can also be enormous (Fitzgerald 1993).

Sara, a well-established faculty member, had brought together several funding sources for a program on campus. When she reported on her activities at a department meeting, the chair commented with a wink, "Well, when we want someone to solicit, we know who to ask." She was humiliated and angry. She resolved not to get involved in future projects with the department, and was effectively silenced during meetings.

The chair later gave her a negative annual review, in spite of positive input from colleagues.

PATHS TO RESOLUTION

Individual resolution needs are as varied as the emotional responses to sexual assault. Many emotional responses, such as stress behaviors and fear, are reduced by time and distance from the trauma. Others, notably guilt, depression, feelings of helplessness, and relationship problems, may continue or grow worse with time, and may need more direct intervention. However, some paths to resolution have been found to help survivors of any sexual assault. Specific counseling approaches and guidance are offered by Quina and Carlson (1989). Some approaches are the following.

1. *Cast the experience as a sexual assault, and recognize its effects.* Survivors frequently use terminology that does not include the word *rape* (Fitzgerald et al. 1988; Russell 1984) or *harassment* (Brooks and Perot 1991). Thus many have difficulty recognizing their experience as victimization. It is helpful to use the words that fit the experience, validating the depth of the survivor's feelings, and allowing her to feel her experience was serious. In some cases, the terminology of sexual assault can help a person recognize the relationship among victimizations, as in Ellen's case. Recognizing past abuses may be important to this process, and in fact a harassment incident can lead the survivor to seek therapy to resolve prior trauma issues.

After her professor's sudden reversal of kindness, Ellen found herself in a prolonged depression. Her relationships with men, including other professors, became more sexual, although she didn't want to have sex with anyone. Finally, through counseling, she told for the first time about a sexual assault by a favorite uncle during her childhood. As she described her uncle's earlier praise and the devastating reversal of feelings she experienced after he assaulted her, she began to see both experiences clearly as sexual assaults rather than seductions. She recognized that she had come to respond to all men with a sense of resigned dread, anticipating a sexual assault. In fact, she interpreted any compliment from a man as a signal he wanted to have sex with her, since that was where compliments had led in the past.

2. *Find others with similar experiences and share stories.* It is essential to know that we are not alone. In therapy groups or just in self-disclosing conversations, or even in reading the stories of others, the sexual assault survivor can discover that she is rational, her reactions are normal, and others have overcome this trauma. Furthermore, as stories are compared, the cultural and social pattern emerges, and individual victim blame becomes more difficult to maintain.

Eventually, Ann went to a campus professional women's function, sitting quietly in the back of the room. A woman faculty member from another department came over to talk, and befriended her. In their discussion, Ann's new friend disclosed that one of Ann's colleagues—the same man who had approached Ann—had acted very strangely toward her. Suddenly, Ann was relieved of all her self-doubts about her situation. She also realized that sexual harassment was a serious problem on campus. She became active in the organization and helped organize a campus "speak-out" on sexual harassment.

3. *Recognize the personal losses of sexual assault, and allow a grieving process.* In addition to betrayals and life changes such as being fired or rejected by friends, the experience of sexual assault constitutes a major personal loss. Recovery from sexual assault often follows the analytic grief process, described by Rando (1984). The mourning process takes time, perhaps a year or more, and involves stages of acute stress, denial, depression, and anger prior to achieving peace with the reality of the loss. Survivors need to appreciate the depth of their feelings of loss, and to allow themselves to mourn, in order to achieve that peace.

Faye spent months being "tough" about her lawsuit—she described it as having to block out all emotions in order to survive (denial). When her mother accused her of shaming the family, her well-crafted armor came crashing down. She found herself unable to get up and get dressed in the morning, and had to seek therapy. Her therapist wisely recognized the signs of mourning and the reasons for Faye's grief, and eased her fears about her normalcy. When Faye did not feel strong enough to pursue the lawsuit, her therapist helped her mourn that loss as well, appreciating that she had done all she could, and helping her feel like a survivor rather than a victim.

4. *Join or form a feminist network and support group, to prevent future traumas for others as well as oneself.* In addition to rich friendships and the feelings of mutual caring in such a group, self-esteem can be raised by helping others, and a good strong feminist support group can provide real empowerment. Some campuses have formed casual support groups for women in general (e.g., "Women in Science"), where sexual harassment might be discussed; some counseling and women's centers provide facilitators for sexual assault survivors' groups. Any format is possible.

I finally left my first job and moved to a department with three faculty women. We started meeting for lunch regularly, just to touch base about ongoing events and to do problem solving when necessary. At least once a semester we went to dinner with the three secretaries, and had an evening of fun, support, empathy, and genuine mutual admiration. Now the number of women faculty in our department (of twenty-four) has grown to ten, our dinners have expanded to include women from related departments, and our empowerment—as well as our deep friendships—are extraordinary. A male colleague confided that he envied our network, because it allowed us to discuss our problems as well as our successes, unlike the men's bonding groups. We helped him form his own support group of gently men!

Notes

1. This framework is laid out in Quina and Carlson 1989, with appreciation to Hazel Temple for her articulation of the model. Other support for this view is found in Reilly, Lott, Caldwell, and DeLuca 1992 and in Stanko 1985.

2. All of the italic paragraphs in this paper are stories based on true situations. The names are fictitious, and details of the stories have been altered slightly to protect the identities of the victims and perpetrators. I am grateful to these women for sharing their deep personal pain with me.

3. Several men friends have described the early inculcation of these images of women—and of what "real men" do to women—especially through peer pressure during adolescence. I appreciate their honesty, and their efforts to overcome their own sexism.

References

Alliance Against Sexual Coercion. (1981). *Fighting sexual harassment: An advocacy handbook*, Boston: Alyson.

Bart, P., and O'Brien, P.H. (1985). *Stopping rape: Successful survival strategies.* Elmsford, NY: Pergamon.

Bartling, C.A., and Eisenman, R. (1993). Sexual harassment proclivities in men and women. *Bulletin of the Psychonomic Society, 31* (3), 189–92.

Benson, D.J., and Thomson, G.E. (1982). Sexual harassment on a university campus: The confidence of authority relations, sexual interest and gender stratification. *Social Problems, 29,* 236–51.

Bingham, S.G., and Scherer, L.L. (1993). Factors associated with responses to sexual harassment and satisfaction with outcome. *Sex Roles, 29* (3/4), 239–69.

Brooks, L., and Perot, A.R. (1991). Reporting sexual harassment: Exploring a predictive model. *Psychology of Women Quarterly, 15*)1), 31–47.

Brownmiller, S. (1975). *Against our will: Men, women, and rape.* New York: Simon & Schuster.

Check, J.V., and Malamuth, N.M. (1985). An empirical assessment of some feminist hypotheses about rape. *International Journal of Women's Studies, 8* (4), 414–23.

Copenhaver, S., and Grauerholz, E. (1991). Sexual victimization among sorority women: Exploring the link between sexual violence and institutional practices. *Sex Roles, 24* (1/2), 31–41.

Crull, P. (1982). Stress effects of sexual harassment on the job: Implications for counseling. *American Journal of Orthopsychiatry, 52,* 539–44.

Dietz-Uhler, B., and Murrell, A. (1992). College students' perceptions of sexual harassment: Are gender differences decreasing? *Journal of College Student Development, 33* (6), 540–46.

Fitzgerald, L.F. (1993). Sexual harassment: Violence against women in the workplace. *American Psychologist, 48* (10), 1070–76.

Fitzgerald, L.F., and Ormerod, A.J. (1991). Perceptions of sexual harassment: The influence of gender and academic context. *Psychology of Women Quarterly, 15,* 281–94.

Fitzgerald, L.F., Weitzman, L.M., Gold, Y., and Ormerod, M. (1988). Academic harassment: Sex and denial in scholarly garb. *Psychology of Women Quarterly, 12* (3), 329–40.

Freeman-Longo, R.E., and Wall, R.V. (1986). Changing a lifetime of sexual crime. *Psychology Today,* March, pp. 58–64.

Gallant, M.J., and Cross, J.E. (1993). Wayward puritans in the ivory tower: Collective aspects of gender discrimination in academia. *Sociological Quarterly, 34* (2), 237–56.

Goodman, L.A., Koss, M.P., Fitzgerald, L.F., Russo, N.F., and Keita, G. (1993). Male violence against women: Current research and future directions. *American Psychologist, 48* (10), 1054–8.

Gordon, M.T., and Riger, S. (1989). *The female fear.* New York: Free Press.

Grauerholz, E. (1989). Sexual harassment of women professors by students: Exploring the dynamics of power, authority, and gender in a university setting. *Sex Roles, 21* (11/12), 789–801.

Groth, A.N. (1979). *Men who rape: The psychology of the offender.* New York: Plenum.

Gutek, B. (1985). *Sex and the workplace.* San Francisco. Jossey—Bass.

Gutek, B., and Koss, M.P. (1993). Changed women and changed organizations: Consequences of coping with sexual harassment. *Journal of Vocational Behavior, 42,* 28–48.

Hamilton, J.A., Alagna, S.W., King, L.S., and Lloyd, C. (1987). The emotional consequences of gender-based abuse in the workplace. *Women and Therapy,* 6 (1/2), 155–82.

Holcomb, D.R., Holcomb, L.C., Sondag, K.A., and Williams, N. (1991). Attitudes about date, rape: Gender differences among college students. *College Student Journal, 25* (4), 434–39.

Holgate, A. (1989). Sexual harassment as a determinant of women's fear of rape. *Australian Journal of Sex, Marriage and Family, 10* (1), 21–28.

Holroyd, J.C., and Brodsky, A.M. (1977). Psychologists' attitudes and practices regarding erotic and nonerotic contact with patients. *American Psychologist, 32,* 843–49.

Jaffe, D., and Straus, M.A. (1987). Sexual climate and rape: A state-level analysis. *Archives of Sexual Behavior, 16* (2), 107–23.

Junger, M. (1987). Women's experiences of sexual harassment. *British Journal of Criminology, 27* (4), 358–83.

Kanarian, M., and Quina-Holland, K. (1981, April). *Attributions about rape.* Paper presented at the meetings of the Eastern Psychological Association, New York City.

Konrad, A.M., and Gutek, B. (1986). Impact of work experiences on attitudes toward sexual harassment. *Administrative Science Quarterly, 31,* 422–38.

Loy, P.H., and Stewart, L.P. (1984). The extent and effects of the sexual harassment of working women. *Sociological Focus, 17,* 31–43.

Malamuth, N.M. (1988). A multidimensional approach to sexual aggression: Combining measures of past behavior and present likelihood. *Annals of the New York Academy of Sciences, 528,* 123–32.

Malamuth, N.M., and Briere, J. (1986). Sexual violence in the media: Indirect effects on aggression against women. *Journal of Social Issues, 42* (3), 75–92.

Meyer, M.C., Berchtold, I.M., Oestreich, J.L., and Collins, F.J. (1981). *Sexual harassment at work.* Princeton, NJ: Petrocelli.

Mosher, D.L., and Anderson, R.D. (1986). Macho personality, sexual aggression, and reactions to guided imagery of realistic rape. *Journal of Research in Personality, 20* (1), 77–94.

Mosher, D.L., and Sirkin, M. (1984). Measuring a macho personality constellation. *Journal of Research in Personality, 18,* 150–63.

Mynatt, C.R., and Allgeier, E.R. (1990). Risk factors, self-attributions, and adjustment problems among victims of sexual coercion. *Journal of Applied Social Psychology, 20* (2, part 1), 130–53.

Pope. K. (1990). Therapist-patient sex as sex abuse: Six scientific, professional, and practical dilemmas in addressing victimization and rehabilitation. *Professional Psychology Research and Practice, 21* (4), 227–39.

Pryor. J.B. (1987). Sexual harassment proclivities in men. *Sex Roles, 17* (5/6), 269–90.
  Quina, K., and Carlson, N. (1989). *Rape, incest, and sexual harassment: A guide for helping survivors.* Greenwood, CT: Praeger.

Rando, T. (1984). *Loss and grief.* Lexington. MA: Lexington Books.

Reilly. M.E., Lott, B., Caldwell. D., and DeLuca, L. (1992). Tolerance for sexual harassment related to self-reported sexual victimization. *Gender and Society,* 6 (1), 122–38.

Reilly, M.E., Lott, B., and Gallogly, S.M. (1986). Sexual harassment of university students. *Sex Roles, 15,* 333–58.

Rosenfeld, A.H. (1985). Discovering and dealing with deviant sex [Report on work of Abel, Becker, and Mittleman]. *Psychology Today,* April, pp. 8–10.

Rubin. L.J., and Borgers, S.B. (1990). Sexual harassment in universities during the 1980s. *Sex Roles, 23* (7/8), 397–411.

Russell, D.E. (1984). *Sexual exploitation.* Beverly Hills. CA: Sage.

Sanford, L.T., and Donovan, M.E. (1984). *Women and self-esteem.* New York: Penguin Books.

Schneider, B.E. (1987). Graduate women, sexual harassment, and university policy. *Journal of Higher Education, 58* (1), 46–63.

Scott, R.L., and Tetreault, L.A. (1987). Attitudes of rapists and other violent offenders toward women. *Journal of Social Psychology, 127* (4), 375–80.

Sheffield, C.J. (1989). The invisible intruder: Women's experiences of obscene phone calls. *Gender and Society, 3* (4), 483–88.

Summers, R.J. (1991). Determinants of judgments of and responses to a complaint of sexual harassment. *Sex Roles, 25* (7/8), 379–92.

Tata, J. (1993). The structure and phenomenon of sexual harassment: Impact of category of sexually harassing behavior, gender, and hierarchical level. *Journal of Applied Social Psychology, 23* (3), 199–211.

Terpstra, D.E., and Baker, D.D. (1988a). A hierarchy of sexual harassment. *Journal of Psychology, 121* (6), 599–605.

————. (1988b). Outcomes ot sexual harassment charges. *Academy of Management Journal, 31* (1), 185–94.

Zaitchik, M.C., and Mosher, D.L. (1993). Criminal justice implications of the macho personality constellation. *Criminal Justice and Behavior, 20* (3), 227–39.

10

Coping with Sexual Harassment

Vita C. Rabinowitz

Wherever it occurs, from the street to the workplace, the experience of sexual harassment defines and limits women in sexual and gender-specific terms. When sexual harassment occurs in the academy, the repository of our best traditions and highest intellectual and moral aspirations, it is experienced by women as a particularly devastating betrayal of trust. Sexual harassment gives the lie to the belief that women compete on the same terms as men for the training and credentials required for professional careers.

This chapter addresses the questions of how female student victims of sexual harassment by male professors in the academy come to label, accept, and cope with their experiences. It begins by considering how students cognitively appraise harassment by faculty and why there is such deep-seated resistance to acknowledging the fact of their victimization. Next, it reviews the literature on the aftereffects of experiencing sexual harassment by a faculty member. Many women display a constellation of cognitive, behavioral, emotional, and physical symptoms following harassment that may persist long after the harassment ends and even change the course of their lives. Finally, it explores the implications of this' analysis for future research in sexual harassment and for those advocates, counselors, and educators who seek to help victims of harassment become survivors.

COGNITIVE APPRAISAL OF HARASSMENT

Most surveys of sexual harassment on college campuses define harassment in ways that include the following behaviors (see Fitzgerald, this volume):

- Gender harassment
- Seductive behavior—inappropriate and offensive but sanction-free sexual advances

- Sexual bribery—solicitation of sexual activity or other sex-linked behavior by promise of rewards
- Sexual coercion—coercion of sexual activity by threat of punishment, and
- Sexual assault—gross sexual imposition or assault

It is a reliible finding in the literature on sexual harassment on college campuses that about 30 percent of undergraduate women experience harassment by at least one of their professors during their four years in college (Dziech and Weiner 1984; Adams, Kottke, and Padgitt 1983). Yet only about 5 percent report the harassment or file a grievance (see Fitzgerald, this volume), and on the average only between 2 and 7 percent of the undergraduates report having directly confronted their harassers (Sexual Harassment Survey Committee 1985; Koss 1990). Many have speculated about why so few women seem to fight their harassment. To understand this, we need to understand the victimization process generally, and how it operates within the particular context of the university.

The Power of the Professorate

Research demonstrates that there is a high level of ambiguity among victims and observers about what causes and constitutes sexual harassment (Fitzgerald 1986; Jensen and Gutek 1982; Somers 1982). Perhaps nowhere is this ambiguity greater than in the academy, and it places female students at a distinct disadvantage.

Unlike employers in the workplace, professors usually do not have the power to hire and fire students, determine the size of their paychecks, or control their prospects for promotion. Their power as classroom instructors, research directors, and academic and career advisors is relatively indirect, and is often more subtly exercised than the power of employers. For this reason, it is easy for students and professors alike to underestimate the power a professor possesses in his interactions with his students. In fact, professors wield a great deal of power over students who depend on them for grades, letters of recommendation, academic and career counseling, and research and clinical opportunities. This is especially true of particular subgroups of students whose power and control in their relationships with their professors are constrained. These subgroups might include the following:

- Graduate students, whose future careers are often determined by their association with a particular faculty member
- Students in small colleges or small departments, where the number of faculty available to students is quite small
- Women of color, especially those with "solo" or "token" status (see DeFour, this volume)

- Students in nontraditional fields for women, like engineering, where women are vastly outnumbered by men (Dziech and Weiner 1984)
- Students who are economically disadvantaged and work at school for pay

Further contributing to the power difference between male professors and female students is the issue of the students' age. For the most part, female college students are younger and less experienced than their professors. They are at that developmental stage in which it is common to question values and standards of behavior and open themselves to new viewpoints and experiences. Professors are among the most available, attractive, and salient role models for undergraduates. Students often look up to their professors with great admiration, and attribute to them such appealing characteristics as brilliance, sophistication, wisdom, and maturity.

It is precisely this interaction of power relations, age difference, and gender stratification that makes the intrusion of sexual interest by male faculty members so problematic in the academy. Dziech and Weiner (1984) have written extensively about the vulnerability in the student status that makes sexual harassment by faculty a most intimate betrayal of trust. They state that sexual harassment by faculty injects a note of "incestuous sexuality" into the faculty-student relationship that shocks the average student. Indeed, research suggests that most students initially react with disbelief and doubt about even the most blatant sexual advances by faculty. And students often continue to believe that they have misinterpreted their instructor's behavior long after the facts warrant an appraisal of harassment (see Zalk, this volume).

Contributing to this ambiguity is the type of harassment that is so common to university settings. To be sure, physical assault, sexual coercion, and sexual bribery exist in the academy. In the UCLA survey (Sexual Harassment Survey Committee 1985), 29 percent of those students who reported being harassed described the harassment as including unwanted touching, sex-related attempted assault, or physical assault. Ordinarily, however, professors exert more subtle pressure on students than many oher authority figures apply to those over whom they have the power, commensurate with their more diffuse power and higher level of sophistication. For instance, their inducements are more gradual and less overtly linked to concree rewards or immediate sexual obligation than employers'. Instructors might, for example, accumulate credit over time for potential sexual favors by extraordinary friendliness, extra help with assignments, lenient grading, and extended deadlines. Benson and Thomson (1982, 243) describe an interview with a male faculty member who characterized some of his colleagues as being "fundamentally dishonest" in their dealings with female students. He noted that they praised female students to render them more vulnerable to future sexual advances and may have laid the groundwork for such overtures through patterns of selective attention and reward. Thus, through the considerable latitude inherent in the faculty role, a professor can avoid the potential danger of a blunt proposition while manipulating his authority over female students.

Despite the ambiguity inherent in most types of sexual harassment on campus, and the initial tendency of most students to give their professors the benefit of the doubt in labeling their behavior as harassment, students who are the targets of unwanted sexual interest will eventually come to acknowledge and manage this sexual pressure (Sexual Harassment Survey Committee 1985; Benson and Thomson 1982). The preponderance of research on harassment is clear in indicating that most harassers are persistent and that harassment rarely ends spontaneously and often escalates in the absence of direct action. But even after students correctly perceive their professors' sexual intent, they rarely come to view themselves as being harassed or victimized (Dziech and Weiner 1984).

Self-Blame among Victims

There is ample evidence that women experience an enormous amount of guilt and self-blame surrounding harassment, just as they do over rape and incest (Dziech and Weiner 1984; Koss 1990; Alliance Against Sexual Coercion 1981). In a society where women are held and hold themselves responsible for arousing men's sexual interest, it is easy to understand how female students can become conflicted about their own motives and behaviors. Students who have been harassed by professors frequently report worrying about what it was that they did to lead their professors on, or wondering what they might have done earlier to discourage him. Like other victims, students also report asking, "Why me?" or "What did I do to deserve this?" Theorists have come to understand these questions as reflecting the victims' search for meaning and control in their victimization, and as having some adaptive value (cf. Janoff-Bulman and Frieze 1983; Wortman 1983). But these questions also give the effect of putting the focus on the victims' behavior and "character-blaming" the victims instead of the perpetrator. Even if the victim could avoid second-guessing her behavior and motives, she knows that others would judge her harshly if the situation became known (Jensen and Gutek 1982; Kenig and Ryan 1986). In cases with sexual overtones, male and female observers typically wonder, "Did she encourage him?" or "Did she enjoy it?" (Dziech and Weiner 1984).

Commenting on the notions that men are at the mercy of their sexual appetites, which women need to curb, Dziech (1985) observed:

I think it's really damning that a handful of people have allowed us to believe that such behavior is normal of men. It's not a woman's job—

it's certainly not an 18-year-old student's job—to control her 40-year-old professor's sexual outbursts. (7)

There are other aspects of harassment by college professors that facilitate self-blame by students. Some students exonerate their professors and blame themselves because they have been flattered by their professors' interest in them. As noted previously, harassers in the academy frequently lay the groundwork for sexual advances by treating potential targets in a special way and convincing them that they occupy a unique place in the professors' thoughts and affections. All of us want to be attractive to others, and enjoy being well-treated. Women of college age may be especially vulnerable to flattery by professors because they exhibit a lesser sense of self-control over their own fates and less self-confidence in their academic abilities than do men of similar age (Kenig and Ryan 1986). It can be an exhilarating experience for a young woman to be the object of attention from someone who holds the prestigious position of professor, someone who might choose any one of a hundred students to favor, but has chosen *her*. It is easy for her to fall into the trap of blaming herself for her normal desire to be noticed and appreciated. Another self-blaming scenario among students, albeit a self-serving one, centers on the belief that the professor's passion is fueled by relatively noble sentiments, like spiritual kinship and romantic love, that she alone inspires. Not surprisingly, research suggests that self-blame is especially prevalent among women who have complied with their harassers in any way (Alliance Against Sexual Coercion 1981).

Rejection of Victim Status

As uncomfortable and distorted as it may seem to blame oneself for unwanted sexual attention, there is much evidence from the literature on victimization that blaming oneself and refusing to acknowledge that one is being harassed or victimized is preferable to claiming the status of the victim (cf. Janoff-Bulman and Frieze 1983). Many women who sustain harm do not perceive themselves as victims. Koss (1985) reported that, of a group of college women, all of whom had had experiences that met legal definitions of rape, only 57 percent regarded themselves as rape victims. Similarly she also, noted that in a national sample, 30 percent of the women who were raped by strangers and 62 percent of the women who were raped by acquaintances did not view their experiences as any type of crime. So common is this refusal to accept victim status among people who have suffered that Estep (reported in Koss, 1990) proposes that people do not become victims simply by virtue of sustaining injury or loss. According to Estep, there are three steps to becoming a victim: (a) sustaining damage, (b) perceiving the injury as unfair and oneself as victimized, and (c) seeking redress. There is great resistance against moving from step *a* to step *b* because almost no one covets the label *victim*. The traditional view of victims, particularly in our society, is that they are losers.

To acknowledge victimization is to acknowledge losses of the following:

- Control over one's future
- The belief in a "just world," where good things happen to good people
- A belief in personal invulnerability
- A belief in the world as safe and predictable
- A positive image of the self

More than anything else, these shattered assumptions may be the vehicle through which negative life events like harassment wreak their damage.

STUDENT COPING STRATEGIES

Denial, Avoidance, and Deceit

Given this cognitive appraisal by student victims, we can now consider the coping behaviors commonly exhibited by students who are compelled to deal with unwanted sexual attention by faculty.

Initially, many victims attempt to deny that unwanted sexual advances took place. Surveys of harassment repeatedly cite such self-statements by students to the effect that the professor could have been just kidding, or lonely, or interested in their social lives, or in being friends, or in trying to be nice, etc. (cf. Benson and Thomson 1982; Dziech and Weiner 1984; Alliance Against Sexual Coercion 1981). Those students who acknowledge the sexual intent early on typically deny the power relations that underly the situation and thus fail to regard those intentions as harassing. Researchers have found that student responses to recognizing this sexual pressure range from the belief that the professor is in love with them to the notion "That's how men are; you can't blame a guy for trying," (Dziech and Weiner 1984; Alliance Against Sexual Coercion 1981). Underlying the first belief is the assumption that the relationship is one between equals, and the student is truly free to behave as she pleases. The second belief is predicated on the notion that sexually harassing behaviors by men are inevitable and normal, if not harmless.

When the coercive nature of the sexual advances cannot be denied, the relationship becomes a distinct source of distress for students. Students attempt to ignore or trivialize unwanted sexual advances for as long as possible (Benson and Thomson 1982).

It is a very common coping mechanism for women to believe, despite evidence to the contrary, that the harassment will stop if they are unresponsive or unavailable. Women receive a good deal of social support from men and other women for denying, ignoring, anl trivializing harassment (Alliance

Against Sexual Coercion 1981; Reilly, Lott, and Gallogly 1986). Reilly, Lott, and Gallogly (1986) cite the report of one victim of sexual harassment in the academy that highlights this problem:

> Her boyfriend told her that "you should expect it, and you shouldn't run in shorts when other people aren't." Others told her: "You should just ignore it, don't respond, don't yell, don't throw things." (147)

Reporting that one has been harassed by a professor may be met with skepticism or ridicule, and attracts scrutiny of one's behavior or motives.

For the vast majority of undergraduate victims, coping with the problem of harassment means using indirect tactics to forestall escalation. Benson and Thomson (1982) report that most women invent other appointments or enlist friends to accompany them to instructors' offices to avoid being alone with their harassers. Many students in their survey cut class and even hid to prevent encounters. Two respondents in the Benson and Thomson study wrote: "I never went to his office hours" and "I no longer went to his section because of the uncomfortable situation" (245). Dressing down, and trying to appear less attractive, is another strategy frequently employed to avoid notice (Dziech and Weiner 1984).

Even when undergraduate women are directly confronted with the bluntest propositions, their management tactics remain indirect. A majority of the students who responded to the Reilly, Lott, and Gallogly (1986) and Benson and Thomson (1982) surveys who experienced the most persistent, coercive harassment reported counteracting propositions by talking about their boyfriends or husbands, expressing reluctance to becoming sexually involved with faculty or married men, or claiming no time for social activities. Students seemingly resort to these tactics to try to keep their professors at bay at the same time that they avoid the dreaded direct confrontation. Yet the mention of a boyfriend or other social concerns as an excuse for a rebuff legitimizes the intrusion of sexual interest in the faculty-student relationship, reaffirms that women continue to be defined in relation to men, and undermines the perception of women as independent scholars and professionals.

Study after study confirms that students rarely express their true feelings in these situations (Kenig and Ryan 1986; Dziech and Weiner 1984; Benson and Thomson 1982; Reilly, Lott, and Gallogly 1986; Jenson and Gutek 1982). The widespread incidence of denial, avoidance, and deceit leads to the inescapable conclusion that, on some level, most students are highly sensitive to the power imbalance between faculty and students. Students do not in fact feel free to refuse unwanted advances. There is evidence to suggest that fear of retaliation by the scorned professor is the paramount reason that students attempt to cope with harassment by indirect means (Dziech and Weiner 1984;

Benson and Thomson 1982). More than one-third of the harassment victims in Jenson and Gutek's study reported that they did not file a grievance against their professors because they "thought it would be held against [them] or that [they] would be blamed" (128).

Some victims do not report the harassment because they feel some sympathy for their harassers. Students frequently express great concern over whether the harasser might lose his job or his family if a complaint is filed against him (Alliance Against Sexual Coercion 1981; Dziech and Weiner 1984). It is not uncommon for harassers to count upon—and play upon—this concern (Dziech and Weiner 1984).

Finally, there is some evidence that students fail to report cases of harassment because they are unaware that the university makes provisions for such complaints and feel powerless to act effectively (Reilly, Lott, and Gallogly 1986).

What do the student victims eventually do? Research suggests that students who have had little prior involvement with a harasser most often try to withdraw from fbture interactions whenever possible (cf. Dziech and Weiner 1984; Benson and Thomson 1982). Missed educational opportunities are the most obvious price paid for this coping strategy. Students quit research teams, drop courses, switch majors, and drop out of college altogether in numbers that we will never know because of what many people perceive as harmless flirtations. Dziech and Weiner (1984) suggest that the extraordinary dropout rates among women in nontraditional fields like engineering are largely due to the high rates of sexual and gender harassment encountered there.

Sexual Advances in Well-Established Relationships

Some of the most severe consequences of harassment appear to be suffered by students who enjoy long-standing professional contact with a faculty member before his sexual interest in them becomes evident (Glaser and Thorpe 1986; Benson and Thomson 1982). Studies suggest that students in these situations come to question the reasons for their previous academic success. They become skeptical about the value of their professor's praise and encouragement. And they tend to become suspicious of male faculty in general, as these students report to Benson and Thomson (1982):

I became disillusioned with academia. [The experience] lessened by confidence on whether it was worth going through with it all.

[With male faculty, I am] more cautious about being open and friendly. (246)

Sexual Intimacies between Professors and Students

The consequences of harassment are apt to be particularly severe when students enter into sexual relationships with faculty members (Alliance Against

Sexual Coercion 1981; Glaser and Thorpe 1986; Reilly, Lott, and Gallogly 1986). Becoming sexually involved with a professor increases the likelihood that the student will report feelings of being in love, being used or betrayed, and of being responsible for her professor's behavior (see Zalk, this volume).

Recent research by Glaser and Thorpe (1986) surveyed 464 female clinical psychologists about their graduate school experience of sexual intimacy with and sexual advances from psychology educators. Consistent with earlier research (cf. Pope, Levenson, and Schover 1979), the results indicated that sexual contact is quite prevalent overall, with 17 percent of respondents reporting sexual contact and 22 percent of recent doctoral recipients reporting sexual intimacy. As Pope, Levenson, and Schover (1979) found, the rate of sexual intimacy with professors was especially high (34 percent) among doctoral candidates who were divorcing or separating during training.

At the time of the sexual contact, 72 percent of the respondents reported receiving unwanted sexual advances from educators that did not lead to sexual contact. The majority of these women declined the advances directly (30 percent) or indirectly (60 percent), suggesting that graduate women may be more likely than their undergraduate counterparts to reject advances directly. But they paid a price for this directness: 45 percent of respondents who declined advances reported not only significant subsequent harm to the working relationship but also punitive damage from educators. These include lowered grades, withdrawal of support and opportunities, and sharply sarcastic criticism of work once praised. Many respondents volunteered that they had seriously considered leaving graduate studies in the face of these pressures.

These findings, along with the results of previous studies on the sexual harassment of students, led Glaser and Thorpe (1986) to issue this stern warning to psychologists:.

> The profession needs to acknowledge and address the reality of a population of women of unknown numbers who after gaining keenly competitive admission to doctoral studies in psychology, take leave of that effort, not through lack of ability or diligence, but through disgust, dissuasion, and misuse. The numbers need not to be large for that to be an appalling and shameful situation. (50)

Sexual Harassment Syndrome

Missed educational opportunities, lost time and effort, and feelings of disillusionment and disappointment are high prices, indeed, to pay for one's victimization by harassment. But they are not the only costs. Tong (1984) has identified a "sexual harassment syndrome" that describes the emotional and physical symptoms suffered by victims of sexual harassment generally. Based on her analysis and the survey data on reactions of student victims in the academy (cf. Sexual Harassment Survey Committee 1985; Reilly, Lott, and Gallogly 1986; Benson and Thomson 1982; Dziech and Weiner 1984; Jenson and Gutek 1982), the following consequences of harassment may be experienced by student victims:

- General depression, as manifested by changes in eating and sleeping patterns, and vague complaints of aches and pains that prevent the student from attending class or completing work
- Undefined dissatisfaction with college, major, or particular course
- Sense of powerlessness, helplessness, and vulnerability
- Loss of academic self-confidence and decline in academic performance
- Feelings of isolation from other students
- Changes in attitudes or behaviors regarding sexual relationships
- Irritability with family and friends
- Fear and anxiety
- Inability to concentrate
- Alcohol and drug dependency

Previous research has not yet systematically investigated the conditions under which victims will experience any of these consequences. There is some evidence to suggest that to the extent that the sexual harassment resembles the trauma of rape or incest, the student may exhibit the characteristics of post-traumatic Stress Disorder as described in DSM-3R (cf. Koss, 1990; Gagliano 1987). These characteristics include intense terror, reexperiencing the event, hypervigilance, helplessness, increased arousal, eating disorders, avoidance of stimuli associated with the event, and numbing of general responsiveness.

DIRECTIONS FOR FUTURE RESEARCH

Clearly, future research needs to address the questions of what factors increase the likelihood that sexual harassment will occur, will persist, and will cause emotional, academic, physical, or other harm to students. We need information about the structural, institutional, and departmental factors that encourage or sustain harassment. We also need further information about the faculty, student, and relationship characteristics that increase the chances that harassment will take place or will be especially harmful to victims. Based on this review of the sexual harassment literature, we can isolate certain characteristics that merit further investigation for their possible contribution to the experience of harassment:

Faculty Characteristics:

- Faculty member is tenured (cf. Sexual Harassment Survey Committee 1985; Dziech and Weiner, 1984).
- Faculty member has senior status in the department (Dziech and Weiner 1984).

Student Characteristics:

- Woman is a graduate student (Glaser and Thorpe 1986).
- Student, if undergraduate, is a graduate school aspirant (Benson and Thomson 1982; Dziech and Weiner 1984).
- Student has returned to school after a hiatus (Dziech and Weiner, 1984).
- Student is divorced or separated (Glaser and Thorpe 1986; Pope, Levenson, and Schover 1979).
- Student is a member of a racial or ethnic minority (DeFour, this volume).
- Student holds traditional, as opposed to progressive, sex-role beliefs (Jenson and Gutek 1982).
- Student is economically disadvantaged (Dziech and Weiner 1984; Alliance Against Sexual Coercion 1981).
- Student is a "loner"—has no visible ties to other students, or to faculty or family (Dziech and Weiner 1984).
- Student is physically attractive (Dziech and Weiner 1984).

Characteristics of the Faculty/Student Relationships:

- Faculty member and student are in the same field (Dziech and Weiner 1984).
- Faculty member has more than the usual amount of power over student's evaluations, outcomes, or prospects (i.e., is a mentor, dissertation advisor, honors sponsor, employer) (Glaser and Thorpe 1986; Alliance Against Sexual Coercion 1981).
- Faculty member and student have had a long, well-established relationship prior to the onset of harassment (Benson and Thomson 1982).
- Faculty member and student have had a sexual relationship (Glaser and Thorpe 1986; Alliance Against Sexual Coercion 1981).

MOVING FROM VICTIM TO SURVIVOR: IMPLICATIONS FOR ADVOCATES AND COUNSELORS

The present chapter conceptualizes sexual harassment in the academy as coercive because it is supported by and can be enforced through the power of the professorate and is reinforced through its confounding with age and gender. The implications of this analysis for the therapeutic treatment of harassment are that victims have suffered from the abuse of power, feel power-less, and need to be empowered.

Specifically, victims need validation of their perceptions and feelings about their experiences. They need to know how common the experience of harassment is, and how common are the tendencies to deny, ignore, and trivialize those experiences. They need to understand harassment in terms of power relations instead of sexual relations, and to debunk the myths about how such behavior is normal among men. Depending upon the particulars of their situation, victims may need referals to psychologists, physicians, college officials, or lawyers. More commonly; however, they may need information about interventions that are inherently supportive and empowering for harass-ment victims. These include skills training, participation in support groups, and the sharing of information about confronting harassers or filing formal complaints against them.

Several therapists and researchers have begun the process of elucidating the specific steps that counselors might take in treating victims of harassment (Gagliano, 1987). The following prescriptions borrow from their work and the present analysis of sexual harassment.

Specific Advice for Counselors, Advocates, and Educators:

- Acknowledge her courage by citing how difficult it is to label, report, and discuss harassment.
- Encourage the ventilation of her feelings and perceptions, and validate them. It is not the role of a counselor to determine whether harass-ment as legally defined has occurred. Female students have little to gain from making false charges of harassment against professors and rarely make them (cf. Fitzgerald 1987).
- Provide information to students about the incidence of harassment to assure her that she is not alone. Communicate the research findings about the consequences—emotional, behavioral, and physical—of harrassment to assure her that the harassment is not harmless to victims and that she is not overreacting.
- Counteract her tendencies to blame herself for the harassment by explaining its origins in power relations. Assure her that she is in no way responsible for her professor's sexual interest in her, regardless of her behavior or dress. Tendencies to self-blame are likely to be strongest in women who have delayed reporting the harassment or who have complied with the harassers in any way. Self-blame is also likely to be high in those who have "voluntarily" entered into sexual relationships that they now wish to end, but cannot because of pres-

sure to continue. These women need to know that their past behavior may well have been constrained, and in any case that past activities do not control future choices.

- Aid the student in her search for meaning in the victimization. She will need to rebuild shattered assumptions. As Koss (1990) notes, the experience of sexual harassment can change people's lives. Cherished, lifelong beliefs about authority figures, men, academia, and the professorate may be lost forever. The student's positive self-image and professional prospects may be blighted. She will need to acknowledge, assess, and "mourn" these losses before she can establish the new beliefs and support systems that will guide her future academic and professional career.

- Monitor the physical, emotional, academic, and interpersonal toll of harassment. The strain of coping with harassment will have some predictable effects on a woman's physical and emotional health. The student may need help in seeing seemingly unrelated problems in her life as the consequences of harassment. The counselor should monitor the use of maladaptive coping strategies like denial and avoidance. The counselor should be cognizant of the incident of illness and emotional distress so that he or she can help the client make the correct attributions about the sources of the problem so that the proper referrals will be made.

- Offer a safe forum for the expression of anger and resentment. Victims sometimes become very angry when they become fully aware of how their lives have been changed by this experience. Many resent how their behavior has been manipulated and constrained by the harasser. Some have experienced reprisals in the form of lowered grades, unfair criticism, and lost opportunities. Anger is an entirely normal and appropriate response to being harassed. Because it is so dangerous to express their anger to the harasser and so unrewarding to seek sympathy from friends and fellow students, it is critical that women have a safe place to ventilate their anger. Without such a place, women sometimes allow their anger to damage their other relationships (cf. Alliance Against Sexual Coercion 1981).

- Offer skills training. Depending upon the particular problems presented by the harassment and the personality of the victim, the student may need training in one of the following areas: assertiveness, problem solving, decision making, self-efficacy, or stress management.

- Teach the student to validate herself. The socialization process turns women into skillful self-discounters. Gagliano (1987) has proposed a way to counteract this pattern through positive "self-talk"—silently repeating to oneself validating, supportive, positive messages. Another of her suggestions is the use of "stoppers." Stoppers are easy and effective behavioral techniques designed to cut off self-blaming, powerless, and other negative cognitions. Clients may receive significant validation and support from participating in self-help groups for victims of harassment or speaking to member of a sexual harassment panel.

The goal of the intervention should be to enlighten the client about her options and support her to make informed choices about her life, even if the counselor disagrees with those choices. This is the crux of empowerment.

References

Adams, J.W., J.L. Kottke, J.L. and Padgitt, J.S. (1983) Sexual harassment of university students.*Journal of College Student Personnel, 24*, 484–90.

Alliance Against Sexual Coercion. (1981) *Fighting sexual harassment: An advocacy handbook.* Boston: Alyson.

Benson, D.J., and Thomson, G.E. (1982) Sexual harassment on a university campus: The confluence of authority relations, sexual interest, and the gender stratifications. *Social Problems, 29*, 236–51.

Dziech, B.W. (1985). Indiana University Women's Affairs Office develops sex education package. *Behavior Today Newsletter*, 15 July 1985, 5–7.

Dziech, B.W., and Weiner, L.L. (1984). *The lecherous professor: Sexual harassment on campus.* Boston: Beacon Press.

Fitzgerald, L.F. (1986, August). *The lecherous professor: A study in power relations.* Paper presented at a meeting of the American Psychological Association, New York.

————. (1987, August). *Sexual harassment: A new look at an old issue.* Symposium presented at a meeting of the American Psychological Association, New York.

Gagliano, C. (1987, January). *Surviving sexual harassment: Strategies for victims and advocates.* Paper presented at the Women in Higher Education conference, Orlando.

Glaser, R.D., and Thorpe, J. (1986). Unethical intimacy: A survey of sexual contact and advances between Psychology educators and female graduate students. *American Psychologist, 41*, 43–51.

Janoff-Bulman, R., and Frieze, I.H. (1983). A theoretical perspective for understanding victimization. *Journal of Social Issues, 39*, 1–17.

Jensen, I.W., and Gutek, B.A. (1982). Attributions and assignment of responsibility in sexual harassment. *Journal of Social Issues, 38*, 121–36.

Kenig, S. and Ryan, J. (1986). Sex differences in levels of tolerance and attribution of blame for sexual harassment on a university campus. *Sex Roles, 15*, 535–49.

Koss, M. (1990). Changed lives: The psychological impact of sexual harassment. In M. Paludi (Ed.), *Ivory Power: Sexual Harassment on Campus.* Albany: State University of New York Press.

Pope, K.S., Levenson, H., and Schover, L. (1979). Sexual intimacy in psychological training: Results and implications of a national survey. *American Psychologist, 34*, 682–89.

Sexual Harassment Survey Committee (1985). A survey of sexual harassment at UCLA. Administrative Report, February.

Somers, A. (1982). Sexual harassment in Academy: Legal issues and definitions. *Journal of Social Issues, 38*, 23–37.

Tong, R. (1984). *Women, sex, and the Law.* Totowa, NJ: Rowman & Allanheld.

Wortman, C.B. (1983). Coping with victimization: Conclusions and implications for future research. *Journal of Social Issues, 39*, 195–221.

11

Addressing Sexual Harassment:
Strategies for Prevention and Change

Maryka Biaggio and *Arlene Brownell*

Recent studies suggest that sexual harassment is a significant problem on university campuses. Dziech and Weiner (1984), after reviewing available surveys, conclude that 20 to 30 percent of female students report sexual harassment during their college years, though rates vary according to specific categories of harassment, such as generalized sexist remarks, seductive behavior, sexual bribery, sexual coercion, and sexual assult (Fitzgerald and Shullman 1985). In some settings (e.g., male-dominated educational institutions), the incidence may be even higher. For instance, a 1994 General Accounting Office (GAO) report found that nearly 60 percent of female Air Force Academy cadets polled by the GAO in 1991 said they experienced one or more forms of harassment a couple of times a month or more, and 90 percent of them said they felt they were harassed because they were women ("Female Cadets Seek Harass-Free Campus" 1994). While ample evidence indicates that sexual harassment is a serious and widespread problem (Till 1980), most instances of harassment go unreported (Swecker 1985). In fact, victims are likely to report only severe harassment (Brooks and Perot 1991; Jones and remland 1992; Sullivan, Redner, and Bogat 1985), even though harassment at any level of severity is not likely to stop without some action taken by the victim (Benson and Thomson 1982; Sandler and Associates 1981). Further, when instances of harassment are confronted or when complaints are filed, it is often difficult to satisfactorily redress the problem or prevent similar recurrences.

Benson and Thomson (1982) note that harassment has numerous adverse effects on female students: self-doubt, loss of confidence in academic ability, disillusionment and cautiousness with male faculty, and suspicion of male instructors. Unfortunately, many victims report that they cope with harassment by avoiding or dropping classes, avoiding the perpetrator, bringing friends to meetings with the professor, mentioning boyfriends or partners to demonstrate lack of interest in the harasser's actions, attempting to ignore the behavior, switching majors, or dropping out of the program (Adams, Kottke, and Padgitt 1983; Benson and Thomson 1982; Dziech and Weiner 1984; Jones and Remland 1992). Thus, harassment can result in significant costs to female students—often limiting their academic opportunities.

This chapter discusses several issues raised when university faculty and student affairs staff address occurrences of sexual harassment of students on university campuses. How do institutional policies and procedures affect the incidence of harassment and disposition of complaints? How can institutions educate about and challenge attitudes that can perpetuate harassment? How should faculty, staff, or counselors who become aware of harassment respond? What are the consequences of reporting, and how can negative consequences be minimized?

Although males may be victims of sexual harassment, the focus here is on female victims. Also, in recent years there has been much publicity and discussion about false reports of sexual harassment. False reports can occur, and such reports can improperly impugn on the reputation of the purported perpetrators. But it appears that underreporting occurrences of harassment is a more insidious problem than is false reporting. In a survey and follow-up interview study of sexual victimization (Biaggio, Watts, and Brownell 1989), it was noted that although most victims told someone they trusted about their sexual victimization experience (including sexual harassment), very few reported the incident to someone in a position of authority. Sullivan, Redner, and Bogat (1985), in a survey of 219 undergraduate women, found that the women believed that victims of harassment were more likely to report to a woman than to a man, and were more likely to report problems to someone outside of the perpetrator's department. It has been the experience of the authors that this is generally true. Thus, it behooves university personnel at all levels, and especially women, to be prepared to deal with reports of harassment. In order to responsibly and effectively address sexual harassment on campus, possible actions must be thought through carefully. In this chapter we will examine issues and possible strategies that can be employed to effectively contend with the problem of sexual harassment as it affects university students. Though the focus here is on strategies that can be employed in the university setting, many of the strategies may be applicable to other settings as well.

Sexual harassment has been defined in a variety of ways. The Equal Employment Opportunity Commission defines sexual harassment as unwelcome sexual advances, requests for sexual favors, and other verbal or physical conduct of a sexual nature and asserts that such occurrences constitute unlawful sex discrimination under certain circumstances. The National Advisory Council on Women's Educational Programs argues, "Academic sexual harassment is the use of authority to emphasize the sexuality or sexual identity of a student in a manner which prevents or impairs that student's full enjoyment of educational benefits, climate or opportunities" (Till 1980, 7). A typical university policy states that "sexual harassment is definfed as: 1) sexual contact of any nature which is not fully and mutually agreeable to both partiets; 2) any verbal written, or pictorial communication of a sexual nature, which has the effect of intimidating the person or persons receiving the communication; and 3) unwelcome sexual advances, requests or contacts of any nature, when such acts are intended to be or have the effect of being the basis for either implicitly or explicitly imposing favorable or adverse terms and conditions of employment or academic standing" (Indiana State University 1981, AH-11). Each of these definitions focuses on the sexual nature of the advance, whether it be physical, pictorial, or verbal, though the extent to which the definitions address legality or possible outcomes varies.

THE EFFECTS OF UNIVERSITY POLICIES ON REPORTING AND PROCESSING

There are a number of ways in which policies can impede or facilitate investigation and fair disposal of harassment complaints. For instance, restrictive and technical definitions of sexual harassment might not take into account the more subtle and insidious forms of harassment. The way in which harassment is defined will affect the institution's policy and procedures.

Definitions of sexual harassment are important because they can educate the community and promote discussion and conscientious evaluation of behavior and experience. Students learn that certain experiences are officially recognized as wrong and punishable; professors are put on notice about behaviors that constitute sexual harassment; and administrators shape their understanding of the problem in a way that directs their actions on student inquiries and complaints. A definition can set the tone for the university community's response to sexual harassment. (Crocker 1983, 697)

For a comprehensive analysis of university definitions of sexual harassment and the implications of these definitions for policy, the reader is referred to Crocker (1983) and Somers (1982). Results of a study by Brooks and Perot (1991) suggest that university officials could facilitate more reporting if public policy statements and educational efforts encouraged potential victims to identify and affirm feelings of offensiveness in response to inappropriate sexual behaviors from faculty members.

According to the Equal Employment Opportunity Commission, it is the employer's responsibility to prevent and redress sexual harassment. On the university campus, the affirmative action office is usually charged with the execution of this responsibility. However, level of commitment to affirmative action principles varies widely, and many affirmative action officers have lost status and influence during the past five years because of the Reagan and Bush administrations' civil rights policies (Evans 1985). Further, since it is typically faculty, staff, or counselors who first learn of specific occurrences of harassment, it behooves them to be aware of university policies and the affirmative action officer's role in the system. Further, university officials receiving complaints should also be aware of any state laws that might make it mandatory to report certian alleged criminal or dangerous behaviors.

It must be recognized that not all universities appoint an affirmative action officer and that, in those institutions that do appoint an officer, she/he might be vested with little authority. And further the affirmative action officer is an employee of the university administration, which is responsible for structuring the officer's role and responsibilities. Thus, affirmative action officers might be perceived as having, and might in fact have, conflicting loyalties in their role that can conspire against their effectiveness.

Legal precedent has been established for hearing sexual harassment grievances under the stipulations of Title IX (*Alexander vs. Yale* 1977, 1980). Further, in 1981 the Office of Civil Rights of the U.S. Department of Education determined that sexual harassment of students is a violation of Title IX of the 1972 Educational Amendments, thereby serving notice that universities are liable if they do not have adequate grievance procedures to handle students' complaints (Adams, Kottke, and Padgitt 1983). Many institutions have responded by articulating policy statements defining harassment and formalizing procedures for processing complaints. In fact, in 1993 the California state legislature amended the state education code to require that all California educational institutions have a written policy on sexual harassment informing students that everyone, regardless of their gender, should enjoy freedom from discrimination of any kind in educational institutions (McKenna and Cuneo Labor and Employment Bulletin 1994). Administrators of universities that have not yet formulated policy statements might be more inclined to do so if administrators viewed the policies as protecting the institution (from negative pulicity, lawsuits, etc.) as well as its students and employees.

However, the mere presence of a policy does not insure its effectiveness. The U.S. Merit Systems Protection Board (1981) recommends specific procedures for addressing harassment: A memorandum from the university president condemning harassment should be distributed; materials should be designed to educate people about their rights, definitions of sexual harassment, and procedures for dealing with complaints; adequate procedures must be developed to handle complaints; and a system to monitor and evaluate these procedures at all levels should be implemented. Policy statements should thus provide a clear understanding of harassment, possibly including examples of different types of harassment, and should spell out procedures for filing complaints and persons to whom inquiries or complaints should be directed.

Many educational institutions will require approval of any institutional policies (including sexual harassment policies) by governance units within the institution. Faculty groups are likely to be concerned about academic freedom, and an instructor's ability to express views or convey knowledge (e.g., about sexuality in psychology classes, or about anatomy in health or medical classes). Given this concern, it would be desireable for descriptions or verbal harassment to be clearly differentiated from communications that are in the service of the educational enterprise. Such a delineation will clarify the goals of the policy for faculty members.

University policies might impede rather than facilitate the processing of harassment complaints. If, as the U.S. Merit Systems Protection Board recommends, a good monitoring system is in place, then there is a means to document inadequacies in the policy and to revise the policy accordingly. If a monitoring system is not in place, then the responsibility for evaluating the policy is diffused and there may be no clear means to address inadequacies in the policy. The implementation of an objective monitoring body with sufficient credibility and support to be effective in changing policy may be critical to achieving an effective policy.

Further, university procedures might conspire against effective disposal of complaints. It must be recognized that harassment charges are embarrassing to institutions, and administrators might wish to suppress reports even though such suppression potentially places institutions in greater legal jeopardy than a direct response to complaints would.

There are a number of ways in which procedures might obstruct remediation. For example, procedures might fail to protect the confidentiality of either the victim, the accused perpetrator, or both. It is difficult to establish reporting and grievance procedures that contain sufficient safeguards for confidentiality to both encourage their use by students and assure the rights of the accused while simultaneously discouraging false allegations (Adams, Kottke, and Padgitt 1983). For instance, the Alliance Against Sexual Coercion, an organization whose sole purpose is to counteract the sexual harassment of women, suggests that a credible grievance procedure will provide four guarantees: confidentiality, impartiality in investigating, protection from retaliation, and an assurance of a viable administrative remedy if the allegation is proved. In addition, the name of the complainant should be known only to the individual investigating the complaint and the person accused during the investigation (Alliance Against Sexual Coercion 1980). This degree of confidentiality theoretically protects the rights of both the complainant and the accused during the investigation. Institutions may consider a "limited identification" policy that would allows the student to protect her/his identity from the professor named in a complaint when certain circumstances are met. (Such a policy has been utilized by Yale University [Dziech and Weiner 1984]).

Students face a number of risks in reporting harassment—for example, retribution, loss of educational opportunities, and identification as a "trouble-maker." Procedures that are insensitive to the risks a student takes in bringing forth a complaint may fail to protect the student's interests during the proceedings. For instance, we know of one university where procedures called for the complaint to be placed in the student's academic file rather than in the accused perpetrator's file. Such practices may promulgate revictimization of the student while protecting the perpetrator. There should be a clear statement that the university does not allow any retaliatory actions to be taken against people filing complaints, and this policy should be strictly enforced (Alliance Against Sexual Coercion 1980). A student who requests to transfer course sections or drop a course should be allowed to do so.

Unfortunately, the prevalence of harassment far exceeds the incidence of reports (Sullivan, Redner, and Bogat 1985). The small number of victims who report sexual harassment suggests that a silent reaction to the harassment is typical; unfortunately, this silence helps to maintain the existence of harassment (Brooks and Perot 1991). Students may believe that their complaint will not be taken seriously, that they will be blamed for the harassment, or that they will be retaliated against (Adams, Kottke, and Padgitt 1983). Yet it has been found that students who complain to appropriate persons or to the harasser about being harassed are more effective in ending the incidents than are those who do not (Benson and Thomson 1982; Sandler et al. 1981). Institutions must provide clear and safe means of reporting harassment and must widely disseminate this information about reporting procedures to students as well as to faculty and staff. The reporting of sexual harassment will serve to change the university climate over time, by alerting university officials to the extent of the problem and by demonstrating to students that their complaints will be taken seriously (Sullivan, Redner, and Bogat 1985).

Grievance procedures should spell out remedies and disciplines for proven charges of harassment. "A clear statement that disciplinary action or remedial action will be pursued if the charge is proved is a clear statement that the university thinks that sexual harassment is wrong and is willing to back up their words with actions" (Alliance Against Sexual Coercion 1980, 18). Further, disciplinary or other actions should not focus on the victim (e.g., allowing the student to leave a course or obtain a grade change), but on the harasser, specifying what disciplinary action will be applied. The range of disciplinary measures—from a reprimand to dismissal—should be spelled out.

Meek and Lynch (1983) and Diamond, Feller, and Russo (1981) recommend that, in addition to formal grievance mechanisms, an informal grievance procedure be made available to students. When such an informal procedure was instituted at the University of Florida, more students reported instances of sexual harassment. Apparently, many students simply wanted to make their experience known and to have someone ask the perpetrator to stop the offensive behavior. However, it is not clear how effective this informal procedure would be in preventing future occurrences of harassment by the same perpetrators or in protecting from retribution those students who have continued contact with the perpetrator.

> Ironically, successful informal mediation deceives the campus community into not knowing or acknowledging that there are harassment problems. Files are not kept, public knowledge is minimal, and sanctions for an offender are limited. Without some form of record keeping, the same professor can abuse individual students one at a time and be given the same "second chance" over and over again. Without an attempt to document the frequency of problems on a campus, the institution can deceive itself into believing that sexual harassment is only a minor issue. (Dziech and Weiner 1984, 175)

Still, the benefits of an informal procedure may make it worth considering as an additional, but not the sole, means to address harassment. Meek and Lynch (1983) recommend that certain professionals in student affairs be responsible for dealing with complaints. They contend that speaking to student affairs personnel is less threatening than reporting the problem in the offender's department. They strongly suggest that these professionals be women, since they assume that female students would be more comfortable talking with women about harassment, an assumption borne out in research by Sullivan, Redner, and Bogat (1985).

An effective policy against harassment will not place all the responsibility on victims to report and thus stop harassment. Clearly, persons with low status are at risk when they report offenses by persons with higher status. Thus, perpetrators must come to understand the inappropriateness of harassment and the harmful effects it can have on victims. Universities might institute preventive or educational approaches in an attempt to increase awareness of the problem among faculty, staff, and students. Workshops or guest lectures that address the specialized concerns of deans, department heads, and faculty can be useful preventive devices (Dziech and Weiner 1984), particularly if units or departments with high incidents of harassment are targeted. These educational programs might deal directly with the problem of sexual harassment, or they might approach it as part of the larger issue of the "chilly classroom climate" to which women students are subjected (Hall and Sandler 1982). Though such programs can be coordinated by the administrative offices on campus (e.g., Affirmative Action), faculty and staff who are familiar with the extent and nature of the problem can serve as valuable consultants or workshop leaders, particularly if they are knowledgeable about effective means to raise awareness about the problem.

Training investigators on how to conduct an effective, legally defensible investigation is also critical (McKenna and Cuneo Labor and Employment Bulletin 1994, 17): "Any educational institution which implements proper training will see immediate dividends. Students will inherently know that the investigation is being taken seriously and addressed professionally when they observe a skilled investigator in action."

ATTITUDES ABOUT SEXUAL HARASSMENT

Dissemination of information will not necessarily affect attitudes that perpetuate victimization. We know that victims' responses to harassment vary as a function of their attributions and attitudes about harassment and gender roles. Even if students recognize the inappropriateness of sexual advances, they may fear that their report will not be taken seriously or that they will be blamed for the event. In fact, Jensen and Gutek (1982) found that women who evidenced behavioral self-blame were less likely than other victims to either report harassment or talk to someone about it. Similarly, women with traditional sex-role beliefs were more likely to blame themselves and other women for harassment. Jensen and Gutek thus suggest that only by changing people's general sex-role beliefs can one affect a change in the attitudes toward harassment.

In recent years researchers addressing victimization have called attention to the relationship between attitudes regarding sexual victimization (adversarial sexual beliefs, rape myth acceptance, etc.) and tolerance of sexual victimization (Biaggio, Brownell, and Watts 1988; Burt 1980; Diamond 1980; Murrell and Dietz-Uhler 1993; Weis and Borges 1973). In effect, such attitudes perpetuate the occurrence of victimization by minimizing its significance, blaming the victim, recognizing only extreme forms of victimization, and conspiring against the reporting of victimization.

Harassment is a pervasive phenomenon, and failure to recognize or report even "mild" occurrences increases the probability it will continue. The provision of a clear definition of the many forms of harassment, however, increases the probability that individuals will recognize and report such behaviors. On most campuses, there is no clear mechanism for disseminating information about problems such as sexual harassment. Thus, universities must address not only the nature of the information to be provided but also the means or forums for dissemination of this information. The Alliance Against Sexual Coercion (1980) recommends the following means of making university policy public: Distribute the grievance procedure annually to all students and include the procedure in the faculty code book; have a committee that specifically reviews the work of the grievance committee or officers; and generate public discussion by annually placing the issue of sexual harassment on the agendas of the governing bodies of the university.

Several myths about harassment serve to minimize the problem. According to one view, a woman should be complimented, not incensed, if confronted with male sexual interest and should accept the fact that men have been genetically selected for sexual arousal (Hagen 1979). Others hold that women use their attractiveness and sexual wile to gain favors from male professors. However, as Benson and Thomson (1982) point out, these views neglect the formal role relationships between superiors and subordinates, and thus fail to recognize the coercive nature of these "attentions." "Rather than having a unilateral 'sex advantage,' female students face the possibility that male instructors may manipulate sexual interest and authority in ways which ultimately undermine the position of women in academia" (Benson and Thomson 1982, 240). Another myth is that female students unjustly accuse their professors of harassment, thus ruining their professors' reputations and endangering their livelihood. We know that most victims do not report harassment (Swecker 1985); contriving a complaint is an even less likely occurrence.

Evans (1978) points out a number of myths about harassment, including that sexual harassment is fun, harassment is trivial, only women in low-status jobs are sexually harassed, and sexual harassment is easy for women to handle. These contentions generally ignore, trivialize, or discount the seriousness of the problem for women. Evans cites survey data from the Working Women United Institute (1978) indicating that women experience negative emotional reactions to harassment, harassment can have serious economic repercussions for women, harassment is pervasive across various employment settings, and women faced with harassment are placed in a double bind or no-win position. Research on the effects of harassment on university campuses reveals that female students experience reactions and difficulties similar to those reported by female employees (Benson and Thomson 1982).

Three constellations of attitudes and beliefs that foster acceptance, and thereby prevent the elimination, of sexual harassment have been identified by Swecker (1985). The first is the point of view that accepts and extends stereotypical heterosexual relationships to the environment at large. According to this belief, men and women are naturally attracted to each other, it is natural for men to pursue their attractions, and men and women both enjoy this "pursuit." This belief leads to a tacit denial of harassment as a problem. The second recognizes a power differential by which superiors gain sexual favors from subordinates. Though this view acknowledges sexual harassment as a power issue, it narrowly defines harassers as superiors and views harassment as normative. The third barrier involves the unquestioning acceptance of gender-role norms that maintain male dominance and female powerlessness. According to this standard, women who react negatively to harassment are stepping out of line and creating problems. To alter the context in which harassment is allowed to occur, systemic prevention, rather than case-by-case remediation, will be necessary to prevent sexual harassment. It is not sufficient to have the proper policies in place. "Administrators must recognize that they are a part of a system which perpetuates the conditions allowing sexual harassment to occur" (Swecker 1985, 6).

A variety of interventions can be implemented in order to challenge attitudes that perpetuate harassment:

1. Key individuals within organizations can be targeted (e.g., residence advisors in dormitories, student government officials, department chairs, unit supervisors, sorority and fraternity presidents) for attendance at workshops; these persons can be informed about the institutional policy against harassment and can be given responsibility to disseminate the information. Swecker (1985) describes a project that was directed toward training administrative personnel both to define and recognize sexual harassment and to effectively respond to sexual harassment. The training approach was interactive and experiential; administrators responded to video vignettes and rehearsed responses to various situations. Unfortunately Swecker did not report on the effectiveness of this project. At the very least, however, the present authors hypothesize that periodic exposure to such workshops would sensitize university administrators to the problem of sexual harassment.

2. New student orieptations are another arena for disseminating information about institutional policies that prohibit sexual harassment. Diamond, Feller, and Russo (1981) recommend that all incoming students be given pamphlets defining sexual harassment and advising students of their rights as well as how to avoid harassment, when possible, and how to handle harassment. Materials on sexual harassment should be included in student handbooks.

3. Some introductory classes (e.g., psychology, sociology, business) might be appropriate places for discussion of sexual harassment, thereby providing students with definitions and information about institutional policies. Such classes as psychology of women or human sexuality are excellent arenas in which in-depth discussions about sexual harassment can occur. Persons who are not employed by the

university are likely to be valuable resources for special presentations in such classes. However, because this strategy can reach only a proportion of students, it should not be the sole means to provide information to students.

4. Items relating to sexist comments or sexual invitations can be placed on teaching evaluations. This format would provide the opportunity for students to anonymously report their perceptions of such classroom behavior, and would serve as a mechanism for feedback to instructors wishing to monitor their own behavior.

5. Student newspapers can be urged to publish articles on sexual harassment, indicating why it is a problem and explaining what the university's policies and procedures are.

6. The names of persons who are known to be chronic harassers can be made public or passed through the student grapevine. Some students do avoid taking classes from people known or rumored to make inappropriate overtures to students (Adams, Kottke, and Padgitt 1983).

7. One interesting tactic comes from the experience of a graduate student. Several women students in a small graduate class discovered upon comparing notes that they had each been sexually harassed by the same professor. They decided to collectively tell him that they found his behavior discomforting. They waited until the next occurrence and then as a group nondefensively but firmly confronted him and requested that he not repeat such behaviors. Apparently the group strategy was effective in this case; the women felt empowered by working together and their strategy nullified any protests of innocence. Obviously not all professors will respond positively to this intervention, but the group process provides support and allows for a collective assessment of the probably outcome prior to taking action.

8. Community activist strategies can be used both to raise public awareness and to protest particular instances of harassment. The strategies suggested by the Alliance Against Sexual Coercion (1980) include these: having a speak-out or protest with press coverage; picketing offending faculty members' classes and using other public humiliation/confrontation tactics; conducting a survey showing the prevalence of harassment at the university and widely publicizing the results; sending warning letters to harassers informing them that they are engaging in illegal, sexually discriminatory behavior and listing the ways they can be legally prosecuted; and blitzing the media with stories and flyers. *Women's Forum Quarterly*, a publication of Seattle Central Community College in Washington, publishes

the winner of the "Sexist Remark of the Quarter Award"; the
purpose is to increase awareness of sexism and bias in the classroom
(Dziech and Weiner 1984). Hall and Sandler (1982) similarly recommend that local statistics be developed to promote recognition of
the specific institution's problem while counteracting the tendency
to avoid or deny the problem. Many of the above tactics involve
naming alleged perpetrators, thus raising the possibility of libelous
activity, and should not be endorsed lightly. On the other hand,
collective and public protest can be quite effective in bringing
problems to the attention of insensitive or recalcitrant offenders
or university administrators.

It is generally more desirable to employ preventive, proactive attitude
and behavioral change strategies than to simply confront individuals. When
university employees and students become fully aware of the problem and
the inappropriateness of harassment, then they will be more likely to monitor
their own behavior and the behavior of those around them. Thus, if a critical
mass of people in a unit or department do not condone harassment, they
may be able to exert pressure to conform on those who fail to recognize or
take the problem seriously.

PROCESSING COMPLAINTS

It is not unusual for university faculty, staff, or counselors to become
aware of instances of harassment through either observation, hearsay, or the
self-reports of victims. Many complicated issues arise at this point.

1. If a student reports being the recipient of sexual overtures but does
not define them as harassment, should these events be defined as harassment
by the person to whom they are reported? It would seem appropriate to label
this experience harassment for the following reasons. Victims typically experience humiliation, embarrassment, and guilt following harassment; a turning
point in their feelings and approach to the harassment occurs when they
recognize that they are not to blame and that the harasser is violating their
rights (Salisbury et al. 1986). Further, Fitzgerald and Shullman (1985) found
that 50 percent of the female students they surveyed reported having experienced at least one incident of harassment when specific behaviors meeting
legal definitions of harassment were described to them without the use of the
term *harassment*. However, when asked directly if they had been harassed, only
1 percent indicated that they believed they had been sexually harassed. Thus,
naming the problem can validate the victimization experience and facilitate
the victim's understanding of the harassment, as well as encourage receptivity

to a range of support services available to counteract the isolation typically experienced by harassment victims.

2. Is it appropriate for a faculty person or student affairs staff member to advise the victim or to intervene on the victim's behalf? Victims are likely to confide in persons that they trust when reporting incidents of harassment. Thus, even though university employees might not be formally designated for this role, they might become involved in harassment cases by virtue of the victim's seeking advice from them. In such instances, we believe that persons confided in should serve as advocates for the victim, even if only to counsel the victim on whom else to approach for further advice. However, advocates should not coach the victim to describe her experiences in a certain way, since this might constitute grounds for dismissing any complaint or for awarding compensation for wrongful charges to the alleged perpetrator.

If there is no established grievance procedure or if the designated procedure thwarts the process and has been ineffective in remedying harassment, then how should the advocate proceed? Eventually the advocate may decide to work for institutional policy reform. Initially it is important to help the victim cope with the harassment. The advocate may be able to suggest a range of adaptive strategies found in the literature or refer the victim to someone who is kowledgeable about coping with specific types of harassment (e.g., the Affirmative Action Officer, an appropriately trained counselor, or someone who has coped successfully with harassment experiences). In addition, the student can be referred to support groups available at the student counseling center or the campus women's center. If there is an effective grievance procedure (formal and/or informal) in place at the institution, then advocates can inform the victim on how to proceed.

If the victim wishes to file a formal grievance, then acting as an advocate means determining how this can be accomplished with minimal risk to the victim. It may be necessary for the advocate to consult—confidentially, and with the permission of the victim—with others on campus who are knowledgeable about how to effectively use the system. If the victim wants the advocate to informally help to prevent further harassment, then the advocate must determine how to effect this end. If the advocate happens to be the administrative superior of the perpetrator, then the advocate can discuss the problem directly with the perpetrator. However, if this is not the case (and it is not likely to be, because the women who are most likely to be sought out for assistance by victims are most concentrated in the lowest academic ranks), then the advocate should encourage the victim to solicit help from a superior who might be sympathetic to the difficulty and who would confront the perpetrator. If the victim is reticent, then the advocate can offer to go with the victim to the superior. If the victim is unwilling to verbally request assistance from another person, then the advocate might suggest that the victim put her request in writing. If the victim refuses to act further on her own behalf, the advocate must decide whether or not to proceed. However, the advocate's case would be quite tenuous unless armed with the victim's complaint. Further, some institutions may not be willing to investigate complaints by proxy, unless the alleged conduct is thought to put the university community at risk. Of course, all of these possibilities should be discussed nrith the victim before any action is taken. We recommend that the advocate document in writing the details of the complaint and hold this documentation in a confidential file in case other victims seek out the advocate with complaints about the same perpetrator. If a pattern of victimization emerges for a particular perpetrator, the university might be more receptive to investigating a complaint by proxy. Also, victims previously reticent to file a grievance might be more willing to do so if they know that others have experienced harassment by a particular perpetrator.

3. Several other practical issues must be considered if a university employee becomes aware of instances of harassment. Should the victim be urged to lodge a formal complaint? To what extent should the possible costs and benefits to the victim of pursuing a formal complaint be presented (e.g., see Adams, Kottke, and Padgitt 1983)? What is the role of the advocate in protecting the victim from further harassment? Obviously, it is important that the victim understand the grievance procedure and its probably impact on her/him. Complaints and lawsuits increase the stress on the complainant and usually do so until final resolution (Salisbury et al. 1986). Victims need to have as much information as possible in order to make an informed decision about filing a formal complaint. Of course, it may not be possible to anticipate all the possible outcomes or problems, but advocates should be thorough in exploring these issues.

If the victim is in a position to be harmed by the perpetrator, steps should be taken to remove the threat of continued harassment or of retaliation for reporting the harassment. The possibility of continued harassment or retribution should be examined in a manner that communicates to the victim that her/his well-being is important. It is not uncommon for victims to worry about retribution, and a sensitive discussion of such a possibility is likely to validate the victim's reactions to the harassment.

Taking steps to minimize negative consequences for the victim usually requires the cooperation of the head of a unit or department. This necessitates disclosure of the harassment and, therefore, must be acceptable to the victim. However, the victim should be made aware of the options and their likely consequences and then be allowed to make the final decision. Special arrangements may sometimes be necessary in order to avoid limiting the victim's access to the same educational opportunities as are provided to other students. For instance, if the student is taking a required course that is taught only by the perpetrator and does not wish to continue with this instructor, then an alternative should be developed by those who are in a position to do so.

4. Should the person to whom harassment is reported urge the victim to gather evidence or document specific events? How can the desire for confidentiality or discretion be balanced with the necessity of providing clear evidence? Diamond, Feller, and Russo (1981) recommend that a written and dated record of all incidents, with witnesses noted, be kept. Gathering information does not mean that a report must be filed, though the investigation of a report is facilitated if specific instances have been documented. Victims can be urged to document instances of harassment but keep the documents in their own possession until they decide whether or not to file a formal grievance.

Some (e.g., Sullivan, Redner, and Bogat 1985) recommend that results of hearings in which someone has been found guilty of sexual harassment be made public. (Institutions might wish to seek legal counsel about the advisability of publishing the names of offenders, however, since this could lead to legal action). This would communicate to students that such charges are taken seriously and that the university administration is handling complaints to the satisfaction of students. Alternately, the numbers and dispositions of complaints could be publicized, without disclosing the identities of involved parties. In any event, if harassment is proved, one potential benefit in releasing the outcome of the investigation is that such publicity sends a clear message about the unacceptability of harassment and might deter subsequent harassment.

DEALING WITH THE CONSEQUENCES OF HARASSMENT

Victims often suffer serious consequences of harassment (Benson and Thomson 1982) or are adversely affected by the proceedings when complaints are filed. Numerous stress reactions have been reported in surveys and in therapy: physical aches and ailments, confusion and self-blame, feelings of humiliation and alienation, reduced ability to concentrate, loss of self-esteem, decreased self-confidence, lessened ambition, sleeplessness, fear, anxiety, depression, anger, and disillusionment with male professors (Benson and Thomson 1982; Safran 1976: Working Women United Institute 1978). It is important that advocates understand the negative effects of harassment; even if victims do not seek counseling, advocates can help them understand the link between the experience of harassment and their stress reactions, thus normalizing their experience.

While evidence suggests that harassment will not stop without some counterresponse on the part of the victim or an advocate, the act of filing a complaint in itself is stressful and can generate adverse consequences (Boring 1978). Following the filing of a report, victims should be prepared to be questioned, blamed, and possibly transferred from the situation in ways that might call attention to them (e.g., having an advisor or course section changed). Advocates should be aware of the possible consequences of filing complaints and should expect to be called upon to provide victims with support during this process. It is not uncommon for victims to experience social isolation from classmates who do not want to be associated with a "troublemaker," or even from friends who are inexperienced in helping others cope with such stress. There is little data on percentages of victims who receive professional counseling as a direct consequence of harassment, though Ginorio (1982) reports that 9 percent of all student victims talked to a counselor or psychologist about sexual harassment. It may be helpful to refer the victims of harassment for counseling, though this should be done in a way that does not imply blame or disturbance on the part of the victim. Salisbury et al. (1986) found that group support was more effective than individual counseling in aiding individuals to cope with the specific effects of sexual harassment, especially in the initial, acute stages of the harassment experience. They report that the group provided validation of the victim's feelings, understanding of the victimization experience, and support, and that the group process was related to changes in self-image, radicalization, activism, and healing.

It must also be recognized that advocates of victims may suffer adverse consequences as a result of supporting victims during either informal or formal compalint proceedings. Advocates may be asked to testify on the victim's behalf, adding a quasi-legal component to their role. Since women are more likely than men to become privy to reports of harassment, and since women are more heavily represented in the lower ranks and are less likely to be tenured (Sandler 1986), they may be more vulnerable than employees who are in higher, tenured ranks.

> Academic women find themselves in a Catch-22. They cannot function as responsible professionals and women if they ignore the sexual harassment of students, but they cannot confront it or be advocates without great risk to their own credibility and status within the institution. (Dziech and Weiner 1984, 154)

When formal complaints are investigated, there will be disruptions in the department or unit. Those who profess ignorance about harassment as well as those who have long observed and come to tolerate mild occurrences of harassment are likely, at a minimum, to experience feelings of ambivalence. They might question the validity of the charge, minimize or rationalize the perpetrator's responsibility for the occurrence, or lapse into victim blaming. Even if they do not want to vindicate a colleague when serious harassment has been charged, they might experience a sense of loyalty to the person they have worked with for years, which further distorts their objectivity. The advocate's role in the process may become suspect, and she/he may be perceived as encouraging a "troublemaker" or being one herself.

Advocates may also find that some colleagues, in an attempt to resolve their own ambivalence, will want to discuss the charge with them. Questions of confidentiality arise here, and the victim's requests must be honored. Advocates should be aware that judicious discussions of the issues are important because they might shape the course that any hearings will take and they can influence future policies in that unit.

CONCLUSION

Faculty and student affairs staff who are in the position of observing and being told about instances of sexual harassment must consider a multitude of issues in determining how to effectively address the problem. It is important that advocates understand the institutional policies regarding harassment and know how to use the grievance procedure that is in place at their university. Many victims might not want to pursue a formal complaint and might simply request the support and guidance of the advocate to whom they are reporting the incident. In either situation the advocate must consider the extent to which she/he can be effective without engendering the resentment of the accused or others. When significant risks are involved for the advocate, she/he might be most effective by requesting that the student also report the harassment to a superior or another colleague who would be sympathetic to the victim and who might be in a better position to act on the complaint. The decision to actually file a complaint should be an informed one; victims have the right to understand the complaint process and difficulties they may encounter. Similarly, the investigation should be carried only as far as the complainant wants it to go (Alliance Against Sexual Coercion 1980).

Perhaps as more university faculty, staff, and students become aware of the seriousness of the problem of sexual harassment, there will be greater recognition of its subtle forms and harmful effects. With this awareness, university administrations might more actively combat harassment on their campuses. We hope that this discussion contributes to awareness, and thus enhances the effectiveness of *all* individuals who become involved in addressing sexual harassment on campus.

References

Adams, J.W., Kottke, J.L., and Padgitt, J.S. (1983). Sexual harassment of university students. *Journal of College Student Personnel*, 484–90.

Alexander v. Yale University, 459 F. Supp 1 (D. Conn.), 1977.

Alexander v. Yale University, 631 Fed. 2d. 178 2nd Cir. (D. Conn.), 1980.

Alliance Against Sexual Coercion. (1980). *University grievance procedures, Title IX, and sexual harassment on campus.* Boston: Alliance Against Sexual Coercion.

Benson, D.J., and Thomson, G.E. (1982). Sexual harassment on a university campus: The confluence of authority relations, sexual interest and gender stratification. *Social Problems, 29,* 236-51.

Biaggio, M.K., Brownell, A., and Watts, D. (1988), March). *Sexual victimization: Attitudes related to victimization.* Paper presented at the Association for Women in Psychology conference, Bethesda, MD.

Boring, P.Z. (1978). *Filing a faculty grievance.* Washington, DC: Women's Equity Action League.

Brooks, L., and Perot, A.R. (1991). Reporting sexual harassment: Exploring a predictive model. *Psychology of Women Quarterly, 15,* 31-47.

Burt, M.R. (1980). Cultural myths and support for rape. *Journal of Personality and Social Psychology, 38,* 217-30.

Crocker, P.L. (1983). An analysis of university definitions of sexual harassment. *Signs: Journal of Women in Culture and Society, 8,* 696-707.

Diamond, I. (1980). Pornography and repression: A reconsideration. *Signs: Journal of Women in Culture and Society, 5,* 686-701.

Diamond, R., Feller, L., and Russo, N.F. (1981). *Sexual harassment action kit.* Washington, DC: Federation of Organizations for Professional Women.

Dziech, B.W., and Weiner, L. (1984). *The lecherous professor: Sexual harassment on campus.* Boston: Beacon Press.

Evans, G. (1985). Affirmative-action officers say their influence on campus is waning, blame Reagan's policies. *Chronicle of Higher Education,* 6 November, pp. 27, 31.

Evans, L.J. (1978). Sexual harassment: women's hidden occupational hazard. In J.R. Chapman and M. Gates (Eds.), *The victimization of women* (203-23). Beverly Hills: Sage.

Female Cadets Seek Harass-free Campus. (1994). *Denver Post,* 9 May, pp. A1, A6.

Fitzgerald, L.F., and Shullman, S.L. (1985, August). *The development and validation of an objectively scored measure of sexual harassment.* Paper presented at the American Psychological Association convention, Los Angeles.

Ginorio, A. (1982). *The sexual harassment of University of Washington students.* Unpublished manuscript.

Hagen, R. (1979). *The bio-sexual factor.* New York: Doubleday.

Hall, R.M., and Sandler, B.R. (1982). *The classroom climate: A chilly one for women?* Washington, DC: Association of American Colleges, Project on the Status and Education of Women.

Indiana State University. (1981). *Indiana State University Handbook.* Terre Haute: Indiana State University.

Jensen, I.W., and Gutek, B.A. (1982). Attributions and assignment of responsibility in sexual harassment. *Journal of Social Issues, 38,* 121–36.

Jones, T.S., and Remland, M.S. (1992). Sources of variability in perceptions of and responses to sexual harassment. *Sex Roles, 27,* 121–42.

McKanna & Cuneo Labor and Employment Bulletin. (1994, March). *Effectively responding to student generated sexual harassment complaints* (16–17). San Franscisco: Author.

Meek, P., and Lynch, A. (1983). Establishing an informal grievance procedure for cases of sexual harassment of students. *Journal of the National Association for Women Deans, Administrators, and Counselors, 46,* 30–33.

Murrell, A.J., and Dietz-Uhler, B.L. (1993). Gender identity and adversarial sexual beliefs as predictors of attitudes toward sexual harassment. *Psychology of Women Quarterly, 17,* 169–75.

Safran, C. (1976). What men do to women on the job: A shocking look at sexual harassment. *Redbook,* 217–24.

Salisbury, J., Ginorio, A.B., Remick, H., and Stringer, D.M. (1986). Counseling victims of sexual harassment. *Psychotherapy, 23,* 316–24.

Sandler, B. (1986). *The campus climate revisited: Chilly for women faculty, administrators, and graduate students.* Washington, DC: Association of American Colleges, Project on the Status and Education of Women.

Sandler, B., and Associates. (1981). Sexual harassment: A hidden problem. *Educational Record, 62,* 52–57.

Somers, A. (1982). Sexual harassment in academe: Legal issues and definitions. *Journal of Social Issues, 38*, 23–32.

Sullivan, M., Redner, R., and Bogat, G.A. (1985, August). *Sexual harassment of university students: Students' perceptions and responses.* Paper presented at the meetings of the American Psychological Association, Los Angeles.

Swecker, J. (1985, August). *Straightening out the power curve: Eliminating sexual harassment in institutions.* Paper presented at the meetings of the American Psychological Association, Los Angeles.

Till, F. (1980). *Sexual harassment: A report on the sexual harassment of students.* Washington, DC: U.S. Department of Education.

U.S. Merit Systems Protection Board. (1981). *Sexual harassment in the federal workplace: Is it a problem?* Washington, DC: U.S. Government Printing Office.

Weis, K., and Borges, S.S. (1973), Victimology and rape: The case of the legitimate victim. *Issues in Criminology, 8*, 71–115.

Working Women United Institute. (1978). *Responses of fair employment practices agencies to sexual harassment complaints: A report and recommendations.* New York: Working Women United Institute.

12

Investigating Complaints of Sexual Harassment

Helen Remick, Jan Salisbury, Donna Stringer, and *Angela Ginorio*

Sexual harassment is a major problem in higher education. Although promulgation of policy and good educational efforts on sexual harassment are effective responses to sexual harassment, they increase the likelihood that complaints of sexual harassment will be brought. How complaints are handled determines whether others will bring complaints and whether legal action will follow. If complaints are handled fairly and in a timely manner, virtually all complainants and alleged harassers will accept the process. Word will circulate that complaints are taken seriously and handled well. An effective complaint process will encourage genuine complaints, discourage complainants from going to outside agencies, and deter potential harassers. Bungled complaints will discourage potential complainants from seeking on-campus relief, sending them to outside agencies, and signal harassers that they can continue their behaviors with impunity.

Sexual harassment is a type of gender-based discrimination and must be understood within the context of power and inequality of opportunity (Stringer et al. 1990; Walker, Erickson, and Woolsey). Because it involves sexuality, the investigation of sexual harassment complaints presents a number of challenges. Sexual harassment is not like other forms of discrimination; the offending behaviors are seen as intimate and sexual, therefore difficult to discuss. While other forms of discrimination often involve rejection of a person, accompanied by a refusal to interact, sexual harassment is typified by a refusal to leave someone alone. Each case is unique, requiring a specially tailored response; it is important to be sensitive to the differences in each situation and to avoid trying to use exactly the same response to each complainant. This emphasis on the need for individualized responses does not preclude an understanding of sexual harassment as discrimination against an entire class of people.

This chapter proposes investigative and organizational strategies to address sexual harassment complaints in the context of sex discrimination. The practices have evolved over a decade, and the authors have applied them in a variety of settings.

Confidentiality

Institutions should be very careful about promising confidentiality to persons involved in complaints. No more should be offered than can be guaranteed. Promises of confidentiality must take into account the initial investigation and what occurs in any possible subsequent appeal processes or legal actions. Parties will also want to understand how much will be told to others during the normal course of an investigation. Institutional policies vary as to how much is told the respondent. We recommend that the respondent be given the name(s) of the persons bringing a complaint as well as details of what is being alleged. The supervisors of both parties will also need to know about the complaints in order to be alert to possible retaliation and to add any relevant information they might have. Witnesses named by either party will also need to know names and sometimes details in order to respond to issues raised in the complaint.

Public institutions need to be aware of the public disclosure laws of their particular state, which may or may not leave investigative files or reports open to public disclosure. In Washington State, for example, the public disclosure law was interpreted in 1990 by *Cowles Publishing v. Brouilet* to mean that investigative files of most state agencies (with exceptions only for those such as the Highway Patrol and the Washington State Human Rights Agency specifically named in the law) are subject to public disclosure. The case in point was brought by a newspaper against the state superintendent of schools, asking for the investigative files of teachers who had lost or relinquished teaching certificates as a result of accusations of sexual misconduct. The state supreme court ruled that the entire contents of the investigative files should be made public upon request, because it is in the public's best interest to know of misconduct by public employees. The lower court from which this case originated interpreted the decision to mean the name of the person bringing the charge could be deleted, as could limited specific identifying information. This court opinion resulted in opening up to local newspapers and any interested parties the contents of investigations undertaken with assurances of confidentiality. Washington residents were able to read details from sexual harassment or sexual misconduct investigations at the University of Washington and by the State Medical Disciplinary Board, among others.

Even though most complaints will not end up in lawsuits and many institutions will not be affected by public disclosure laws, it is important to keep in mind that written documents, including informal notes, can become public under certain circumstances. Investigators should make only those notes they will not mind reading in disciplinary procedures, legal proceedings, or the newspaper.

Assurances of confidentiality are often seen as central to any good complaint procedure. However, in the face of increasing litigation or the use of appeal procedures by those accused of sexual harassment, it is unrealistic to assure anyone making a complaint that his or her name will remain confidential. And it is not always the case that the complainant wishes to have his or her situation remain confidential; at the University of Washington, for example, the first case to have widespread publicity did so when a complainant took the investigative report of her case to the student paper. Respondents as well may bring cases to public attention.

Confidentiality applies when the complainant is known to the investigator, but efforts are made to limit knowledge of the name of the complainant to those who need to know. Anonymity, when the name of the complainant is not known, presents other issues. EEOC guidelines indicate that employers are responsible for sexual harassment about which they know or should know. Anonymous complaints serve as notice. Named respondents should be notified that an anonymous complaint has been received; simply keeping such complaints in a secret or confidential file without notification has an unacceptable "Big Brother" aspect to be avoided. However, action on anonymous complaints beyond notifying someone that an anonymous complaint has been made presents great difficulties. Rarely will someone respond to an anonymous complaint with a full confession and willingness to take whatever disciplinary action is to be meted out. And without a witness, disciplinary action can rarely be undertaken. Because of these complications, institutions can only be advised to proceed with caution with anonymous complaints.

Investigative Procedures As a part of Institutional Procedures

Investigations comprise only a small part of institutional procedures and must fit well with other, related ones. There are numerous aspects to processing a sexual harassment complaint, and some portion of the pieces will be considered to be part of the investigation and others not, depending on specific institutions. For example, the first stage is the investigation and ascertaining of facts. Second comes a legal analysis and determination of whether a violation of policy has occurred. Third, in cases where a violation has occurred, is determination of appropriate disciplinary action against the harasser and appropriate remedy for the complainant (these actions may take place in separate arenas). Lastly is any appeal right of the harasser against disciplinary action taken, and sometimes an appeal right of the complainant if the complaint was not sustained. Procedures may vary within an institution relative to the status of the accused or the complainant (e.g., faculty various kinds of staff, or students). That is, if the accused person is a faculty member, the investigators might only determine the facts, while a faculty committee might analyze the facts and determine any disciplinary action. Or a complaint procedure might determine facts and whether discrimination has occurred, but not take the disciplinary action or serve as the appeal body

Whichever portion of the entire procedure is labeled as the complaint procedure, it should mesh seamlessly with the remaining parts. Written documents should be appropriate for use in all stages and should be complete enough to avoid duplication of effort. Investigators will need to be ready to do their part, then turn over the case to the persons conducting the next stage. Unions contracts present an added dimension to the investigative procedure. Administrators with responsibility for sexual harassment should carefully read and understand the union contracts. Notification rights should be identified. Typically contracts give members the right to have a union representative at any meeting, including investigatory interviews, that could lead to a disciplinary action.

In sexual harassment cases, it is important to keep in mind, the role of the union is to represent its members in disciplinary actions taken by administrators. Investigations take place *before* any disciplinary action and have as their purpose to ascertain whether discipline is appropriate. Union members can certainly have a union representative present during the investigatory interview, but there is otherwise no role for the union until disciplinary action is proposed. At that point, administrators should be sure to follow the processes outlined in the union contract, as it would be to follow procedures determined by a faculty senate, civil service rules, or other formal procedures (Olswang 1994).

Most unions will examine both the facts and the process used in a case. If the union believes a member has been guilty of sexual harassment, it would most likely advise the member not to pursue an appeal or a grievance. If, on the other hand, the facts clearly indicated that the union member had committed sexual harassment but had been disciplined too severely or without appropriate process, the union would defend the member in an appeal of the discipline or process. If the member wishes to pursue an appeal against the advice of the union, the union is obligated to defend the member.

Sexual harassment charges put unions in a difficult role. Unions represent members in disputes with employers; this means that the union is bound to represent the alleged harasser. Other union members, especially women, are often outraged when the union takes this position in a sexual harassment case. Unions need to take special care in explaining what their role is and to take other actions, such as special training for shop stewards, to indicate that they oppose sexual harassment in the workplace.

Administrators should work with union leadership to establish relationships such that the union will bring sexual harassment issues to management's attention when reported first to the union. Some unions may wish to handle complaints of sexual harassment of members like any employee grievance. This approach has several important drawbacks. First, the persons charged with responsibility for union grievances are unlikely to have the special sensitivities necessary in many sexual harassment complaints. Second, grievance procedures usually have very short limitations on timeliness of complaints; very often complaints must be made within fifteen or thirty days of the time of the alleged offense. Experience with sexual harassment complaints indicates that many are not brought that rapidly. Third, to limit complaints to such a short time period creates a conflict with the federal laws allowing for complaints of discrimination within six months of the alleged offense. Administrations would do best to negotiate with the unions to allow sexual harassment complaints to go through institutional, not grievance, procedures.

Institutional Placement

The person with responsibility for hearing and/or investigating charges of sexual harassment must have sufficient credibility and access to power so that appropriate actions can be taken. It is helpful as well if they are in jobs where students and others are likely to look for them. Biaggio, Watts, and Brownell (1990) indicate that affirmative action offices are usually the offices with these responsibilities, and suggest widespread efforts on campus to let others who might get reports of sexual harassment know which office has responsibility.

Affirmative action officers are appropriate to receive complaints against faculty only if they have responsibility for faculty matters and have enough credibility within the system that a finding of sexual harassment would be taken seriously and result in appropriate action. Where affirmative action officers do not have responsibilities for issues related to faculty or are otherwise not appropriate, a tenured faculty member or senior administrator, with appropriate release time to meet these additional responsibilities, should be appointed to deal with complaints against faculty.

It may also be appropriate to have separate persons or offices responsible for informal as opposed to formal complaints. At the University of Washington, for example, a faculty member with 50 percent release time listens to informal complaints against faculty members. The affirmative action officer, who reports to the provost, is responsible for taking all other complaints. See discussions below on formal and informal complaints.

GENERAL APPROACHES

Committees

We recommend against the use of committees to investigate sexual harassment complaints (Remick 1986). Committees are a familiar part of campus life and seem to be preferred for dealing with sexual harassment where some groups on campus do not trust the administration to handle complaints effectively. A committee can be useful in identifying administrative policy problems and solutions, but should not be used for individual complaints.

Committees have several drawbacks. First, such a process assumes that no special skills are needed to counsel those with complaints or to conduct an investigation. Second, committees never respond rapidly to complaints: Meetings must be arranged to deal with cases, people are busy and have schedules that are difficult to coordinate, meetings may seem impossible during semester breaks or summers, and so forth. Third, having a committee as the initial contact for describing an harassment charge may discourage potential complainants. Fourth, too many people know what has happened or is alleged to have happened, and it is very difficult to maintain appropriate levels of confidentiality. Dziech and Weiner (1984, 159–60) give an excellent example of pitfalls of committees.

If the campus community does not trust administrators to investigate sexual harassment, then that is the issue to be addressed. If the fault lies with an affirmative action officer who is not trusted, then that person should be replaced. If an investigation can be competently conducted but no action taken, then look for ways to make the top administration more responsive to the issue.

Administrators who have groups clamoring for a committee should appoint a responsible person or persons to investigate sexual harassment complaints. They should then be prepared to support these persons when they investigate a complaint and take appropriate action if there is a finding that harassment has occurred. In order to build campus trust, administrators should make periodic informal reports to an appropriate group (e.g., the faculty senate or the committee on the status of women), recognizing the need for protection of names but letting them know that action has been taken. These steps will relieve pressure for committee structure by establishing trust that the administration will take appropriate action.

In cases where faculty members are involved, committees are very likely to be part of the process that either determines or reviews disciplinary action. Investigators must be prepared to present information to faculty committees and to defend all aspects of the investigations. As faculty have become increasingly aware of the serious repercussions of sexual harassment charges, attention has focused on investigations. The widely placed advertisement by the National Association of Scholars (see, for example, the *New Republic*, 14 March 1994) lists the following as one of many problems with sexual harassment policies and procedures:

> mid-level administrators with meager academic experience but a strong commitment to fashionable causes are frequently accorded a major role in drawing up harassment regulations, interpreting them, counseling complainants, investigating charges, administering hearings, and determining guilt and penalties. Sometimes one and the same person performs all of these functions and, in addition, encourages students and other to make harassment charges. This leads to violation of academic due process.

Investigators should expect even more strongly worded criticisms of their investigative work and personal beliefs during hearing procedures.

Use of Investigators

Investigations take special skills. In-house complaints may or may not end up at an outside enforcement agency or in court. Whoever conducts investigations should be aware of the standards applied by outside agencies and the reasons for them and should be aware of when and why he or she deviates from the standards. (see, for example, Lebrato, 1986; College and University Personnel Association 1986; Equal Employment Opportunity Commission 1990).

Each complaint and investigation brings something new to one's knowledge of sexual harassment and investigative techniques. If possible, the same persons should have responsibility for investigation so that they can learn from each experience and improve their methods. Small campuses may want to assign these duties to the same person for each complaint, while large campuses will probably want to have full time investigators.

Formal and Informal Complaints

Many institutions appear to consider complaints to be informal if they are not committed to writing, and to require a written complaint for formal action. In this approach, institutions might take the position that they cannot act on a sexual harassment complaint unless the victim is willing to submit a formal written complaint. The reasoning given is that if the victim is not willing to come forth and have his or her name attached to the complaint, then the institution has no grounds for proceeding. To act on an unwritten complaint, it is assumed, would violate the rights of the alleged harasser.

This reasoning ignores the legal guidelines. The U.S. Equal Employment Opportunity Commission (EEOC) guidelines on sexual harassment and subsequent policy guidance (EEOC 1990) make clear that in the employment area, the employer is liable for any harassment by a supervisor, whether or not the employer has knowledge that it has occurred. Further, the employer is liable for harassment by co-workers or outsiders when the employer knows or could reasonably be expected to know that the harassment has occurred. (EEOC regulations do not always apply directly to relationships between faculty and students, because there may not exist an employment relationship; however, it can be assumed by analogy that such laws as Title IX of the Education Amendments would apply similar standards ["Office of Civil Rights Interpretation of Title IX" 1992; Jaschik 1994]). This means that once a situation is brought to the attention of the institution, whether to an affirmative action officer, someone in personnel, or a department chair (among others), the institution then knows of the situation and legal liability exists. Should a person refuse to sign a statement, then later sue, claiming that the institution knew of the situation but did nothing to keep it from continuing, the institution would be hard pressed to say that it has a policy on the issue, knew of this complaint, but did not act because their procedures for formal complaints were not exactly followed.

Legal requirements do not rule out the possibility of informal actions. We would instead differentiate informal and formal actions by their outcomes and whether there is an investigation. Informal complaints may or may not be written, are not investigated, and do not result in formal disciplinary actions. Persons complained against might agree to actions such as apologies, demotions, or voluntary resignations, without going through formal disciplinary procedures. Formal complaints, on the other hand, must be written, whether by the complainant or by someone else, and agreed to by the complainant, require an investigation, and result in formal disciplinary action if it is found that harassment has taken place. Price Spratlen (1994) says that informal complaints can best be characterized as educational in intent for both the complainant and the alleged harasser, while formal complaints are more legal in nature.

Institution-Initiated Complaints

If the complainant hesitates to proceed with a complaint but all indications are that a serious problem exists, consider an institution-initiated complaint. In cases of serious allegations where we had difficulty getting an individual to bring a complaint, we have initiated complaints on behalf of the institution. These were cases in which we had reason to believe there was a problem, and the investigation took place on the institution's behalf, in order to assess whether liability existed. This shift of responsibility for the initiation of the investigation from the individual to the institution relieved the fears of alleged victims such that they fully cooperated with us even though they had been reluctant to bring a complaint. This procedure protects the institution in those situations where a problem has been brought to its attention, thus creating potential legal liability. If a problem exists, the institution then has sufficient information to proceed with corrective action, and if the allegations are unfounded, the institution can demonstrate that it has investigated the situation and has reason to believe no action is necessary.

Ombudsman

An ombudsman can play an important role in listening to and resolving informal complaints against faculty. We offer the following as a model that has been very successful for us (Price Spratlen 1994). Such a person should be a female tenured faculty member with a background providing counseling skills. The ombudsman can be available by phone or in person to talk about possible sexual harassment situations. Some complainants will choose to use phone contact only in order to preserve their anonymity. The ombudsman helps the complainant clarify the issues surrounding the harassment, defines terms, listens, and provides advice. At the time of an in-person meeting, the ombudsman may ask the complainant to write down what has happened, so that the complainant and the ombudsman can better understand what happened.

Most often, when the harassment is not of a serious nature, the complainant will only want to talk to a knowledgable person and plan what action to take herself or himself. In these cases, the ombudsman will give advice; she also will follow up by phone in several weeks to be sure the situation is resolved.

When more intervention is needed, the ombudsman will agree to talk to the faculty member and his or her chair. In this procedure, the ombudsman calls the faculty member to her office; she explains the behavior that has been described to her and asks whether the faculty member agrees that it occurred. In our experience, faculty members agree on the stated behavior about 95 percent of the time, though there is usually disagreement on what the behavior meant.

The ombudsman may ask the faculty members to write down their version of the situation as well; some are willing to do so, while others may agree to read the statement made by the complainant and signed that they agree that the situation was as described. Because of confidentiality concerns, all written materials are returned to each writer at the end of the process. The ombudsman looks for resolution of the situation, as appropriate: Sometimes nothing more is required than this conversation, and sometimes she holds meetings bringing together the faculty member, the complainant, and the chair of the department or dean. In the latter meetings, the ombudsman offers the complainant a "safe" place to let the faculty member know how he or she feels about the behavior and what effect it had on his or her well-being. If serious harassment is described or the harasser is a repeater, official disciplinary action might be called for, and the ombudsman turns the case over to the provost for formal investigation.

Formal Investigations

Formal investigations are necessary whenever (1) a formal complaint has been received; (2) the complaint (formal or informal) is about an alleged harasser against whom previous charges have been filed; or (3) when the nature of the complaint (formal or informal) is of such a nature that the alleged sexual harassment may lead to disciplinary actions. Because higher education institutions often have little experience with formal investigations, this topic is treated in detail below.

CHARACTERISTICS OF A GOOD INVESTIGATOR

Institutional Considerations

The investigator or investigative unit should report directly to the person who will determine the institutional response. It is essential that the investigator be aware of and try to minimize his or her departmental loyalties or dislikes when carrying out investigative responsibilities. At the same time, the investigator must also be sensitive to the "culture" of the institution and recognize that persons in certain kinds of jobs or at certain levels will need to be treated differently to get to the same end (i.e., resolution Of a complaint). For example, an investigator can usually get pictures of nude women off the walls in the motor pool by going to a supervisor who can order the pictures removed, but will need a different approach to get a faculty member to remove from his door an art print showing people in fifty coital positions.

Investigator Credibility

A key to effective investigations is the credibility of investigators. Investigators must conduct their inquiries, write their reports, and make recommendations in objective, clear language so that the institution, the alleged harasser, and the alleged victim can trust that they are being treated fairly.

Credibility will be achieved largely by remaining neutral while providing necessary support to all involved. This means that an investigator cannot allow any of the parties to pressure her/him to reveal confidential information, to become an advocate for anyone involved, or to "take sides" in a final report or recommendations. Language in written material should be based on findings as they relate to the law and the facts, not to an investigator's personal feelings.

The investigator must also be honest. If the institution has failed, management must be so informed. If the investigation yields information that an employee has experienced poor treatment but not discriminatory harassment, the complaining employee should be told this in straight-forward language which does not lead her/him to believe or hope that allegations will be supported in a final report. While employees never like being told their allegations are without support, our experience is that they prefer to have this information as early and as candidly as possible so they don't continue pursuing a "lost cause."

The need for credibility suggests that a primary criterion for good investigators is the ability to be fair and candid, without allowing personal feelings to interfere with effectiveness. Once an investigator has achieved a reputation for fairness, both the investigative office and the institution will become a place where members of the university community will go to resolve sexual harassment situations.

Sensitivity to Hierarchy

Dealing with complaints of sexual harassment requires a delicate approach. Some may argue for egalitarian treatment, where all complaints are handled in the same fashion. This will not work. The rules associated with disciplinary action against faculty are different from those against staff or students, and treatment of sexual harassment must parallel existing procedures. It is difficult enough to approach someone who has been accused of sexual harassment, because of the personal nature of the complaint and the need to watch for false accusations; one does not need to compound the situation by breaching the written code and social etiquette of the institution. Faculty members should be approached on these topics by other faculty members, persons with Ph.D.'s, or others seen as peers, because status inequality can have subtle but strong effects. For example, if the investigator is too deferential to faculty and does not ask hard questions, the investigation will be hampered because essential information may not be uncovered. On the other hand, a faculty member who feels educationally superior to an investigator may accuse anyone questioning his or her authority of being a bully or violating his or her civil rights; likewise, an investigator who feels inferior to a faculty member might try to bully him or her to demonstrate power. Thus an investigation might be hampered by either friction or deference resulting from status inequality.

Persons investigating complaints against or by staff persons must be aware of any civil service, other personnel or union rules. These rules will set limits on procedures and possible remedies.

Sensitivity to Issues

Investigators *must* be able to relate well to a wide variety persons, so that complainants and respondents will talk to them. First, they should have the ability to think and talk about sexuality and deviant behavior. Because of the high incidence of sexual abuse in our culture and the associations sexual harassment brings to this abuse, the investigators must be prepared and able to listen to stories about incest, rape, and battering. Second, the investigator must not criticize the complainant for not being aggressive enough in response to the alleged harassment, openly identify with the complainant, or apologize for or criticize the behavior of all men. Third, a knowledge of psychological theory appears helpful, though those with counseling training must exercise care not to become a "counselor" to persons who clearly need help. Investigators must maintain a distance from all parties so that they can make a reasoned judgment about the nature, legal issues, and resolution of the complaint, *and* be upheld as objective by others such as judges and hearing officers.

Men or Women As Investigators

The question inevitably arises as to whether males or females should do the investigating. Sexual harassment is about sexual behavior, attitudes, and beliefs about sex. There is a strong reluctance on the part of many women to discuss sexual matters with men, especially ones they do not know. We found this reluctance to be so strong that it interfered with the investigation. For example, women are likely to tell a man that another man has propositioned her; she is more likely to tell another woman that the harasser repeatedly asked her "if she wanted to fuck." Propositions come in many forms and are more or less socially acceptable. If the complainant is unwilling or unable to tell an investigator what actually happened, the investigator cannot judge the seriousness of the event.

In addition, men and women do not necessarily share the same sense of how severe or damaging a behavior has been (Gutek, 1985 and Fitzgerald 1993). For example, in one case the harasser had on several occasions grabbed a woman's hand and placed it on his erect penis. On another occasion, he had propositioned a woman in an elevator, she had said no, he had followed her to her room, grabbed and forcefully kissed her, and then left. Men tended to see the first behavior as the more offensive, while women tended to react to the second as a scenario for rape and therefore far more serious and frightening.

We have found that men are also more comfortable talking to women investigators. Heterosexual men who have been harassed by men or women often feel shame at not having stopped the harassment in a "manly" way, and seem to be able to discuss their conflict with women with less loss of face. Gay men seem also to prefer not to discuss difficult sexual matters with men, gay or straight.

We have concluded that when staffing and workload permit, the best approach to investigating sexual harassment is to have an interview team of a male and female, which provides the benefit of both perspectives simultaneously. Outside of the interview situation, each can use the other for occasional reality checks and for support. "Mixed" teams do not seem to interfere with reporting; the interviewee simply tends to make eye contact with the same-sex person while answering sensitive questions. For the female complainant, the team approach offers a "safer" environment than talking about sex to a strange man.

Personal Needs

Investigators must not go into this kind of work if they have a strong need to be liked or to have their work appreciated. No matter what the outcome of a case is, someone, and possibly everyone, will be angry. The alleged harasser may continue to deny that he or she did anything wrong and may accuse the investigators of being overzealous, on witch hunts, man haters, etc. The complainant may be satisfied with the outcome but anxious to forget everything about the situation, including the work of the investigator. The complainant may not be satisfied with the outcome and may blame the investigator for not doing more. Sometimes the final outcome determined by the institution will be less than the investigator recommended. The investigator must take comfort in knowing that he or she did the best that could be done. If the investigator finds that he or she too often does not get management support in these cases, the investigator should consider why: Has the investigation been badly done; are reports clear enough; does management have a poor understanding of the psychological and legal aspects of harassment; or does management not care? In cases where management remains unresponsive, the investigator may need to consider a new employer.

Investigation of sexual harassment complaints, especially where the complainant has a past history of victimization and/or the alleged behavior of the harasser is far beyond acceptable bounds, can take a high toll on investigators. The investigators as well as the complainants are often forced to relive past traumas. It is common for women to experience anger not only at the alleged harasser, but also for any harassment or sexual trauma they had experienced in the past. We found that women investigators tend to take their anger home and to experience varying levels of difficulties in relationships with men in their personal lives. This effect seems to be more pronounced in heterosexual women than in lesbians. Men often become confused by what cultural heroes like Burt Reynolds, Errol Flynn, or Don Juan have modeled as manly and what the law now defines as illegal. Male investigators may therefore experience a kind of "collective guilt" for the destructive behavior of men; they may feel guilty for past actions or fantasies. Like women investigators do, male investigators take this guilt home, and it complicates their personal relationships. The men in the lives of the women investigators sometimes experience the same kind of guilt as do the men investigators. For these reasons, using a supportive team approach to investigating and resolving sexual harassment is helpful for personal survival and professional effectiveness.

INVESTIGATIONS

Investigator Autonomy

Institutional leadership must be prepared to give investigators the autonomy and power they need to do a good investigation. It is important for the investigator to remember his or her role: on behalf of the institution, the investigator is trying to find the facts and remedies in order for the institution to make the best possible decision as to how to respond to the complaint. Institutional interests include maintaining morale and productivity as well as limiting legal liability, decisions to cover up incidents of sexual harassment, or failure to find or take seriously existing problems are not in the best interest of the institution. While he or she works on behalf of the institution, the investigator does not represent the complainant or the respondent (the person accused of discrimination). In the gathering of facts and assessment of the situation, the investigator should strive to be seen as a fair, neutral third party; it may be necessary to remind others involved in the investigation of this neutral role.

Complaint Intake

If an investigator knows from initial phone contact that a person with a sexual harassment complaint is coming in, he or she should set aside a two-hour period for the first interview. If two persons will be investigating the complaint, both should be present at the initial interview. This interview should ascertain the following: what behaviors occurred and approximately when; who else knows about the behaviors or may have experienced similar incidents; who in management or supervision has been notified of the situation and what they did; and what the complainant expects as an outcome (e.g., for the behavior to stop, counselling, back wages). The investigators should be prepared for this session to be very emotional. This emotional level may be the result of trauma created by the sexual harassment. The complainant may also have concerns about the effects of reporting on work place inter-actions, the responses of friends and family, and the possible impact on his or her career and personal reputation.

Complainants may have other experiences that add to the trauma of sexual harassment. Because the incidence of sexual abuse is so high in the general population, many complainants, especially women, may have been sexually abused at some previous time in their lives. Sexual harassment of a person who has previously experienced abuse will often cause that person to relive those traumas. In addition, many harassers seem to choose vulnerable persons as their victims. It is very common to find that complainants are in the midst of such major life changes as divorce, a recent death in the family, or a move to a new town and/or job with the accompanying isolation from friends and relatives.

Investigators should ask complainants not to discuss the complaint with others in order to lessen the probability of retaliation and to avoid influencing other witnesses. Even after such advice, the complainant is likely to talk to others. This breach may have several outcomes. First, other victims and/or witnesses often come forward after they hear that someone else has initiated a complaint. Second, the emotional effect on other witnesses is often lessened if they are expecting to be contacted as a witness and have had time to prepare themselves to talk about the alleged harassment.

Most complaints are serious, yet complainants will often conclude their recitation of facts with a request that nothing be done—they don't want to hurt the harasser or endanger their own situation (Brooks and Perot 1991; Gutek 1985). Investigators should make it clear that the institution has an obligation to make the environment free of such situations and that legally the investigators cannot ignore the complaint nor can they ignore their knowledge of the situation even if a complaint is not brought formally. The parties may decide at this time whether to pursue the complaint as a formal one requiring a written resolution, or as an informal complaint.

We discuss with the complainant how he or she is likely to feel about having filed the complaint. On the next day, he or she may want to withdraw the complaint, and will likely have several changes of heart during the process. Such discussion has lowered the incidence of attempts to drop charges; instead, later conversations consist of confirmations of vacillations and ranges of emotion. For example, the investigator will need to explain that he or she takes the complaint seriously, that the alleged behavior is not acceptable to the institution and should not be occurring in the work environment, and that the institution wants it to stop and will proceed with an investigation, either formal or informal. The legal liabilities of the institution do not give investigators the option of ignoring a complaint once it has been brought to their attention. If the investigator assures the complainant that the issue is important and that the investigator will offer as much protection as possible against retaliation, the complainant will usually agree to proceed and be willing to attest to the discriminatory acts.

Notification

Notification should be limited to a need-to-know basis. For example, the appropriate supervisors of the complainant and alleged harasser should be notified that a complaint has been received and an investigation is taking place, because he or she need to know why the complainant's performance or emotional state might not be up to usual standards, that no disciplinary actions should be taken against the complainant or alleged harasser without consultation with the investigators, and that investigators may be talking to other members of the department. Should the immediate supervisor be the person accused of harassment, then that person's supervisor should be the person informed. If the alleged harasser is in a different department from the complainant, his or her supervisor should be notified as well. This notification is essential because the supervisor should know that the complainant and alleged harasser will be absent for interviews and may have changes in their performance; watch for further situations of harassment; prevent retaliation against the complainant; and be given a chance to give to the investigator any information of other incidents of harassment.

The respondent should also be notified that a complaint has been lodged against him or her. He or she should be asked to meet with the investigators at the investigators' office as soon as possible. The investigators should prepare for the meeting by reviewing the material from the intake interview and making a list of items to be covered. The list should include that the institution takes complaints seriously and that a complaint has been brought against the respondent. Describe the behaviors alleged by the complainant and ask the respondent whether the described behaviors occurred. In our experience, the respondent often admits that the behaviors occurred, though there may be some difference in interpretation of intent or severity. After the behavior has been described and possibly agreed to, *then* it should be labeled as sexual harassment and unacceptable.

Interviews

Interviews are rarely as straightforward as the above descriptions might indicate. Investigators should be prepared to take the time to establish rapport with whomever they are talking to and to allow the conversation to "wander" on occasion. The idea is to get the needed information at some time, not to get it as fast and "efficiently" as possible. These interviews will be stressful to all involved. In order to reduce the stress and improve the effectiveness of the process, the investigators should allow time for getting acquainted and should expect a limited amount of small talk.

The investigator should contact other persons named by the complainant as possibly having information about the harassment. A list of items to be covered should be prepared before the interview, so that no important issues are missed. Again, however, the investigator should avoid overly structured interviews; important new information can come out during the discussion if the interviewer is able to establish an open, safe forum for conversation.

Others in the environment should be interviewed as well, to see whether they have observed or experienced any harassing behavior. When asking questions, do not ask whether they have seen or experienced sexual harassment; the definition is so different to each individual, that specific behaviors should be referred to instead. For example, in interviews we have had persons say that they had not experienced sexual harassment from a certain person, while at the same time stating that he had regularly propositioned them, touched them or others, or told offensive jokes. The interviewer should be sure that by the end of the interview the interviewees understand the legal definition of sexual harassment and which behaviors are not acceptable; this is best done by giving the interviewees a written definition and taking time to explain any part of it that may not be clear.

The use of tape recorders is not recommended; they make most persons self-conscious and uncomfortable even under the best of circumstances, and these interviews will be tense enough without an added impediment. Acceptability of note taking depends on institutional culture, the perceived status of the interviewers, and the type of person being interviewed. For example, note taking is routine in many professional settings and might not be noticed, while in blue-collar settings a notebook might be viewed with mistrust. With two interviewers, it is possible for one to be asking questions while the other is taking notes without being too obvious; it is important that they alternate in these roles so that the notetaker is perceived as a professional part of the investigative team, not a secretary. Be sensitive to what is acceptable and appropriate.

Referrals to Counseling

The complainant is likely to be very emotional and in need of strong support. The best support an investigator can provide is information on the process, acknowledgment of the legitimacy of emotions felt, and referrals to appropriate resources. The investigator may wish to ask the complainant whether she or he has people outside of the institution to talk to and may suggest that the person seek emotional support, even including counseling, if necessary—making it clear that she or he is not crazy but will need support because of their feelings about the harassment and because the investigation and resolution process will be stressful. Investigators should be very careful that this referral is not seen as validation that illegal sexual harassment has occurred, since at this point no conclusion has been reached. The investigators should be sensitive to the response of the complainant to the suggestion for counseling. There are wide differences in acceptability of counseling as an aid to problem solving, based on such factors as education, race, age, social class, religious background, and individual preference. Complainants who are not interested in counseling should not be pushed to receive it.

Institutions with employee assistance programs (EAPs) or student counseling programs may wish to make referrals of complainants and/or respondents to these services. Before this is done, evaluate whether the program is qualified to handle sexual harassment cases. For example, if the primary purpose of an EAP is alcoholism counseling, the staff may not be sensitive to the issues surrounding sexual harassment.

Commitments to Complainants

Investigators should beware of making commitments to the complainant. During investigations, investigators should not commit their institution to specific actions. Investigators will rarely have the authority to make such decisions, and those who can will want to wait until they have assessed whether sexual harassment has actually taken place and, if so, what the appropriate remedy is. An early commitment may be difficult to undo even should the investigators find later that the complaint has insufficient merit. If the investigation leads to the conclusion that counseling, for example, is appropriate, the employer can always pay for the counseling already received. While one may want to do what is best for all as rapidly as possible, one is dealing with a legal issue with potential liability. At the same time, should the early stages of investigation indicate that a serious problem exists and immediaie corrective action is needed, it should be taken. This early commitment to solution will very often mitigate further economic and psychological damages and head off legal action by complainants.

Commitments by the Institution

Institutions must be willing to stay out of the way of the investigation and avoid pressuring the investigators to find no discrimination. The results of the investigation should be evaluated with an open mind, and no retaliation should be taken against the investigator for finding evidence of sexual harassment. Ignoring the situation after an investigation has shown harassment increases employer liability, and actions against the investigator can result in suits by the investigator as well as the complainant.

A good investigation lays the groundwork for a good resolution. An institution with the facts can clearly determine whether a problem exists and what, if any, actions are appropriate. Should corrective actions be needed, the institution can determine what to do for the complainant and with the respondent. Whether or not the institution concludes a discriminatory act has occurred, administration may want to take actions to lessen tension in the department.

Complaint Resolution

External investigators are motivated to find the facts and make a clear finding of guilt or innocence that will hold up in a court of law. Their process tends to be to accumulate every fact, talk to every possible witness, and then to make a judgment. Internal investigators also need to know the facts, but only need to know enough to move to in-house resolution of an institutional problem. If resolution is not possible, then internal investigators must proceed to exhaustive external standards.

It is expedient to resolve complaints before a formal finding must be written. After several interviews, it usually becomes obvious whether there is a problem of sexual harassment. If the alleged harasser agrees that certain behaviors or incidents took place (even if he or she does not label them as harassment), or if the harasser disagrees but several other credible persons say that they experienced the same behaviors or saw them directed at someone else, then there is enough evidence to go forward (and too much not to act). If there is a situation of an allegation of one-on-one harassment that cannot be verified, then one can still act, but in a different fashion, usually by educating the alleged harasser as to what behaviors of his or hers may be open to misinterpretation and by warning the person as to what will happen if further reports are received. In these cases, the exact response made often depends heavily on the investigator's professional judgments regarding the credibility of each party.

Each complaint should be treated on its own merit and in its own context; there is no formula or standard way to solve a problem. The investigators should assemble the facts and present them to the person in the position of authority. If all agree that they should proceed, they have several choices, depending on the severity of the harassment, the level or kind of complainant (e.g., civil service, unionized, management employees, student, or user of services), the institutional culture, and the damage if any to the complainant and/or the institutional environment.

The nature of the harassment is an important factor in determining the damage to the complainant. The role power of the harasser over the complainant can also make a big difference in how hurt the complainant is by the harassment. The attitude of others, both in the institution and acquaintances, and personal factors such as sources of stress and past history of sexual abuse add to the impact of sexual harassment. A harassment situation can be devastating or merely annoying. The investigators must listen and observe closely and be prepared to see very different reactions to seemingly similar situations.

DISCIPLINARY ACTION AND FOLLOW-UP

Disciplinary Action

If the situation is characterized by offensive remarks, with no threats implied, and a complainant who is annoyed but not damaged, one may act rapidly and simply. Tell the harasser to stop. Tell him or her that further reports will result in disciplinary action. Warn against any retaliatory action directed at the complainant. Follow up the conversation with a letter saying the same thing. In such a situation, this is the outcome that most complainants want and, in our experience, is very often enough. Sometimes this action can make place in the interview with the respondent; he or she agrees that the incidents took place (though, of course, there was no intent of harassment). There is then no need for further investigation, since there is no conflict over what took place.

If there are multiple victims of harassment or someone who has been badly hurt, stronger actions are called for. Consider suspension, transfer, or termination for the harasser and paid counseling or transfer for the victim. The courts have taken a dim view of solutions that require all of the change by the victim (e.g., the victim is put in a new, perhaps less desirable, job, while the harasser stays put). Careful documentation is in order for disciplinary situations, to protect against legal action by the harasser and to show positive actions taken, should there be legal action by the complainant.

Do not be driven by fear of legal action, especially by the alleged harasser. In our experience, they frequently threaten to sue; with many Americans, this threat has replaced the threat of bodily harm. No one can be stopped from suing. In dealing with the alleged harasser, the goal is not to avoid suits, but to avoid losing them. If an institution has done its homework well and has good documentation, it is not likely to lose a suit by a harasser.

If the serious harasser is also famous or a high producer, don't protect him or her. Other famous persons or high producers are in the labor market who are not harassers and therefore do not create a liability for the institution. The adverse publicity and the legal expenses of a sexual harassment case can far outweigh any other positive contribution of an individual.

In situations where the institutional culture prefers resignations, because firing is either difficult or "not done," call a meeting with the harasser, the investigators, and the responsible administrator. Suggest that the harasser bring along his or her attorney. Tell the harasser that the purpose of the meeting is to discuss the allegations informally, before a final report is prepared, and to review what has been discovered to date. Present the harasser and his or her attorney with a summary of findings: three promises of promotion in return for sex, five threats of failed examinations, one forced kiss and fondling, etc. here is no need to mention names. We have found this approach to be very successful. The harasser may or may not continue to deny the situation, but his or her attorney will be able to make a judgment as to what is in the best interest of the client. Resignations have followed these meetings.

Our resignations are not without ramification. During this session, we present to the harasser and the attorney a draft of a statement that we will give whenever asked for a letter of recommendation. The text is "You should know that at the time Dr. X resigned, he/she was under investigation for a charge of sexual harassment. Because of the resignation the investigation was terminated and there was no finding." Attorneys have agreed with this wording. The statement has two effects: it protects the organization from legal liability should an ex-employee go on to harass at a new job, and it protects the harasser by limiting what will be said to prospective employers. That is, we instruct the harasser's immediate supervisor, and others likely to be asked for recommendations, that the statement is *all* that should be said; they are not to discuss any details about any allegations of harassment.

The investigator may find that the department or institution wants to take action against a harasser that appears disproportionate to the harassment incident. This most often occurs when the harasser has many deviant behaviors and work-related problems, only one of which is sexual harassment. Alcoholism, drug abuse, and/or mental illness are often involved and make these cases very complex. In these cases, the manager has been observing problems for a long time but has taken no action, usually out of a lack of information or ability with disciplinary actions. The harassment charge involves investigators from outside the department and gives the manager something specific on which to take disciplinary action. It is important that the sexual harassment program not get labeled as too punitive, overzealous, etc., because disciplinary actions are out of proportion. One should limit the discipline to that which is appropriate to the case in hand, and initiate separate disciplinary actions against the person for other, nonharassment problems.

The Effects of the Investigation

Any investigation, and especially one involving discrimination such as sexual harassment, disrupts the particular setting. The act of interviewing sensitizes people to the general issue of sexual harassment and to their work or educational environment. They are forced to think about their attitudes and behavior and report their perceptions about the specific situation. They often feel obliged to "choose sides." It may be unavoidable that people will questionion the character, motivations, and competence of both complainant and respondent.

Initiating an investigation raises the expectations of the complainant. While the person who complains knows intellectually that the outcome of the investigation may or may not support his or her allegations, there is an emotional expectation that the complainant's needs will be met. Even if the complaint is validated and appropriate actions are taken, the actions may not be enough for the complainant to feel vindicated.

In the course of conducting an investigation, the investigators may have disappointed, outraged, and offended some people. For instance, some people look at sexual harassment as a purely interpersonal conflict, and they feel that a formal legal investigation serves only to blow a small personal problem out of proportion. At the very least, many people resent outsiders investigating their group and take the asking of questions as an accusation of collective guilt. Professors are especially likely to see any questioning as inappropriate infringements to their autonomy and perhaps their academic freedom.

The effects of an investigation process on the alleged harasser vary greatly. The response might vary from social withdrawal to resignation or taking a leave of absence. The person might also aggressively lobby for himself or herself and against others now identified as disloyal troublemakers.

Investigative contacts can include education about sexual harassment, investigations, and legal responsibilities and can do a great deal to help those involved to have realistic expectations and a more cooperative attitude. Moreover, it is important for interviewers to give specific guidelines to interviewees about what can be said about the interviews, to whom, and why.

Investigators cannot solve all of these problems. However, they can be prepared and should report to appropriate administrators the kinds of problems they uncovered and suggest that steps be taken to solve them. Each institution will have its own approach to such issues, sometimes depending upon available funds, other times upon local customs. Actions can include bringing in organizational development specialists to look at unit functioning, referring individuals to counseling, bringing in counselors to work with the unit, special training programs either for individuals or the unit, or unit meetings to discuss problems. What is most important is that people surrounding an investigation be aware that problems will arise and that an effort be made to restore group cohesiveness and effectiveness.

Investigations have effects upon the investigators as well. We know several investigators who have lost their jobs after making unpopular findings. Others have been sued or brought before faculty panels by men in cases where no cause was found, on the basis that the investigator had too vigorously done his or her job; one such case resulted in a $15,000 judgment against an individual investigator and an equal amount against the institution. (The institution paid the entire amount because the investigator had, in its opinion, carried out her job duties appropriately.

CONCLUSION

Handling a complaint of sexual harassment in an institution of higher education requires a complex set of investigative organizational procedures and resources. This chapter describes a system of investigation that might be most likely to resolve a situation fairly, prevent further harassment, and mitigate harm to a complainant and liability to the institution.

References

Biaggio, M. K., Watts, D., and Brownell, A. (1990). Addressing sexual harassment: Strategies for prevention and change. In M. Paludi (Ed.), *Ivory power: Sexual harassment on campus*. Albany: State University of New York Press.

Brooks, L. and Perot, A. (1991). Reporting sexual harassment: Exploring a predictive model. *Psychology of Women Quarterly, 15*, 31–47.

College and University Personnel Association. (1986). *The lecherous professor*. Boston: Beacon Press.

Dziech, B. W., and Weiner, L. (1984). *Sexual harassment: Issues and answers*. Washington, DC: College and University Personnel Association.

Fitzgerald, L. F. (1993). Sexual harassment: Violenc against women in the workplace. *American Psychologist, 48* (10), 1070–76.

Gutek, B. A. (1985). *Sex and the workplace*. San Francisco: Jossey-Bass.

Jaschik, S. (1994). New focus on civil rights: An aggressive Education Department goes after colleges for violating anti-bias laws. *Chronicle of Higher Education*, 22 June 1994, pp. A27–A31.

Lebrato, M. T. (Ed.). (1986). *Help yourself: A manual for dealing with sexual harassment*. Sacramento: Sexual Harassment in Employment Project of the California Commission on the Status of Women.

Office of Civil Rights interpretation of Title IX. (1992). *Synthesis: Law and Policy in Higher Education*, 310.

Olswang, S. (1994). Personal communication, Vice Provost, University of Washington.

Price Spratlen, L. (1994). Personal communication, Ombudsman for Sexual Harassment, University of Washington.

Remick, H. (1986). Issues in implementation of a sexual harassment policy. In L. Price Spratlen *Prevention of sexual harassment in academe*, (17–25). Seattle: University of Washington Office for Equal Employment Opportunity.

Stringer, D. M., Remick, H., Salisbury, J. and Ginoria, A. B. (1990). The power and reasons behind sexual harassment: An employer's guide to solutions. *Public Personnel Management 19* (1), 43–52.

U.S. Equal Employment Opportunity Commission. (1990). Policy guidance on current issues of sexual harassment. Notice No. N-915-050, 19 March.

Walker, G., Erickson, L., and Woolsey, L. (1985). Sexual harassment: Ethical research and clinical implications in the academic setting. *International Journal of Women's Studies*, 8 (September/October), 424–33.

13

Institutional Strategies:
Creating a Sexual Harassment Panel

Dorothy O. Helly

GENERAL BACKGROUND

In 1981 a process began at Hunter College of the City University of New York that brought together faculty, counselors, staff, and students to discuss and propose ways of dealing institutionally with sexual harassment on campus. That process was effected by the federal legislation making sexual harassment illegal and by directives from the City University to come into compliance with such legislation. The result was a policy statement and guidelines and a Sexual Harassment Panel representing all sectors of the Hunter College academic community. The process was neither easy nor swiftly accomplished, but in the course of pursuing it, the participants educated themselves and began to educate elements of the campus community to increased sensitivity to the meaning of sexual harassment. Sexual harassment has long been a phenomenon in which the victims have been blamed for their victimization, the most subtle and pervasive exercise of power over the structurally subordinate that has made even the victims doubt their own right to accuse their victimizers and claim justice for themselves.

To understand the context in which the Sexual Harassment Panel was created at Hunter College, it is necessary to know some general facts about the college itself. Founded in 1870 as New York City's first public normal school for women, Hunter College by 1914 was a free-tuition municipal women's college offering a liberal arts degree. Into the 1960s its undergraduate student body numbered between 4,000 and 5,000; and though it became coeducational in 1964, women students have never made up less than 70 percent of its enrollment. From the mid 1960s to 1980, however, the percentage of women on the faculty and in positions of faculty and administrative leadership declined, despite the appointment of its first women presidents.[1]

From the early 1960s Hunter College became part of the City University of New York, one eventually of ten senior (four-year) colleges, seven community (two-year) colleges, a graduate school for Ph.D. programs, an affiliated medical school and, more recently, a law school. With the inauguration of a City University policy of "open admissions" in 1970, the size and composition of the student body at Hunter College radically changed from under 5,000 students, predominantly white and white ethnic in background, to between three and four times that size, 60 percent being of African American, Hispanic and other Caribbean, and Asian heritages. The imposition of tuition and further modification of "open admissions" in the mid 1970s did not alter this trend.

Hunter College, situated in the heart of Manhattan, is representative of a complex urban society, for which it serves, as it has traditionally done, as an important avenue of social advancement. Surveys in the late 1970s indicated that 40 percent of its students were not born in the United States. By the 1980s records also indicated that 25 percent of Hunter College students were older, returning women students.

From 1980 to 1988, affirmative action during the Hunter College presidency of Donna E. Shalala increased both the number of women and the number of African Americans, Hispanics, and Asians on the faculty. By 1985 Shalala's leadership and a college community responsive to affirmative action guidance had resulted in women faculty again numbering some 41 percent of the total. When Karen Bogart visited the college in 1983, as part of her preparation of *Toward Equity: An Action Manual for Women in Academe*, she found seventeen programs and policies she could include in her list of "Exemplary Programs and Policies That Promote Sex Equity in Postsecondary Education." Taken together, these programs and policies made Hunter College an outstanding example of equity at the university level. One of these seventeen policies was its Sexual Harassment Procedures.[2]

HISTORY OF THE PANEL

Student unrest in the spring of 1970 led to changes in the college governance system. The new academic senate at Hunter College was composed of faculty students, and administrators, and an office of ombudsman was instituted. The third incumbent in that office sent out a memorandum in October 1981 addressed "To All Who Expressed Interest" in meeting to consider a policy and procedure for sexual harassment. What had precipitated it? In May of the previous spring term, when making his annual report to the senate, the ombudsman had commented on a special category of case he had dealt with that year. A student had sought the ombudsman's help in difficulties she was having with one of her professors, and had cited among her troubles with him his general denigration of women in the classroom. What sort of remark had the student complained about, the ombudsman was asked. He replied, the professor referred to women by such stereotypes as "dumb blondes." In response, there was an outburst of laughter among the members of the senate.

As an associate dean at the college in charge of the evening session and graduate services, I was an *ex officio* member of senate. My reaction to the senate response elicited by the ombudsman's report was anger and dismay. I made an appointment to see him. We had worked on many committees in the past and I trusted his common sense and integrity completely. Since I could be forthright with him in expressing my concerns, we shared a frank discussion about what we both knew about the issue of sexual harassment at the college. We then agreed to explore the question further, each promising to talk with others among the faculty and staff who might share our concerns. The ombudsman followed up with a memorandum raising the question of forming a working committee on the subject. I suggested doing so early in the fall term.

The ombudsman's 22 October memorandum invited recipients to meet in his office early in November and included two enclosures. The first was a copy of the Standford University *Campus Report*, dated 14 January 1981; the second was an article from *The Chronicle of Higher Education*, dated 4 May 1981. The Stanford *Campus Report* announced a recently adopted formal policy on sexual harassment. Previously announced informal procedures had been formalized to meet the requirement of a federal Equal Opportunity Employment Commission policy for universities announced in 1980. A committee made up solely of college officials had formulated Stanford's policy, which defined sexual harassment as "repeated and unwanted sexual behavior, such as physical contact and verbal comments or suggestions, which adversely affects the working or learning environment." The policy included informal and formal procedures to be used by faculty, staff, and students "subjected to offensive sexual behavior."

The *Chronicle* article ("Accused of Sexual Harassment, Male Professor Sues Female Complainants for $23.7 Million") dealt with a Clark University sexual harassment charge made by two women faculty against a member of the sociology department. The complainants complained that university officials were not dealing with the specific issues of sexual harassment and sex discrimination they had raised. The university's resolution of the case was to settle it out of court with the accused faculty member. That left him free to enter his own suit against his accusers. The issues of institutional responsibility and the rules under which the Clark administration operated were central of the concerns of the women complainants.

At Hunter College, the concern at this stage among those discussing sexual harassment was specifically the nature of responsibility of the institution to set up procedures to protect those who believed themselves sexually harassed. This focus brought help from the new chair of the Department of Romance Languages, recently hired from Yale University. At Yale, as the head of a residential college, he had taken part in the university discussion of procedures for handling sexual harassment cases. Learning of our concern to familiarize ourselves with what other institutions were doing, he shared with us materials that explained what had precipitated the Yale Advisory Committee on Grievance Procedure. He was also able to supply us with a written record of how Yale went about setting up a committee to pursue the various issues involved in establishing a statement of policy and procedures. We also examined the resulting handbooks for the faculty and students, which were aimed at dissemination information on Yale's policy.

The chair of Romance Languages also put me in touch with the associate dean at Yale who was convener of their committee. In a long telephone call in mid December 1981, she outlined her experiences in introducing these issues into the Yale community. She agreed to visit Hunter College to speak on this topic.[3] When she came, she explained to interested administrators and faculty members her role in setting up a sexual harassment procedure at Yale.

Examining the Issues

In response to the ombudsman's October 1981 memorandum, four of us began a discussion of the materials already in hand. This core group included the ombudsman, a member of the counseling staff (another Hunter colleague with whom both the ombudsman and 1 had often worked and on whose judgment we could depend) a woman student who was a psychology major working with the ombudsman and interested in this topic, and myself. In addition to the Stanford University and Yale University sexual harassment procedures (including working notes on the Yale committee's work), we had available a "Sexual Harassment Fact Kit" assembled by Robin Diamond, Lynn Feller, and Nancy Felipe Russo (1981) for the Federation of Organizations for Professional Women.

In our discussion, we raised the following points for consideration in terms of our policy and procedures and our overall strategies for dealing with sexual harassment at the college: (1) counseling victims of sexual harassment; (2) educating faculty to the implications of the power they wielded in their relationships with students; (3) disseminating the legal definition of sexual harassment as coercion and threat involving sexual behavior; (4) investigating what official college actions might follow if an allegation of harassment were substantiated; (5) finding out what must be done to protect accusers and to insure due process for the accused; (6) and finding ways of informing every sector of the academic community about this issue. This working committee included, from time to time, the department chair with the Yale experience and the new counsel to the president. As the work of the committee took focus, we kept the dean of students apprised of our progress.

We decided that Hunter College needed formal guidelines and procedures. Not only were they required by law we believed they would also be essential for dealing with the problem at the college. We further decided that these guidelines could be initiated by our group so long as it had the full support of the president of the college, the personnel office, the faculty union, and the student governments. The question remained, at what point should these other individuals and agencies be brought into the process? Our initial decision was to formulate draft guidelines as the basis for discussion.

The ombudsman prepared a preliminary "cut and paste" set of draft guidelines, culled from the available sources. His initial model included (1) a general introduction to the problem; (2) a definition of sexual harassment; (3) informal procedures—step 1; (4) informal procedures—step 2; and (5) formal disciplinary procedures: (a) the Yale version; (b) the CUNY board of trustees disciplinary policy for students; and (c) the faculty union contract on disciplinary procedures. The committee used this draft to discuss whether there should be available both informal and formal procedures, the latter leading to formal action when necessary.

As we worked and discussed this issue with members of the office of student services, there was considerable interest in making sure counselors were prepared to handle problems connected with sexual harassment. The principal concern among counselors was the effect sexual harassment had on those who experienced it. At that time one of the members of the counseling staff was designated as the college psychologist; in mid January 1982, he arranged a workshop for the staff and trainees on counseling victims of sexual harassment. The speaker was a social worker and therapist in analytic training who worked with rape victims at a hospital center in New York. She was also an activist in a rape intervention program. What is clear in retrospect is how little research had been done specifically on the victims of sexual harassment.

A CITY UNIVERSITY OF NEW YORK POLICY STATEMENT

As these consultations took place on 25 January 1982, the Board of Trustees of the City University of New York adopted a formal policy prohibiting the harassment of employees or students on the basis of sex, calling for prompt, confidential investigation of allegations "to ascertain the veracity of complaints and [take] appropriate corrective action." The board made it a violation of university policy to engage in sexual harassment or to take action against any individual for reporting sexual harassment. The definition adopted included "unwelcome sexual advances, requests for sexual favors, and other verbal or written communications or physical conduct of a sexual nature" when submission implicitly or explicitly became a condition of an individual's employment or academic standing, when submission or rejection became the basis for employment or academic decision, or when "such conduct has the purpose or effect of unreasonably interfering with an individual's work performance or creating an intimidating, hostile, or offensive working environment."

The board guidelines charged the presidents of the colleges of the university with implementing their policy, directing all deans, directors, chairs, administrators, and supervisors to undertake responsibility for both implementation and dissemination. The board suggested that students report harassment to the dean of students, who, after informal confidential investigation, should report findings to the president, consulting the Title IX coordinator in the process. Employees covered by collective bargaining procedures "which include gender discrimination as a ground for grievance" were to use them; those who did not were to have recourse to a panel instituted by the president. The first efforts by such a panel were to be both informal and confidential; if no informal resolution were achieved, the panel member was to submit written recommendations to the president, who was to take appropriate action, including initiating disciplinary proceedings. Allegations were to be made within thirty days of alleged occurrence, "except for extenuating circumstances." Two days after the board issued these procedures, the counsel to the president sent a copy to the ombudsman for distribution to the working committee.

By this time the Hunter College working committee had formulated a working draft of its own statement on sexual harassment, including a definition, and the beginning of a set of procedures that might be proposed through the informal stage. Aware of the board of trustees statement of policy, they proceeded on the assumption that their work supplemented the university procedures and could readily exist within the framework established by them. By late March 1982 the committee had a first draft of a statement of policy of procedures for the college and realized that once they had come to some agreement it would be necessary to confer with the dean of students and the legal counsel to the president.

THE FINAL STAGE OF WRITING THE GUIDELINES

The discussions of the draft guidelines for policy and procedures went slowly, but some fundamentals were established. It was decided that the panel should consist of faculty, staff, and students, both undergraduate and graduate, so that individuals in each segment of the community would find someone on the panel they would feel comfortable approaching. Taking this further, it was decided that the panel should include a mix that reflected the variety in the campus community in terms of gender, ethnicity, race, and sexual orientation as well as different disciplines and areas of campus life, such as the clerical pool, counseling, and the library. Not every panel could have every possible type of member, but an effort to maintain a mix was clearly important.

Deliberations moved at an academic pace: slowly and with complexity. In the fall of 1982, the president issued an "Open Line" to the college community, citing the elements of the resolution passed by the board of trustees the previous winter and formally establishing a Sexual Harassment Panel. The terms of membership were two years and the panel members' additional responsibilities were "to consult regularly with the counsel, the vice president for student affairs and the president about the effectiveness of the policy in preventing sexual harassment" and "to recommend methods for educating the campus community about sexual harassment." Eight faculty and staff and three students were appointed to the panel, with the college ombudsman serving as an advisory member.[4] There were five faculty, consisting of one male faculty member in the English department, two women faculty in anthropology and educational foundations (a psychologist), a woman instructor from Academic Skills, and myself (an historian), listed as "Evening." The three staff members were one librarian, one counselor, and one secretary, all women. The students were all women: one sophomore and two juniors. One of these members was Black and one was Hispanic; none was identified with a homosexual orientation. Three were closely allied with the women's studies program. The panel's makeup was not yet ideal, but we now existed.

Our first problem lay in the wording of the president's "Open Line," which followed the board of trustee's resolution closely, directing students to report sexual harassment to the vice president for student affairs and "employees covered by collective bargaining agreements which include gender discrimination as a ground for grievance" to use the grievance procedure provided under those respective agreements. Thus the panel's existence seemed to be only for "employees not covered by a collective bargaining agreement or covered by an agreement which does not include gender discrimination as a ground for grievance." The members of the working committee had conceived of a Hunter College panel as a body that would function in the first instance for all three categories of the campus community, students, faculty, and staff.

Related to this problem was a proposal from the counsel to the president that the students on the panel serve only "when student claims are involved." Within a few weeks a protest had arisen jointly from all the students who had been consulted about being nominated to the panel. They cited the Hunter College practice of including students on all administrative search committees and in the evaluation of administrators and protested the implied creation of two standing committees or panels instead of one if the student members were restricted to which cases they might serve on. The initial procedure suggested by the working committee, which treated all members of the panel equally, was adopted.

THE FIRST SEXUAL HARASSMENT PANEL

On 1 October 1982, the vice president for student affairs requested that I convene the first meeting of the Sexual Harassment Panel. On 7 October, the counsel to the president sent a memorandum to the vice president with some literature she thought the panel might find useful. She also indicated that she wanted to meet with the panel "to discuss the legal issues of which they should be aware." Her concluding remarks indicated that, like the initiators of the process at Hunter, she was concerned about introducing this matter to the academic community: "We should also schedule a series of workshops (1) to educate chairs and deans as to their responsibilities and (2) to educate students and faculty about preventive measures and reporting procedures."

I invited to the first meeting of the Hunter College Sexual Harassment Panel the members named by the president, the vice president for student affairs, and the counsel to the president. The agenda I listed reflected the three areas that needed to be sorted out before the panel could begin its business: to set its policy and procedures in light of the "Open Line" from the president; to allow the counsel to the president to raise legal issues; and to take up the issue raised from the beginning of our discussions, that of educating the college community about sexual harassment.[5] In the interim, one of the students appointed indicated that she could not serve, and she was replaced by a member of the financial aid staff, a Hispanic man who was also homosexual. Thus when we met we better approximated the kind of representative spread of the college community that we had hoped the panel would achieve in our earlier discussions.

At our first meeting, on 28 October 1982, the instructor in Academic Skills, a black woman who had some interest in academic administration, was elected chair of the panel for a two-year term. For the benefit of new members, there was a brief review of the history of the panel. The counsel to the president presented a number of procedural and policy issues for the panel's consideration and distributed a set of proposed procedures; she also shared with the panel a copy of Rutgers University's policy on sexual harassment issued in July 1980. The ombudsman shared with the panel a clipping of a sexual harassment case at Harvard University, reported in the *New York Times* for 21 October 1982, in connection with which Harvard's Board of Overseers received a confidential report. The report urged that victims of sexual harassment be informed of the details of the resolutions of their cases, an action not previously required. The confidential report had been occasioned by student dissatisfaction over this issue, and by the lack of an appeals process, a timetable for an investigation, and an automatic procedure for examining a student's grade in a course where she or he had suffered sexual harassment.

The panel agreed that its members needed to educate themselves about a number of issues involved in procedures and to discuss ways in which to bring them to the attention of the college community. A subcommittee was formed to complete the draft of a statement of policy and procedures, using the working committee's version as its basis and dealing with the issues raised by the counsel to the president. The work of this drafting committee took a long time and involved consultation with existing formal grievance and disciplinary bodies that dealt with issues involving students, faculty, and staff. Out of the process emerged guidelines that ensured everyone's rights to confidentiality and due process while pressing for speedy action. What also emerged was a Hunter College model of procedure that allowed the panel to investigate cases raised by students, faculty, and staff. The panel sent the product of their labors to the counsel to the president in mid January 1983. The review process continued until mid April 1983. The college counsel suggested a system of investigation of complaints, informal and formal, by subcommittees, which could then report to the full panel for final action. This was the system adopted.

A final version of the Statement of Policy and Procedures of the Sexual Harassment Panel of Hunter College emerged 13 April 1983. It was now almost two years since the issue was raised by the ombudsman in the academic senate. The first two introductory paragraphs declared:

> An atmosphere of mutual respect among members of the academic community is necessary for the university to function as a center of academic freedom and intellectual advancement. Any violation of mutual trust, any form of intimidation or exploitation, impairs the institution's educational process because it undermines the essential freedoms of inquiry and expression. Students and teachers must feel personally secure in order for real learning and intellectual discovery to take place.
>
> As a place of work and study, the college must be free of sexual harassment and all forms of sexual intimidation and exploitation. All students, staff, and faculty must be assured that the college will take action to prevent such misconduct and that anyone who engaged in such behavior may be subject to disciplinary procedures.

The procedures encouraged any student, staff member, or member of the faculty to discuss incidents of possible sexual harassment with any member of the Sexual Harassment Panel and indicated a choice of informal or formal complaint procedures that might be initiated to bring about resolution of complaints. The difference between the two lay essentially in the emphasis in the informal procedure on ending the situation complained about through informal discussion and, in the formal procedure, on the requirement of a written statement and formal investigation. In the latter case, after investigation, the decision of the panel was to be referred to the president when the case involved a faculty or staff member and to the vice president for student affairs when it involved a student. Basically, the findings of the panel were advisory to the president, to whom, after investigation, the circumstances and action recommended were forwarded. The intent was always to resolve the complaint by correcting or remedying the injury, if any, to the complainant and to prevent further harassment. Any action taken by the president would be governed by CUNY bylaws.

EDUCATING THE PANEL; EDUCATING THE COMMUNITY

While the draft process continued, the panel members attempted to learn how to conduct an interview with a complainant. The counselor on the panel distributed some written suggestions and undertook some role play for the benefit of the members. She emphasized the need for a quiet place without interruptions, the importance of body language, the use of silence and the right pitch of voice, the way it was possible to listen nonjudgmentally, and how to ask one question at a time. She also made clear the need to assure the complainant of the confidentiality of the interview to let the complainant know what her or his rights are according to the informal and formal procedures, to explan the role of the panel, and to discuss the complaint in terms of when, where, witnesses, and the usefulness of keeping a journal to record details. Eventually the panel evolved a uniform recordkeeping form to aid in the process.

One of the primary goals in the setting up of the Sexual Harassment Panel was that its members should be representative of the campus community in order to encourage all with concerns and complaints to come forward and make them known. Very early in the discussions of the newly constituted panel in the fall of 1982, therefore, it was decided to design a flyer to acquaint people with the panel's existence and the names and telephone numbers of its members. As a beginning, the counselor in the office of student services demonstrated how a simple one might be not together on her own typewriter. By folding an ordinary sheet of paper twice, we created a front panel with the words "SEXUAL HARASSMENT IS A PROBLEM" in large type. Underneath came: "Now there is something you can do to stop it!" Inside, under the title "WHAT IS SEXUAL HARASSMENT?" came a definition drawn from our Policy and Procedures. The middle panel was devoted to "WHAT TO DO ABOUT IT," which referred readers to the panel's informal and formal complaint procedures, urging the reader to explore the issue with a panel member. The third inside panel summarized information about sexual harassment in brief terms, and on the last side was listed the names of the panel members with identification and college telephone numbers. A thousand of these could be duplicated immediately and piles of them placed in appropriate places around the college where they would be noticed and picked up. It was a beginning.

Other kinds of educational techniques were developed as the panel continued in existence. The president agreed to issue an "Open Line" on the college policy concerning sexual harassment at the beginning of each semester, listing the panel members. The dean of students enabled the panel to buy a videotape produced at the University of Indiana at Bloomington, called "You are the Game," illustrating sexual harassment incidents on a college campus. This was shown, and flyers on common myths about sexual harassment were distributed, on several occasions. The electronic bulletin board in the student cafeteria was employed to advertise these showings. Students working for the student newspapers were encouraged to write articles about the sexual harassment panel and the issue of sexual harassment on campus. Several such articles were written over the ensuing years. At one point a questionnaire was devised by some of the panel members, including the ombudsman, to establish to what extent our students believed themselves involved in situations that are legally defined as sexual harassment.

Although these efforts yielded some results, the panel members continued to feel that they had not yet found the way to raise the consciousness of the college community as a whole to the issues involved. A brochure directed toward students evolved from the first simple flyer and one directed toward faculty, the idea for which was borrowed from work done by a similar committee at California State University at Northridge. When later members of the panel, both faculty and students, made sexual harassment the focus of their scholarly research, however, these efforts took on a new dimension and greater visibility began to be achieved.

From the first, members of the panel, though responsible as a group for shaping the policy and procedures to guide effort against sexual harassment, understood that individually they had much to learn about handling cases. To aid this first group, the vice president for student affairs brought forward one of the women administrators who reported to her. She was willing to talk with us about an incident of sexual harassment involving a male administrator in order to allow us to use her remarks as our first testing ground for issues. The counselor in student services who had been on the committee since its first formation facilitated the interview at which the entire committee was present. The discussion proved important. It raised such issues as how to deal with incidents that had no witness, how to evaluate information from a complainant in a nonjudgmental way, and what to advise those who came forward about keeping records of further incidents. In their discussion, the panel members raised classic questions about "enticement," "unconscious provocation," and power relations. It was important for the group to discuss their views in order to discover the areas about which disagreement might arise among them in implementing the policy and procedures they had just completed. It was also important to understand the way society, and especially an enclosed community such as a campus society, had made it easier—and more comfortable—to blame the victim of sexual harassment than to make difficult decisions against peers and colleagues. It was also important to discuss where the priority of the panel lay: upon the rectification of wrongs or upon the penalties and sanctions to be invoked against wrongdoers.

These early discussions led to the decision not to include the names of persons involved in complaints in panel minutes. Similarly, panel members considered how to identify patterns of behavior on the part of particular members of the campus community on the basis of repeated incidents. As a matter of record keeping, this idea proved troublesome. Records of names meant confidential files, and if the files were truly confidential, by whom and when would they be seen in order to establish that such a pattern of behavior existed? In the end, no such formal record keeping was entertained; instead, the long-term members of the panel became the memory of the panel. It was not an ideal solution, but no better one presented itself. Individual panel members saw students, staff, or faculty who wished to speak with them infor-mally. Since the object of the discussion was to resolve whatever was bothering them, if that goal could be accomplished without recourse to anything as structured as an informal complaint, the matter ended there.

CATEGORIES OF CASES HANDLED

The most common case the panel expected was some form of sexual harassment experienced by female students at the hands of their male faculty. For many reasons, this has not been borne out. First of all, it has become increasingly evident that many students who are sexually harassed do not know that the behavior that leaves them so uncomfortable may be so defined. In addition, students at urban, commuter schools bring into the classroom an expectation about dominant male behavior that accepts their responsibility for learning to maneuver around obstacles like sexual harassers. Such attitudes work against holding harassers accountable; instead the message handed along the student grapevine about potential faculty harassers is, "If you want to take their courses, just make sure you keep out of their way." This leaves the most unwary, unselfconscious, more readily victimized student available as target. Such students are convinced that they, not the harasser, are at fault and are more likely only to blame themselves should they find they have a problem. Such students are the least likely to come forward for help, which they equate with more personal humiliation.

The cases that do materialize, therefore, are often those brought by the maturer student, one whose life experiences or academic courses in women's studies have made her more self-confident and aware of her rights to equity of treatment in and out of the classroom. At Hunter College, it is noteworthy that the larger number of female student–male faculty cases handled by the panel in its first decade involved at least slightly older woman students. An interesting subset of such cases involve what the Sexual Harassment Panel now calls "gender harassment," using a term introduced to it by Michele Paludi. In these cases, the more mature woman student, often in her mid or late twenties, refused to put up with behavior that her younger female colleagues did not openly question.

For example, a returning woman student came forward to a member of the panel to complain about the climate in a science classroom that was exemplified by a "joke" that the instructor told, the butt of which was the size of his penis. The joke was met by guffaws by the male students. The protesting woman student, however, was angered, because she believed such a joke gave permission to the men students in the class to exhibit "jock" behavior. As evidence, she cited the fact that shortly after this incident of the "joke," she observed the men at the back of the class whistling at the return of a young woman who had temporarily absented herself. The protesting student spoke to her instructor, trying to tell him that his remarks offended her, but he did not take her seriously. She therefore appealed to the Sexual Harassment Panel, and the coordinators interviewed the instructor and, at his request, arranged a meeting between him and the protesting student. Together, in the presence of the two members of the panel, they struggled to clarify for each other their differing perceptions of the situation. The instructor acknowledged his surprise and slightly wounded feelings: to be told that what he had intended as "putting the class at ease" had come across to one woman student, and perhaps others in the class as well, as productive of tensions, not easing them. Once he listened and established the gap between his intentions and the act, he indicated a willingness to revise his behavior.

Another case brought to the attention of the panel involved more explicit classroom behavior. It was handled by a subcommittee, which reported their findings to the panel. A woman student complained that the climate of learning in her humanities class was disrupted for her by the instructor's insistence on paying special attention to her in the classroom, exacerbated by asking her to visit him in his apartment, which he used as an office. She had withdrawn from the course without completing it and brought her case in hopes of being allowed to take the course with another instructor, without penalty, because of the sexual harassment she had experienced. The subcommittee investigated her complaint and discussed her charges with the instructor. His response was that he was only showing keen interest in her that he exhibited in all his students, and he made clear he believed that, by his attentiveness, he was being a good, supportive teacher. In this case, what occurred looked different to the less powerful person, who was faced with the choice of either "appreciating" a degree of attentiveness that she did not want or resisting it, and opening herself to whatever retaliation her instructor chose, since he retained the power of grading her work. She resolved her dilemma by dropping the course and appealing to the Sexual Harassment Panel for redress. The subcommittee recommended that the student be allowed to take the course again with another instructor, without penalty, and that the instructor be informed that his actions were deemed sexual harassment and asked to confine his advisement of students to the college premises.

In a third instance, the older woman student bringing a charge of gender harassment against a full-time faculty member, who was a department chair and senior professor at the college, was deemed twice to have failed to uphold her charges. In this case, striking because it went through both unofficial and official procedures pursuing the same bill of complaint, a further novel element dealt with the use of tapes. These class discussions were entered as prime evidence, on the grounds raised by the complainant that transcripts alone failed to capture the tone of voice that conveyed the sexist nature of remarks that she alleged conveyed the pattern of gender harassment. On advice of college counsel, the panel subcommittee handling the case allowed the use of the tapes because the professor had originally allowed them to be made by the student in the class. The case posed difficulties for the panel because the complainant herself broke confidentiality and made various members of the college administration aware of her complaint, necessitating an unusual procedure once the judgment had been reached on each occasion, of informing those administrators of the nature of the panels's negative advisory recommendation.

Although at least two cases involving staff members only were brought to the panel, they were matters that were clearly part of issues being handled in other adjudicatory bodies as well and the one that proceeded to the formal complaint stage was not found to have evidence to sustain it. No case involving a faculty complainant about other faculty has come before the panel. There are many possible reasons for this failure. Michele Paludi suggested some of them in a series of workshops for faculty and staff at Hunter College in spring

1988. Women faculty facing a specific problem of sexual harassment are more likely to ask advice from friends and colleagues or attempt to deal with the problem themselves, rather than bring it to the college panel. These issues may be particularly stressful for women faculty, as Darlene DeFour suggests elsewhere in this volume, who are African American, Asian American, or Hispanic, conscious of the toll their marginality in the professoriat takes on them in so many other ways. Women faculty in general tend to believe that it is part of their professional task to cope with such problems informally and on their own. Certainly my own discussions with women faculty colleagues bears out this predilection. Women faculty are concerned that any action they take of a formal nature to counter sexual harassment will harm their careers because they will be labeled "boat rockers." They do not expect support from other women on the faculty, and their realistic appraisal of their situation at most institutions cannot be denied. It takes courage of a high order and perhaps just plain grit to take on personally the established male hierarchies of academic life. What is needed is a well-established female support system, as many male faculty sympathizers as possible to back one's cause out loud, and a powerful, respected, administratively supported sexual harassment panel in place.

One final category of case, that which occurs between female and male students, has many faces. Date rape may be a straightforward issue, but the emotional stakes are complex and on them depend whether the woman is willing to pursue her complaint. Similarly, when women students experience being "hassled" by male students, most decide that it takes less energy simply to avoid the hassler. Most notable for our panel, however, was a case involving gender harassment that flourished in a climate of outright misogyny and sexism among some of the population at our dormitory. A woman student protested the graffiti-filled posters which covered the outside of a bedroom door, and investigation showed how poorly the college's own guidelines on sexual and gender harassment were understood by the administrators and resident assistants in this area of campus life. Her protest led directly to instituting workshops at the residence hall to better acquaint personnel there with their responsibilities regarding harassment issues and the availability of members of the panel for consultation.

SOME PROBLEMS OF IMPLEMENTATION

Implementation of sexual harassment policy and guidelines remains difficult in academe. The expectations of those in subordinate and powerless positions about the prerogatives and privileges of those in power in the academic community work against it, whether we focus on the professor in the classroom, the administrator supervising staff, or the male student who reflects the privilege of being part of the dominant group in society. Those in power give grades, write recommendations, hire, fire, and can by all these means fundamentally affect careers and future lives. Those who occupy the lower steps on a clearly marked hierarchically defined pyramid of power *expect* to be treated as lesser beings. They are socialized to believe in the system that so defines them, and they play to the roles assigned them as dependent creatures, supporters of and subordinate to the greater beings whose lives they often admire and whose words they obey. This is a heady atmosphere, and rare is the senior faculty member or administrator who does not succumb to its blandishments and its pitfalls of easy arrogance. (And too few are the male students who resist these models of behavior offered to them.) As Sue Rosenberg Zalk points out elsewhere in this volume, too few are the male professors who can resist the ease with which a man may be either or both a sexist or asexually exploitative tyrant, depending upon his psyche. Since he is expected to exercise his will at the expense of lesser mortals (and whatever else they are, lesser mortals are generally female), he is rarely held accountable when in doing so he harasses them sexually or creates a classroom climate that harasses them because of their gender.

This same academic climate breeds complaisance among peers and colleagues, female as well as male. The practical result runs the gamut of attitudes from "There but for the grace of God go I" and "Don't blow the whistle" to "Live and let live," "No harm done," and "That's life," to a, more cheaply cynical "She was probably asking for it" and "What are pretty women for, anyway?" Such views represent the urge of those at the top to keep the boat from rocking in order to continue to enjoy the "perks" of power, such as they are in academe. They also imply a conviction that the fate of those in positions at the top affects others similarly placed, threatening to bring them all down like a house of cards if too many whistles are blown from too many sides. This point of view is critical when chairs are asked to discipline senior faculty or deans are asked to discipline chairs. All would deny it, but there is an element of the life raft: it is important to pull together lest all go under in the storm.

Finally, there is the real and realistic concern of the person involved in bringing charges against someone higher up in the hierarchy that the results will not be worth it. The deep conviction, based on a sense of the academic hierarchy and the academic climate, is that the culprit will not suffer for his actions in the end, but rather that the victim will be still further victimized. As I have already noted in discussing some cases dealt with by the Hunter College Sexual Harassment Panel since its inception, it is more often the older, more mature woman student who is willing to undertake the arduous task of bringing charges against someone in power. Such a student, either from life experience or from learned analysis of the structures of society in women's studies courses, has a fair understanding of both the power realities facing her and her chances of success. Younger women students, as Vita Rabinowitz points out in another chapter in this volume, tend to resist labeling themselves as victims and therefore avoid circumstances where this will occur. Thus the most vulnerable woman students, the younger and less sophisticated ones, are the most exposed to the potential of sexual harassment and the least likely to take any useful recourse against it, including seeking aid from a member of the Sexual Harassment Panel.

The most difficult problem of implementation may have to do with the restrictions necessarily invoked to safeguard the rights of the accused. At CUNY, this means that after the panel has completed its investigation and submitted its findings to the president and/or the vice president for student affairs, any decision by the president to take disciplinary action against a faculty or staff member must go through two more stages of disciplinary procedure under union contract and board of trustee guidelines. These of course are important in safeguarding the rights of the accused, but they also mean that the complainant, even after initial investigation has sustained her, may have to be prepared to face repetition of her bill of particulars to yet other bodies of investigators. If she is the least bit vulnerable (and who is not in such circumstances?), the problem becomes whether the results are worth the toll they take on her emotionally.

POSSIBLE SOLUTIONS: FUTURE WORK

To deal with the problem of sexual harassment and the academic complexities that make work in this area generally a slow process, it is necessary to begin with institutionalized procedures. Institutionalization means written procedures, setting out clear, well-defined, and judicious actions to be taken by the complainant and those in charge of investigating the complaints made, ensuring that the institution meets its obligations to protect the rights of the accused as well as to pursue the rectification of the wrongs done victims of harassment.

To deal effectively with the charges made, such procedures must be undertaken by a cross-section of respected members of the university community whose judgment can be relied on to press cases on behalf of the victimized and to guard their interests without creating *causes célèbres* that might polarize the community. These panel members must be trained to be able to handle problems, to resolve them if possible short of bringing charges, and to aid any complainant who wishes to bring charges to do so. Panel members must always act as intermediaries who are investigating a situation, and only after investigation should they express an opinion as to whether the charges brought should be sustained. It is necessary when a panel acts as an advisory body to recall that its members have no power other than advisory and to make sure that the complainant and accused are aware of this as well.

To make the panel's work effective, however, it must have two essential supports. One is an available counseling system to which complainants may turn for the kind of psychological support necessary in going through the hazards of "bucking the system," and the other is the absolutely reliable support of higher administration. A counseling system ideally might include peer counseling for students, faculty, and staff which might be attached to student services, employee assistance programs, and faculty organizations. If panel members must maintain a neutral, open stance, it is critical that they be able to recommend to complainants who are finding the process difficult specific counselors who will be able to give them emotional support. Similarly, if the panel's findings are not upheld and those found guilty of misbehavior not disciplined in some appropriate way, the panel itself loses all effectiveness. Only a close working relationship between this advisory panel and the administrator to whom it gives advice can ensure that actions taken will constitute a real warning to would-be sexual harassers that such actions will no longer be tolerated at that institution. The panel cannot tie the hands of the administrator to whom it is advisory, but it can expect the kind of support that will make its work effective rather than the reverse.

Finally, what is needed throughout the university community in the professoriat, among administrators and staff members, and in the student body is carefully planned-out education to inform each and all of the issues involved in sexual and gender harassment. This is much easier said than done. A few institutions have produced films and videotapes concerning sexual harassment, but none yet addresses the problems of a large heterogeneous student body in an urban commuter college. Even if they did, the resistances to hearing the messages involved are legion: Students do not define what happens to them as sexual or gender harassment unless they really make an effort to understand the process by which these phenomena work. The larger number of faculty and administrators similarly wish the issue would go away, and do not see the need to spend their own time dealing with it.

A few faculty consider the whole issue an invasion of their "academic freedom." It is a stance rarely taken in the academic community when the issues deal with equity and race, but still openly made when the subject is equity and gender. It is critical, therefore, to raise the consciousness of the entire academic community to the way sexual and gender harassment—sexism not less than racism—can poison the learning climate for all women students and constitute a threat to their right to an equal education. Effective change in an academic community occurs when the balance is tilted in favor of it; therefore, we must educate the academic community about sexual and gender harassment. We at Hunter College hope our experience will prove helpful to efforts elsewhere. The current emphasis on sexual harassment research may hold the seeds to greater success for us all. The more we understand about what we are up against, the better we can devise strategies to counter it.

Notes

I wish to thank Professors Richard Barickman, Sam Korn, Sally Polakoff, and Ruth Smallberg, members of the first Sexual Harassment Panel at Hunter College, who read an earlier draft of this chapter and offered corrections and comments of a very useful nature. Sam Korn and Sally Polakoff formed that earliest discussion group out of which this institutional response to sexual harassment took its shape. My co-coordinator on the panel from 1984 to 1988, Richard Barickman, worked from its formal inception on the shaping of its guidelines. Ruth Smallberg has long acted as our "memory bank."

1. Dorothy O. Helly, "Coeducation at Hunter College: Curricular and Structural Changes since 1964," in *Towards Equitable Education for Women and Men: Models for the Next Generation* (Saratoga Springs, N.Y.: Skidmore College, 1985), 51–62.

2. The seventeen programs and policies were listed in eight areas in Karen Bogart, *Toward Equity: An Action Manual for Women in Academe* (Washington, D.C.: Association of American Colleges, Project on the Status and Education of Women, 1984): (1) Admissions ("Career Explorations: Summer Employment for Minority High School Students," 74); (2) Financial aid ("Financial Aid for Returning Women Students," 84); (3) Academic programs ("Women's Studies Program That Produced a Textbook," 90: "Faculty Development to Integrate Scholarship on and by Women into the Curriculum of Introductory Courses," 104; and "Public Service Careers for Women and Minority Students," 133); (4) Student development ("Hunter College Women and Housing Seminars: A Mentorship Program for Students," 139); (5) Support services ("Ellen Morse Tishman Women's Center," 160; and "Hunter College Child Care Center," 165); (6) Employment ("Affirmative Action at a City University," 177): (7) Professional Development ("Stipends for Writing Grant Proposals in Women's Studies," 184; "Promoting Women in Higher Education Administration," 186; "Women and Minority Faculty Development Program," 190; Humanizing the Personnel System," 193; "Employee Assistance Program," 195; and "Career Mobility Program for Clerical Staff," 196); and (8) Overcoming subtle discrimination ("Formal and Informal Procedures for Addressing Sexual Harassment of Students by Faculty," 216).

3. I invited her to speak at a monthly meeting of the Hunter College chapter of ACENIP (American Council on Education's National Identification Program for Women in Higher Education Administration). For the way this group formed part of a larger strategy of women's equity programs at Hunter College, see under PROFESSIONAL DEVELOPMENT in note 2 above.

4. The ombudsman raised with the president the question of whether his membership on the formal Sexual Harassment Panel was as a faculty member or in his official capacity. She stated that it was the latter and named him as a special advisory member.

5. Specifically, my memorandum of 14 October 1982 listed the proposed agenda as election of a chair; panel procedures; legal issues; publicity; and workshops for college administrators, faculty, and students.

Training Counselors in Issues Relating to Sexual Harassment on Campus

K. C. Wagner

Academia is currently addressing the prevention of sexual harassment both as an educational institution and as an employer. Models for informal and formal resolution of complaints (Wagner 1990; Rowe 1990; New Jersey Supreme Court 1993; *Lehman v. Toys 'R Us*) within institutions have emerged along with changes in case law impacting educational institutions (Wetherfield 1990; NOW LDEF 1994). Many campuses have been initiating training and educational programs (*Initiatives* 1990; National Association of Student Personnel Administrators 1992), with students and activists joining forces to organize community responses (Women Tell The Truth Conference, Hunter College, 1991). Researchers and the media continue to capture the complex realities of sexual harassment. (Siegel 1992).

The following materials were adapted from the Working Women's Institute Counseling Program and represented, at the time, eleven years of collective experience[1] in fighting workplace sexual harassment. They were used to train a faculty committee that was designated as "support counselors/advocates" for students on their college campus. This was meant to provide some limited training to a cross section of faculty members, who would be the initial contact for many students. These support counselors were not meant to replace student counseling services or other institutional avenues of redress such as the dean or office of affirmative action.[2]

This two-day workshop followed a film and general discussion on the topic. It was meant to provide some basic interview and counseling skills with experiential practice exercises to meet the particular role and responsbility of the support counselor/advocate.

The materials included are of two sorts: (a) role-playing instructions and case examples, and (b) interviewing and counseling reference materials.

Notes

1. With much appreciation to my sisters who made a difference: Peggy Crull, Julie Goldscheid, Karen Sauvigne, Katy Taylor, and Joan Vermeulen.

2. Issues of confidentiality, organizational notice, and liability vary depending on the institutional role and responsibility of informal and formal complaint handlers.

3. See listings in Siegel 1992. Also, some campus and local theater groups (e.g., Cornell Players, Ithaca, N.Y.) have interactive performances on preventing sexual harassment.

4. Billie Dzeich and Linda Weiner popularized this concept in their pioneering book *The Lecherous Professor* (Boston: Beacon Press, 1984).

5. Bernice Sandler was instrumental in exploring and documenting this issue as founder of the Project on the Status and Education of Women for the Association of American Colleges.

6. For perspectives on this issue, see Susan Faludi, *Backlash* (New York: Crown, 1991); Camille Paglia, *Sexual Personae: Art and Decadence from Nefertiti to Emily Dickinson* and Katie Roiphe, *The Morning After: Sex, Fear, and Feminism on Campus* (New York: Little, Brown, 1993).

References

Initiatives Special Issue: *Sexual Harassment (Part 2)*. *Initiatives* (Journal of the National Association for Women Deans, Administrators and Counselors) 52, no. 4 (Winter 1990). (Contact at 1325 18th St. NW, Suite 210, Washington, DC 20036-6511.)

Lehman v. Toys 'R Us. New Jersey Supreme Court 1993.

National Association of Student Personnel Administrators. (1992). Confronting sexual harassment on campus. Teleconference 12 November. (Contact at 1375 Connecticut Avenue, NW, Suite 418, Washington, DC 20009-5728.)

NOW Legal Defense and Education Fund (1994). Representing plaintiif in *Patricia H. v. Berkley Unified School District*. (Contact: NOW LDEF, 99 Hudson Street, New York, NY 10013.)

Rowe, M. (1990). The ombudsman as part of a dispute resolution system. *Negotiation Journal*.

Siegel, D. (1992). *Sexual harassment: Research and resources.* New York: National Council for Research on Women. (Contact 530 Broadway, 10th floor, New York, NY 10012).

Wagner, K. C. (1990). Programs that work—Prevention and intervention: Developing campus policy and procedures. Initiatives. NAWDAC. Winter.

Wetherfield, A. (1990). Sexual harassment: The current state of the law governing educational institutions. Initiatives. NAWDAC. Winter.

WORKSHOP AGENDA

I. Introduction
    A. What is a support counselor?
        1. Qualities
        2. Functions
        3. Expectations
        4. Organizational and legal liability
        5. Organizational protections for counselor
    B. Policy of college/university
        1. Overview of campus policy and procedures
        2. The law and educational institutions
    C. Record keeping
        1. Philosophy
        2. Issues of coniidentiality
        3. Logistics
            a. Counselor documentation
            b. Institutional record keeping
II. Sexual harassment on campus
    A. Definition
        1. Scope, range, impact
        2. Intersection with other issues (e.g., race, sexual orientation, physical difference, campus rape)
    B. The lecherous professor
        1. Roles they assume
        2. The reasons
        3. The context
    C. The chilly climate for college women
        1. Campus political climate
        2. The learning environment
        3. Individual responses
        4. Individual strategies

III. The initial interview (see role-play A)
    A. Principles
    B. Group excercise
    C. Feedback
IV. Problem solving and interview Techniques (see role play B)
    A. Purpose
    B. Sequence
    C. Outcome
V. Developing Options
    A. The next step
       1. Philosophy
       2. Small-group problem solving
    B. Role-play presentation
    C. Feedback
VI. The follow-up
    A. Time frame
       1. Crisis intervention
       2. Short-term options
       3. Long-term options
    B. Educational function
       1. Forums
       2. Faculty meetings
       3. Curriculum
       4. Ongoing training for support counselor

Role-Play Materials: Objectives and Format

Objectives:

To provide support couselors with an opportunity to
- practice skills
- clarify their role and responsibilities
- learn from each other
- develop a peer network of support and resource sharing

Format:

Small-group role-playing in triads (actors and observor) with a large-group debriefing

and/or

Fish bowl
    A dyad enacts a situtation and a facilitator does a "freeze frame" approach and asks other group members to take over in the role to continue the role-play, with the group acting as observors.

or

    A dyad enacts a situation and a facilitator asks actors to stay in role and observor audience asks questions about the process (e.g., asks counselor about strategies in interview, asks student about impact of certain interactions observed).

Role-Play Materials: Sample debriefing instructions for observors
(Adapted from materials developed by K.C. Wagner for Cornell-ILR EEO Studies Program, Metropolitan District Office, New York City)

Observers Guide

During the role-play, observe the interaction between the players and complete the questions below, annotate if appropriate. You will be giving this feedback *second.*

Your first task is to *debrief* by asking each player to stay in character.

For the counselor:

- — What they liked about what they did
- — What would they have done differently

For the student:

- — What made this process work or not work for you?
  (e.g., What made you un/comfortable? More/less defensive?)
- — Based on your interests, how would you evaluate the outcome?
- — Did you feel it was a safe and open process?

Give your Feedback

As a small group *decide on an issue from your discussion* that would benefit the larger group.

Skills Guide

1. Did the counselor/administrator understand what the student was trying to say?

                                               YES   NO   SOMEWHAT

Intellectually
Emotionally

2. Did the student believe that the counselor/administrator understood what s/he was saying?

                                               YES   NO   SOMEWHAT

Intellectually
Emotionally

3. Did the counselor make the student comfortable?

                                               YES   NO   SOMEWHAT

Intellectually
Emotionally

4. Did the counselor

                                               YES   NO   SOMEWHAT

Define their role

Address confidentiality

Present the process in a
  complete and understandable way

Offer viable solution(s)

Role-Play Materials: Sample role-play case situations

Role-Play One: The First Interview

Situation: A college student has made an appointment to "check out" the Sexual Harassment Committee. This is a first meeting, and there is no information available about the student or the nature of the situation.

Counselor: This is your first contact with a student. Your goal is to fully explore the situation, discuss the stress impact (e.g., emotional, physical, school-related), what the student would like to see happen, and develop approapriate strategies or next steps.

Student: Assume one of the roles as described (see student description A, B, or C).

Student—Female

You are very frightened of telling anyone about a series of incidents with your professor that made you feel uncomfortable. This included stares during class, comments about your looks as a greeting each morning, and touching you under the chin as you were asking him a question after class one afternoon. While you were alone in his office discussing your term project, he suggested that you go out for coffee "sometime." You have not given any verbal response but have demonstrated your objections by moving away or blushing. You feel very guilty, since you felt flattered by his attention at first. However, the incident in his office made you think there were strings attached. It's midway through the term and you just want to get this to stop. You are very anxious about being alone with him and you are afraid your grade will be negatively affected by this.

Student—Male

You are very angry about the fact that the "girls" in your lab seem to get favorable treatment by your professor, who is always flirting with them. You feel that his flirtation with them in class takes time away from your questions. You think that the C you received on your lab project was proof that you didn't get your fair share of his attention. You have even seen the professor walk out with a group of girls in the class and have seen them talking in the parking lot. You want your grade changed and his behavior to stop. You think that all a girl has to do to get a good grade is to look pretty.

Student—Female

You say you are coming out of your concern for a friend, who is unwilling to come forward herself, but you are really talking about yourself. Call your friend "Eileen" and say that she has confided in you about a problem she is having with her math professor, Mr. Green. You recount the following story:

Eileen was failing math, and Mr. Green offered to work with her after class. At first they met in the library and then on two occasions met on a Saturday in his home. Eileen really appreciated his help, since she planned to attend a 4-year college the following fall. After their last meeting Mr. Green suggested they go out for lunch to celebrate her progress. Eileen enthusiastically agreed to his idea, and Mr. Green suggested that he drive his car there. Eileen expected to go to a nearby diner and was surprised that he drove to a small café in another town. While they were at lunch Mr. Green started touching her hand and speaking in low, romantic tones. Eileen successfully changed the topic and left feeling panic stricken. She missed her two classes the following week and had another student pretend to be her mother and say that she was ill. Eileen felt that Mr. Green was really nice to help her and didn't want to get him into trouble but felt sick about the situation and wondered if she had encouraged him without realizing it.

Finally you blurt out that you are talking about yourself and are terrified about facing him and unable to concentrate on studying for your finals.

Role-Play Two: The Counselor's Next Step

Suggestion: Role-play the logical next step based on the role-play situations described in student situation A, B, or C.

Counselor Reference Materials: Draft Intake Form

CONFIDENTIAL

Date of call   Counselor   Case No.

_____   _____   _____

Name _____   Sexual Harassment

_____ current

_____ past

Address: _____   Other _____

_____

_____

_____

Telephone (H) _____

(W) _____

Appointment Date _____

Follow-up:

Description of sexual harassment problem—student status, nature of incident, description of harasser, school-related consequences.

Stress Reactions—emotional, physical, school related.

Counselor Impressions—personal, options, strategies to pursue. Be aware that you may have to show these records to others; avoid any statements that could be used against the student. Example: vague and potentially harmful: "Student was hysterical." Safer comment: "Student displayed anxiety as is a typical reaction to this type of behavior."

Other critical facts:

Strategies	Done to Date/Outcome	Discussed/Will Do
Contact with other students		
Verbal objection		
Written objection		
Keeping log		
Complaints (Check) — to harasser — chair of department — dean — Sexual Harassment Committee — Affirmative Action — other		
Consult(ed) with MD, Attorney, Therapist		
Status of Parental Involvement		
Other:		

Follow-Up Contacts:

Date	Who Called	Content	Counselor

Counselor Reference Materials: Initial Interview

Introduce committee/task force, its name, and affiliation within college community:

  its philosophy—its role—discuss extent of confidentiality and your role as support counselor.

Establish guidelines for the contact:

  type and nature of contacts;
  goal of meetings;
  student's responsibility regarding decisions.

Conduct meeting:

> process to explore situation, provide information and options; initiate exploration (what, when, where, how); explore stress impact (personal and school related); nonjudgmental, active and observant listening; guided movement (ventilation, validation, clarification, partialize, practice); establish short- and long-term goals; summarize status of situation to date; schedule follow-up.

Follow up:

> contact with student;
> explore other referral sources, if appropriate;
> contact with support counselor network;
> contact with other administrative supports.

Counselor Reference materials: Interview Techniques

Individual into Group Context as Student

"The stress that you have described is, of course, very debilitating but it is a common feature of sexual harassment."

"Although each individual is unique in terms of how they respond to stress, there are some common symptoms shared by those who experience sexual harassment."

"Some common stresses experienced by women dealing with sexual harassment are . . ."

Clarification Statements

"Let me see if I understand the situation, you are saying that . . . "

"It sounds like . . ."

"Are you saying that you want to get the harassment to stop but you are afraid to jeopardize your grade?"

Reality Statements

"It's not an easy choice to make, but research shows that ignoring sexual harassment doesn't make it go away."

"It's really up to you to decide on a strategy, since you have to follow through with it."

"My role is to provide you with information on the issue, on your rights and options as a college student."

"We all have expectations of how the situation should be resolved, but to be most effective it's important for you to use the steps that the college has put into place."

Supportive Statements

"You have been under much stress and you have handled it the best you could."

"I know how frightening it is to make a decision without having any guarantees."

"You are in the best position to make judgments about your situation. Trust your instincts."

"I know how overwhelming it feels to face the entire situation; let's break it down into parts."

Action-Oriented Statements

"Let's brainstorm about all the possible things you could say to express your objections."

"A suggestion would be to list the low- and high-risk strategies with the possible consequences of each."

"Let's move to a discussion of your rights and options as a student."

Interviewing People Skills

Listening: Hearing what another person is saying
- Give the person enough time to talk freely or answer you questions. Pay attention to what they are saying.
- Indicate your attention by verbal and nonverbal gestures that would encourage the person to talk.
- Look the person in the eye and sit in a way that communicates your interest in what the person has to say.

Support: Communicating your interest in another's experience
- Indicate your interest in trying to understand by restating in *your words* what the *person has said to you.*
- Make sure tht your verbal and nonverbal responses are nonjudgmental.
- Ask informational or open-ended question that help the person understand their feelings or situation.

Empathy: Communicating your understanding of another's experience
- Watch for nonverbal messages communicating feelings (such as crying, clenched fists, lowered head and eyes, tapping fingers, shaking of legs, voice tone).
- Try to identify in words what the person appears to be feeling; although you might be wrong, it gives the person a chance to express their feelings.

Problem Solving: Help the person sort out their situation, identify short- and long-term options,, and learn about resources
- Help the person break down their problems into smaller part.
- Help the person focus on what can be resolved immediately and what needs more time to handle.
- Help the person identify all their resources and work out a strategy.

Counselor Reference Materials: Thoughts on Options

There is no one best option for any situation; what will work depends on the
- individual (her/his personal profile and interpretation of the problem)
- situation (what seems possible, given the setting)

Every strategy has potential risks and benefits. It is a good idea to have each student spell out what s/he thinks s/he might gain/lose when considering an option.

Often a student will be reluctant or fearful to act. Unless s/he is in physical danger, there is usually time to carefully think through the strategy that makes most sense. Try to facilitate how to define the situation on her/his own terms. A good first step is amost always to encourage a written log, to get a clear sense of what exactly has happened, as well as to develop documentation that may be helpful. Identify other students, past and present with similar problems.

Develop a series of coping strategies to enable the student to deflect remarks.

Role-play verbal responses with students to give them confidence that they can object to the behavior (i.e., change subject, avoid one-to-one contact, social events, take another student along).

Encourage a log to keep dated records of incidents and attempts to deal with the situation. This log should include names of witnesses, copies of pictures, notes, etc.

Legitimize stress reactions by defining typical patterns.

When in the middle of the problem, it is hard to see the supports that may exist. Students should be encouraged to think about supportive students who would be available to them during class or the school day, or groups of students who would get together and let a professor know about his offensive behavior.

Timing is an important factor in discussing options. A letter objecting to the harassment may be seen as inflammatory if it comes out of the blue, but may effectively show that you're serious if it follows a discussion.

It is not uncommon for related issues (sexual assault, the need for long-term counseling, etc.) to surface in the course of a discussion of options. If appropriate, make referrals to campus or community groups.

Resources for Policies and Procedures

Michele A. Paludi

SAMPLE POLICY STATEMENT AGAINST SEXUAL HARASSMENT

Members of an academic community must be able to work in an atmosphere of mutual respect and trust. Any violation of trust, any form of intimidation or exploitation, damages the college's process by undermining the essential freedoms of inquiry and expression.

As a place of studying and work, _____ College should be free of sexual harassment and all forms of sexual intimidation and exploitation. All individuals must be assured that _____ College will take action to prevent such misconduct and that anyone who engages in such behavior may be subject to disciplinary procedures.

It is therefore the policy of _____ College that all individuals have a right to work and learn in an environment free of sexual harassment.

_____ College strongly disapproves of sexual harassment of its members in any form, and states that all individuals at all levels must avoid sexually harassing behavior and will be held responsible for insuring that the campus is free from sexual harassment.

What Is Sexual Harassment?

Sexual harassment is legally defined as "unwelcome sexual advances, requests for sexual favors, and other verbal or physical conduct of a sexual nature" when any one of the following criteria is met:

- Submission to such conduct is made, either explicitly or implicitly, a term or condition of the individual's employment or academic standing.
- Submission to or rejection of such conduct by an individual is used as the basis for employment or academic decisions affecting the individual.

- Such conduct has the purpose or effect of unreasonably interfering with an individual's work or academic performance or creating an intimidating, hostile, or offensive work or learning environment.

Examples of the legal definition of sexual harassment include, but are not limited to the following behaviors:

- Unwelcome sexual advances
- Requests for sexual favors, whether or not accompanied by promises or threats with regard to the professional relationship
- Using sexually degrading words to describe an individual
- Sexually suggestive objects, books, magazines, posters, photographs, cartoons, or pictures

These behaviors constitute sexual harassment if they are committed by individuals who are in a supervisory positions or by peers. And these behaviors constitute sexual harassment if they occur between individuals of the same sex or between individuals of the opposite sex. _____ College prohibits these and other forms of sexual harassment.

Sexual Harassment versus Flirtation and Other Welcomed Behaviors

There are high costs of sexual harassment to individuals. The outcomes of sexual harassment can be examined from three main perspectives: learning/work related, emotional, and health-related.

Learning work-related outcomes. Research has documented decreased morale, absenteeism, decreased job/learning satisfaction, performance decrements, and damage to interpersonal relationships with colleagues.

Emotional outcomes. Being harassed can have consequences that are devastating to individuals' emotional health, including depression, helplessness, strong fear reactions, loss of control, disruption of their lives, and decreased motivation.

Health-related outcomes. The following physical symptoms have been reported by individuals who have been sexually harassed: headaches, sleep disturbances, disordered eating, gastrointestinal disorders, nausea, weight loss or gain, and crying spells.

Thus, sexual harassment is not welcomed behavior; it is unwanted and unwelcome, and it interferes with individuals' ability to get their work or studying done.

What Should Individuals Do if They Believe
They Are Being Sexually Harassed?

Members of the _____ Campus community who have complaints of sexual harassment by anyone on campus, including any supervisors, faculty, or students, are encouraged to report such conduct to the _____ Officer so that he/she may investigate and resolve the problem. The _____ Officer will give advice and guidance on both formal and informal procedures for resolving the problem. They will make a record of the contact, but all information will be kept confidential.

Individuals who feel subjected to sexual harassment should report the circumstances in writing within 90 days to the _____ Officer.

Individuals covered by Collective Bargaining Agreements should feel free to be accompanied by their Union representative in any and all meetings with the _____ Officer regarding a sexual harassment complaint.

Complainants and those against whom complaints have been filed *will not* be expected to meet together to discuss the resolution of the complaint unless this procedure is requested.

Resolutions of Informal Complaints

Any individual may discuss an informal complaint with the _____ Officer. If the person who discusses an informal complaint is not willing to be identified to the person against whom the informal complaint is being made, the _____ Officer will make a confidential record of the circumstances and will provide guidance about various ways to resolve the problem or avoid future occurrences.

If the person bringing the complaint is willing to be identified to the person against whom the complaint is made and wishes to attempt informal resolution of the problem, the _____ Officer will make a confidential record of the circumstances (signed by the complainant) and suggest and/or undertake appropriate discussions with the person involved.

When a number of people report incidents of sexual harassment that have occurred in a public context (for example, offensive sexual remarks in a classroom setting or an office) or when the _____ Officer receives repeated complaints from different people that an individual has engaged in other forms of sexual harassment, the person complained against will be informed without revealing the identity of the complainants.

Resolutions of Formal Complaints

A formal complaint of sexual harassment must include a written statement signed by the complainant specifying the incident(s) of sexual harassment.

The statement may be prepared by the complainant as a record of the complaint.

The complaint must be addressed to the _____ Officer, who will then investigate the complaint, and present his/her findings and recommendations to the President.

Formal complaints will be investigated in the following manner:

If the circumstances warrant an investigation, the _____ Officer will inform the person complained against of the name of the person making the complaint as well as of the substance of the complaint. The investigation will be limited to what is necessary to resolve the complaint or make a recommendation. If it appears necessary for the _____ Officer to speak to any people other than those involved in the complaint, she/he will do so only after informing the complaining person and the person complained against.

The _____ Officer will endeavor to investigate all complaints of sexual harassment expeditiously and professionally. To the extent possible, the investigation will be completed within 15 days from the time the formal investigation is initiated.

The _____ Officer will also make every attempt to maintain the information provided to them in the complaint and investigation process as confidentially as possible.

If an individual making a formal complaint asks not to be identified until a later date (for example, until the completion of a course or a performance appraisal), the _____ Officer will decide whether or not to hold the complaint without further action until the date requested.

If a formal complaint has been preceded by an informal investigation, the _____ Officer shall decide whether there are sufficient grounds to warrant a formal investigation.

After an investigation of a complaint, the _____ Officer will report his/her findings with appropriate recommendations for corrective action to the President or report to the President its finding that there is insufficient eidence to support the complaint.

Following receipt of the report, the President may take such further action as he/she deems necessary, including the initiation of disciplinary proceedings.

Recommended Corrective Action

The purpose of any recommended corrective action to resolve a complaint will be to correct or to remedy the injury, if any, to the complainant and to prevent further harassment. Recommended action may include written or oral reprimand of the harasser; suspension, dismissal, or transfer of the harasser; or other appropriate action.

If the complainant is not satisfied with the attempts to resolve the sexual harassment, the claimant may seek resolution through other sources, for example, the _____ State Division of Human Rights or the United States Equal Employment Opportunity Commission.

Retaliation

There will be no retaliation against individuals for reporting sexual harassment or assisting the _____ Officer in the investigation of a complaint. Any retaliation against an individual is subject to disciplinary action.

False Complaints

If after an investigation of any complaint of sexual harassment it is discovered that the complaint is not bona fide or that an individual has provided false information regarding the complaint, the individual may be subject to disciplinary action.

Remember:

- Sexual harassment is illegal.
- Sexual harassment is not flirtation; it is unwelcomed behavior.
- Complimenting an individual is not sexual harassment.
- Sexual harassment naay result in disciplinary action up to and including dismissal.
- Sexual harassment is harmful to all individuals involved and to the effective functioning of the campus.
- Retaliation for filing a sexual harassment complaint is prohibited and is subject to disciplinary action.
- Sexual harassment is prohibited at _____ College.
- _____ College is committed to dealing with sexual harassment in an effective, confidential, and caring manner.

For additional information regarding sexual harassment, contact:

_____

_____

_____

General Guidelines for Investigating
Complaints of Sexual Harassment

- Investigators must make it clear to all parties involved in the investigative procedure that the campus has an obligation to make the environment free of sexual harassment and free of the fear of being retaliated against for filing a complaint of sexual harassment.
- Every complaint must be kept confidential.
- No conclusions about the veracity of the complaint should be made until the investigation is completed.
- The investigation must be thorough and fair.
- Every step of the investigation must be completely and accurately documented and in a form that can be defended to others.
- Investigations must be completed in a timely fashion.
- The complainant must be interviewed in detail.
- The person complained about must be interviewed in detail.
- All witnesses must be interviewed and assured confidentiality.
- Each complaint against the same individual must be handled independently.
- Provisions must be made for individuals who wish to wait until they receive a grade or a performance appraisal prior to filing a complaint.
- Closure must be provided for all parties involved in the complaint procedure.

Who Should Investigate Complaints of Sexual Harassment?

Each college selects the individual who will be responsible for hearing and investigating charges of sexual harassment. The individual who is responsible for investigating complaints should meet the following criteria. She/he must:

- have sufficient credibility in the area of sexual harassment, including knowledge and formal training;
- be readily accessible for students, faculty, employees, and administrators;
- must have skill in relating to people and eliciting information from them;
- not be uncomfortable in discussing matters of sexuality and sexual deviancy, incest, battering, and rape;
- be fluent in languages in addition to English (or have a co-investigator who can meet this need);
- be tenured and a full professor to avoid potential problems with their tenure and promotions review decisions;

- report directly to the President;
- not permit and of the individuals in the complaint procedure to pressure them to reveal confidential information, to become their advocate, or to "take sides" in the final report of the investigation;
- be honest and candid, without permitting personal feelings to interfere with effectiveness;
- be sensitive to civil service rules, collective bargaining agreements, and other personnel rules;
- be a calming force for emotional discussions;
- set up a "safe" atmosphere for the compainant, alleged harasser, and witnesses to discuss their perspectives without the fear of being ridiculed or judged;
- maintain a distance from all individuals involved in the complaint process so that (1) a reasoned judgment can be made about whether to sustain the charge of sexual harassment and (2) she/he can be upheld as objective by individuals such as hearing officers, judges, parties involved in complaint process.

Some Tips for Graduate Teaching Assistants

- Behavior rules for the outside, voluntary social environment do not always apply in the involuntary college environment where people are a "captive audience."
- Teaching Assitants who communicate their clear stand against sexual harassment help prevent incidents of sexual harassment.
- Sexual harassment is not an expression of sexual interest. It is an abuse of power and is a form of control.
- Changing a college culture from one that encourages sexual harassment to one that prohibits and punishes it takes the burden off of individuals and lessens the college's exposure to charges.
- Graduate Teaching Assistants are viewed as resource people—individuals to consult when students need advice on issues relating to sexual harassment.

Resources for Education/Training

Michele A. Paludi

Sample Workshop Materials for Training College Employees

Goals of Training Program

- Provide information concerning liability
- Define *quid pro quo* and hostile environment sexual harassment
- Discuss psychological issues involved in dealing with sexual harassment
- Discuss the physical and emotional reactions to being sexually harassed
- Provide a psychological profile of sexual harassers
- Discuss peer sexual harassment
- Discuss means of resolution for complaints of sexual huassment

At the conclusion of this training program, individuals will be able to:

- Assess their own perceptions of the definition, incidence, and psychological dimensions of sexual harassment
- Adequately label behaviors as illustrative of sexual harassment or not illustrative of sexual harassment
- Asssss why individuals choose to report or not report sexual harassment
- Identify peer sexual harassment
- Identify employees' rights and responsibilities under Title VII

Topics for Presentation and Discussion

Part 1. Introduction to Training Session and Goals of Seminar
Trainer welcomes participants to seminar
Trainer summarizes goals of seminar
Participants introduce themselves and state their goals

Trainer writes these goals on the flipchart/chalkboard
Trainer summarizes goals

Part 2. Perceptions vs. Realities in Sexual Harassment

Trainer provides case study of employee situation in a college setting
Trainer asks for responses to questions concerning the case study
Trainer summarizes responses

Part 3. Definition of Sexual Harassment

Summary of case law on *quid pro quo* and hostile environment sexual
   harassment
Behavioral examples of sexual harassment
Peer sexual harassment
Trainer makes summary comments from this unit

Part 4. Incidence of Sexual Harassment

Trainer lectures on incidence of workplace sexual harassment
Trainer discusses individuals at risk for sexual harassment
Trainer discusses the relationship between incidence and reporting of
   experiences
Trainer makes summary comments from this unit

Part 5. Impact of Sexual Harassment on Individuals and Campus

Trainer lectures on the impact of sexual harassment on employees
Trainer lectures on the cost of sexual harassment for the workplace
Trainer identifies impact of sexual harassment on students
Trainer makes summary comments from this unit

Part 6. Causes of Sexual Harassment

Trainer lectures on explanatory models of sexual harassment
Trainer lectures on psychological profiles of harassers
Trainu makes summary comments from this unit

Part 7. Preventing Sexual Harassment

Trainer lectures on the campus's sexual harassment policy
Trainer identifies campus's grievance procedure with respect to sexual
   harassment
Trainer asks employees to identify individual responses they can make
   to ensure a workplace environment free of sexual harassment
Trainer introduces college administrator charged with investigating
   complaints
Trainer makes summary comments from this unit

Part 8. Summary Comments and Review

Trainer lectures on 'myths and realities' of sexual harassment
Trainer leads general discussion of sexual harassment
Trainer reviews participants' goals that were generated at the beginning
    of the session period
Question and answer period

Sample Workshop Outline for Faculty

Goals of Training Program

- Provide information concerning liability
- Define *guid pro quo* and hostile environment sexual harassment
- Discuss psychological issues invoked in dealing with sexual harassment
- Discuss the physical and emotional reactions to being sexually harassed
- Provide a psychological profile of sexual harassers
- Discuss peer sexual harassment
- Discuss means of resolution for complaints of sexual harassment

At the conclusion of this training program, faculty will be able to:

- Assess their own perceptions of the definition, incidence, and psychological dimensions of sexual harassment
- Adequately label behaviors as illustrative of sexual harassment or not illustrative of sexual harassment
- Assess why individuals choose to report or not report sexual harassment
- Indentify peer sexual harassment
- Identify students' and employees' rights and responsibilities under Title IX and Title VII
- Design educational programs for their campus to deal with sexual harassment, including peer sexual harassment

Topics for Presentation and Discussion

Introduction to Training Session and Goals of Seminar/Workshop
Definition of Sexual Harassment

Summary of case law on *quid pro quo* and hostile environment sexual
    harassment
Behavioral examples of sexual harassment
Peer sexual harassment

Incidence of Sexual Harassment
    Measurement considerations
    Underreporting of incidences
    Individuals at risk for sexual harassment
    Relationship between incidence and reporting
Impact of Sexual Harassment on Individuals and Campus
    Sexual Harassment Trauma Syndrome
    Internal and external coping styles
    Break
Causes of Sexual Harassment
    Explanatory models of sexual harassment
        Organizational power
        Sociocultural power
    Psychological profiles of harassers
Preventing Sexual Harassment on Campus
    Pedagogical techniques for classroom use
    Campus-wide educational programs
Summary Comments and Review
    "Myths and Realities" of sexual harassment
    Question and answer period

Training College Students

Goals of Training Program
- Define *quid pro quo* and hostile environment sexual harassment
- Discuss psychological issues involved in dealing with sexual harassment
- Discuss the physical and emotional reactions to being sexually harassed
- Provide a psychological profile of sexual harassers
- Discuss peer sexual harassment
- Discuss means of resolution for complaints of sexual harassment

Objectives of Training Program
    At the conclusion of this training program, students will be able to:
- Assess their own perceptions of the definition, incidence, and psychological dimensions of sexual harassment
- Adequately label behaviors as illustrative of sexual harassment or not illustrative of sexual harassment
- Assess why students choose to report or not report their experiences of sexual harassment
- Identify peer sexual harassment
- Identify students' right and responsibilities under Title IX

- Understand their college's policy statement against sexual harassment and grievance procedures for dealing with sexual harassment
- Design educational programs for their campus to deal with sexual harassment, including peer sexual harassment

Part 1. Introduction to Training Session and Goals of Seminar/Workshop

Trainer welcomes participants to seminar/workshop

Participants introduce themselves and state their goals for the training session

Trainer writes these goals on the flipchart/chalkboard

Trainer summarizes goals of participants

Part 2. Definition of Sexual Harassenent

Trainer lectures on definition of sexual harassment

Summary of case law on *quid pro quo* and hostile environment sexual harassment

Behavioral examples of sexual harassment

Peer sexual harassment

Trainer makes summary comments from this unit

Part 3. Incidence of Sexual Harassment Among College Students

Trainer lectures on the incidence of academic sexual harassment

Measurement considerations

Underreporting of incidences

Individuals at risk for sexual harassment

Relationship between incidence and reporting

Trainer makes summary comments from this unit

Part 4. Impact of Sexual Harassment on Students and Campus

Trainer lectures on the impact of sexual harassment on students

Trainer lectures on the cost of sexual harassment for the college/university

Trainer makes summary comments from this unit

Part 5. Causes of Sexual Harassment

Trainer lectures on explanatory models of sexual harassment

Trainer lectures on psychological profiles of harassers

Trainer makes summary comments from this unit

Part 6. Preventing Sexual Harassment on Campus

Trainer lectures on components of an effective policy statement for students

Trainer distributes copies of college's policy statement against sexual
  harassment
Trainer introduces college representative charged with enforcing policy
  statement (optional)
Trainer discusses policy statement
Trainer asks students to list potential educational programs for their
  college/university campus
Trainer writes these responses on the flipchart/chalkboard
Trainer makes summary comments from this unit

Part 7. Summary Comments and Review
Trainer lectures on "myths and realities" of sexual harassment
Trainer leads general discussion of sexual harassment of college students
Trainer reviews students' goals that were generated at the beginning of
  the session
Question and answer period

Part 8. Evaluation of Training Program
Trainer distributes copies of seminar/workshop evaluation form
Trainer meets individually with students who wish to speak to her/him
  privately

Discussing Sexual Harassment in Psychology Classes

Some Examples
Statistics/Experimental
Methodology used to obtain incidence rates of sexual harassment
Reliability and validity measures of sexual harassment surveys
Scaling of scenarios depicting sexual harassment for severity
Examples of feminist methodologies
Social Psychology
Interface of gender, race, and power involved in sexual harassment
Social policy applications of research on sexual harassment
Attitudes toward victim blame and victim responsibility
Developmental Psychology
Incidence of sexual harassment among children and adolescents
Socialization agents contributing to acceptance of sexual harassment
Clinical/Counseling Psychology
Symptoms associated with Sexual Harassment Trauma Syndrome
Relationship between sexual harassment and Post Traumatic Stress
  Disorder
Therapeutic interventions with victims of sexual harassment

Educational Psychology/I/O Psychology
    Sexual harassment as a barrier to career development
    Management issues involved in dealing with sexual harassment
Psychology of Women
    Relationship between sexual harassment and incest, battering, and rape
    Manifestations of power abuses in educational and work settings

Index